Praise for *Graduate to a Great Career*

"One thing you don't learn in college is how to get a job. Don't panic. Catherine Kaputa's new book will provide you with a graduate degree in the subject. Don't go job-hunting without it."
> **—Al Ries, author, *Positioning: The Battle for Your Mind***

"In her latest book, Catherine Kaputa shares the secrets of personal branding, the skill that will set you apart from the other job candidates in your field. *Graduate to a Great Career* will ease your anxieties about the job search and set you on the right career path for you."
> **—Daniel H. Pink, author of *Drive* and**
> ***The Adventures of Johnny Bunko***

"Catherine has crafted a "must read" resource for new grads seeking their first career-launching role. Even better, seasoned professionals will find the content highly beneficial, especially if they are not 'digital natives.'"
> **—Beverly Tarulli, PhD, Vice President, Human Capital**
> **Strategy & Workforce Analytics, PepsiCo**

This book is filled with wisdom, cutting-edge personal branding advice and stories from real first-time job seekers. It shows you how to differentiate yourself from your peers, unlock the "hidden market" of unadvertised jobs, deftly navigate online job posts, leverage internships and ace the interview. In today's highly competitive and challenging market for new graduates, you need to read this book—today.
> **—William Arruda CEO, Reach Personal Branding and author**
> **of *Ditch. Dare. Do! 3D Personal Branding for Executives***

We all know it's hard to get experience without experience. Catherine Kaputa addresses this dilemma with easy to follow advice for writing your own career story and turning it into a brand that's in demand. This is one of those *must reads* for young professionals entering the workplace to navigate their career from the driver's seat.
> **—Julia Brandon, PhD, Senior Director, HR Centers of**
> **Excellence, GlaxoSmithKline**

Whether a STEM or Liberal Arts major, today's student must learn how to connect their interests and skills to employment opportunities. Catherine's book outlines both how and why to begin your career search early as a first-year student, and provides step-by-step instructions of how to market oneself in a complex employment marketplace. Its teachings will turn students from passive individuals applying to jobs into active networkers connecting with companies and organizations.

> **—Mark Presnell, Ph.D., Executive Director, Career Advancement, Northwestern University**

"As a human resources professional, I see the common mistakes and pitfalls that new career professionals often make when trying to land their first job in today's ultracompetitive market where employers are only looking for top talent. Catherine Kaputa's book takes the guess work out of the process and gives young professionals the strategies to maximize their career search and land the job!"

> **—Carrie A. Weaver, PHR, Senior Vice President, Human Resources New York City Economic Development Corporation**

"Job hunting has changed dramatically in the past decade. *Graduate to a Great Career* shows young professionals how to succeed in the social media era and develop a personal brand that will attract the right employers to them."

> **—Dorie Clark, author of *Stand Out and Reinventing You*, and adjunct professor, Duke University Fuqua School of Business**

"The ideal time to master personal branding is at the start of a career. *Graduate to a Great Career* has a variety of gems appropriate for the generation of young professionals who will work well into mid-century, from developing a T-shaped career and presenting your experience visually to applying to online systems via a 'trifecta' of supportive strategies. New grads are lucky to have Catherine Kaputa in their corner."

> **—Alexandra Levit, author of *They Don't Teach Corporate in College* and *Blind Spots: 10 Business Myths You Can't Afford to Believe.***

"In today's competitive marketplace, having a great education and resume is not enough to land a good entry-level job. *Graduate to a Great Career* introduces a breakthrough process for finding your career path, branding yourself so you stand out and executing a successful job hunt. I wish I could have read it when I was starting out."

—**Harvey Cohen, SVP Chief Marketing Officer,**
   Empire State Development

"As a marketing professional and now a professor of marketing, I have seen with first-hand experience how important branding is—and how effective it can be for individuals as well. In business school we prepare our young graduates with knowledge and skills but don't do as much as we could with preparation for the job world. Ms. Kaputa's new book will be essential for all young people looking to launch their careers. Branding is character and finding your brand gives you a great competitive advantage."

—**Peter Johnson, Ph.D., Assistant Professor of Marketing,**
   Fordham University

"*Graduate to a Great Career* is the quintessential "go-to" guide for the college (or high school) grad. Practical advice and guidance, partnered with stories and examples, accompanied by exercises at the end of each chapter, make this book highly impactful. Catherine has crystalized down to the essence the steps a job seeker in TODAY's market needs to take to be successful. Only someone who intimately knows today's job market could do this with the expertise that Catherine has."

—**Laurie Sedgwick, Director of Career Management, Executive**
   MBA Programs and Alumni Support, Cornell-Johnson

My students, undergrads, MBA candidates as well as recent graduates, will derive great benefit from Catherine's *real world* advice on branding and launching your most important product—*you!* The book is impressively broad, covering how to research and find the right job, pitch yourself in an interview and fast-starting your career.

—**Howard Geltzer, Adjunct Professor, New York University,**
   Stern School of Business; University of Southern California,
   Marshall School of Business

"Catherine's book should be handed out at Freshman Orientation: It's never too early to start learning and incorporating the prodigious information in this book. Most university career services departments are too generic in their approach to be truly useful to most seniors. An undergraduate who reads this work early and often will not just navigate his/her college career more effectively, but get a head start on the realities of building a life-long career. Even if you're not graduating from college and have been in a career for decades, "How to Graduate to a Great Career" will help you refresh and refine your personal branding."
—Beth Adler, CPC, JD, MBA, Executive Coach

"In today's innovation-driven business world, you not only have to be a creative thinker on the job, you have to be a creative, innovative thinker to GET a job. The advice in Catherine Kaputa's illuminating book, *Graduate to a Great Career*, will show you how. I highly recommend this book to anyone seeking to land their dream job."
—Mitchell Rigie, author of *Smartstorming: The Game-Changing Process for Generating Bigger, Better Ideas.*

Catherine Kaputa teaches you to look at your strengths in a marketable fashion. This book gives new graduates the tools to get the job they want, to set the course for career success. Catherine shows you how to stand out from the competition in the job search race.
—Randi Rosenbluth, M.Ed., Manager of Learning and Development, Society of Women Engineers

This book should be your #1 gift for every college student and new graduate you know. What got you ahead in academia is not what's needed to find a good job and ace the interview. This book will teach you everything you need to do to market yourself well in today's job market beginning with learning how to pitch yourself well over the phone, in letters and emails, in person and on the Internet.
—Jeffrey LaRiche, CEO, Castle Worldwide

Catherine Kaputa is one of the most knowledgeable professionals in the area of personal branding. Her insights and guidance are grounded, clear, and empowering. Her books are eye-openers about what you need to do to launch your career in the 21st century. Filled with strategies and tactics you're not likely to learn at any university, this book is the handbook every college student, young professional and new business owner needs to start a fulfilling career.

—**Nomi Bachar, author of** *Gates of Power: Actualize*
    Your True Self

Catherine Kaputa's job hunting and career ideas are captivating, persuasive, strategic, empowering and never more apropos. Now I'm telling all the young women I mentor: Read this book and learn how to launch a successful career and Brand You.

—**Elizabeth Hitchcock, Director of Strategy and**
    Innovation, AT&T

No matter your native country or country where you want to work, this guide is for you because it transcends cultural differences. This superb guide on how to land a great job in any country works because it teaches you how to leverage your strengths and out market your competitors with a winning job hunting and personal branding process.

—**Carol Spomer, Business & English for Non-Natives Coach**

GRADUATE
TO A
GREAT
CAREER

HOW SMART STUDENTS, NEW GRADUATES, AND YOUNG PROFESSIONALS CAN LAUNCH
BRAND YOU

CATHERINE KAPUTA
WHAT YOU NEED TO KNOW THAT YOU DIDN'T LEARN AT COLLEGE

NICHOLAS BREALEY
PUBLISHING

BOSTON • LONDON

First published by Nicholas Brealey Publishing 2016

53 State Street, 9th Floor
Boston, MA 02109, USA
Tel: + 617-523-3801
Fax: + 617-523-3708

3-5 Spafield Street, Clerkenwell
London, EC1R 4QB, UK
Tel: +44 (0)20 7239 0360
Fax: +44 (0)20 7239 0370

www.nicholasbrealey.com

Special discounts on bulk quantities of Nicholas Brealey Publishing books are available to corporations, professional associations, and other organizations.

For details, contact us at 617-523-3801

Printed in the United States of America

20 19 18 17 16   1 2 3 4 5 6 7 8 9 10

ISBN: 978-1-85788-640-5

E-ISBN: 9781857889970

Library of Congress Cataloging-in-Publication Data

Kaputa, Catherine—author.
Graduate to a great career : how smart students, new graduates and
   young professionals can launch brand you / Catherine Kaputa.
1 Edition. | Boston : Nicholas Brealey Publishing, 2016.
LCCN 2015044835 | ISBN 9781857886405 (paperback)
LCSH: College graduates—Employment. | Career development. |
   Vocational guidance. | BISAC: BUSINESS & ECONOMICS /
   Careers / Job Hunting. | EDUCATION / Counseling / Vocational
   Guidance. | REFERENCE / Personal & Practical Guides. | BUSINESS &
   ECONOMICS / Marketing / Direct.
LCC HD6277 .K367 2016 | DDC 650.14—dc23
LC record available at http://lccn.loc.gov/2015044835

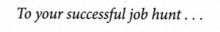

To your successful job hunt . . .

The People and Stories in *Graduate to a Great Career*

The stories in the book are authentic stories shared by college students, new graduates, young professionals, HR directors, recruiters, and hiring managers. My personal career stories are true stories told to the best of my recollection.

So many stories were generously shared, including job pitch emails, phone conversations, interview notes, cover letters, and other marketing materials. I only wish that I could have included them all. In the book, I have sometimes used first names only, often changing the names to protect privacy. For narrative flow, I have chosen between the pronouns "she" and "he" at random.

The tips and advice I propose in the book are my views based on a long career; my work as a personal brand strategist advising a wide range of people, both first-time job seekers and seasoned executives; and, of course, tips from students and new grads on what worked for them in today's dynamic and ever-changing job marketplace.

Contents

Introduction

I t's up to you now.

The umbilical cord might have been cut twenty years ago, but now it's time to be born again. You truly become an adult when that parental cord of support and identity is severed. Your childhood identity, shaped by others, will become history.

Your adult identity may be similar or radically different, but it can't be the same. Everything is different now. You're embarking on a new course, a world outside of university and parental dependency.

It's a once-in-a-lifetime opportunity!

Arguably, the most important features of your personal identity will be shaped by the choices you make in your career. A successful career depends on developing a successful personal brand, just as the company or organization you will work for depends on a successful brand to prosper.

This book will teach you all the skills you didn't learn in college that are needed to graduate to a great career. Its mission is to remove all the mystery surrounding professional life after graduation. The modern graduate or job seeker must face a baffling array of choices and pitfalls, but this book will give you the tools you need to survive.

You'll also learn how to use the "personal branding" approach to land your dream job. This includes finding and clarifying your brand idea, or *unique selling proposition* (USP), just as marketers do in the commercial world. Your USP is the basis of your job pitch, your resume, and your online social media profile. You want to represent something special, what you stand for and can do that sets you apart from others. A strong brand idea shows how you will be effective in achieving professional and personal life goals, but it is also true to yourself and brings more of your personality into the equation.

The branding world also provides a template for effective marketing and networking, as well as a cornucopia of tactics, principles, and tools to help you stand out from the competition.

Bottom line: *You* are your most important asset. You are the only asset that no one can take away. And your ability to maximize that asset in the eyes of others will play a major role in your success.

In many ways, this launching period is the most important moment in your career. It's the time when you can create tremendous value for yourself out of very little.

As a bootstrapping job seeker, you will create many personal and career assets that set the course for career success. You will meet new people and make career contacts. You will start to build a reputation and identity for yourself, both in person and online.

It's a time for exploration. You will learn who you are and what the marketplace values. By exploring different possibilities, you might even discover new career paths that you weren't aware of before.

You're finally out of the reality distortion field that one can get caught up in at college. Now, you're in the real world. You're making decisions for yourself, maybe for the first time.

Looking for your first job can also be incredibly frustrating. You'll be forced to define yourself in terms of your talents and interests. Maybe you've had some really dark moments of unemployment and are unsure of your future career.

But this is also your most valuable time, both creatively and strategically. The experience forces you to look at yourself honestly. You must focus completely on who you are and who you can be.

"Destiny" is a dramatic word, but this first phase sets up your career destiny, too. By choosing a path and moving forward, you will learn how to define your abilities, the special sauce that you—and only you—can bring to a professional situation. What are the assets you have to work with? What core principles do you stand for? How can you make meaning in the world?

Your first years out of school are special for economic reasons, too. People who graduate in years of low unemployment have better career prospects and typically make considerably higher wages throughout their lives than those who graduate in times of high unemployment. And it's a wage advantage that lasts for decades or more, according to economists.

As an enterprising job seeker, don't feel limited by a tough economy or discouraging statistics. Most is not all. There are always exceptions, and when the job market gives you lemons, plan on making lemonade. By thinking optimistically and following the advice in this book, you'll discover fresh opportunities and new paths to success.

The magic is in you. But you must take charge and use your passion and drive to discover your career destiny. Become emotionally and intellectually engaged in launching your career and your life journey. Start to create your own luck and opportunities.

Wherever you are on your career journey, the best (and only) time to start is now. The good news is that you don't have to major in marketing to launch Brand You into the career world. This book will show you how.

CHAPTER 1

Welcome to the Job Hunt, Twenty-First-Century Style

Do you recognize this new graduate? She could be your college room-mate. He could be your son. Or she could be the person looking at you in the mirror.

As a college student, "Erin Jones" was bright-eyed and optimistic. A psychology major, she loved her classes and university life. Now that she's out looking for a job, she's frustrated, anxious, and at times downright miserable.

No matter what job she applies for, somehow she seems to lack the right stuff. Erin spent days preparing to talk about her courses, internships, and personal strengths for a job interview in the marketing department at a well-known company. The interviewer's first question: "What do you think about the story in the *Wall Street Journal* today about our company?" Ouch! She was so busy preparing answers to the most commonly asked questions that she neglected to be up to date on the very latest company news. Bombing on that first question led to a chain reaction of poor answers as her confidence plummeted. Erin knows she can perform better than this.

Edward Bellin, a recent MBA in international business from a French university, is frustrated, too. He spends hours each day scouring the web for entry-level jobs in the EU, primarily France and the UK, and internships and sponsorship in the US. But the recruiting process seems terribly broken. His job applications often get lost in resume cyberspace known as *the black hole*. Even when he's scored an interview, he's had to deal with off-the-wall questions like "If you had to explain 3-D printing to your grandmother, how would you do it?" "Am I supposed to know that?" he wonders. "I'm not a techie." It's frustrating, but Edouard knows he's talented, qualified, and hardworking.

Gradually, they both were hit with the realization that something was very wrong. The career world was not what they imagined or prepared for. Much of the knowledge they learned in school was not transferable to the career world. Erin wonders if she made the right choices beginning with her major. Edouard wonders why there are so few job choices.

Like so many recent graduates and young professionals, they both feverishly tried to find a job but found it wasn't easy. They were all dressed up with no job in sight.

Finding a job is unlike any exam you've ever taken. Even if you prepare day and night, you still might not pass if you don't know how to market yourself.

I'm going to tell you why.

There are too few jobs, especially full-time entry-level positions. Perhaps Erin's major or Edouard's coursework was not what companies were looking for; perhaps it was the way they marketed themselves. They came to realize that there were many others from all over the world angling for the same opportunities. Credentials are important, but they must become better at job hunting—and networking and personal branding, too—if they expect to succeed.

Plus, nowadays, Erin and Edouard have to deal with the *gig economy*. Employers can get away with "temp to permanent" job offers, or they can hire you as a consultant, freelancer, or part-time worker with no benefits or commitment. Employers can make you jump over hurdles. The first hurdle is likely to be a machine, not a person. It's the automated *applicant tracking system* (ATS) that many companies use to screen applications digitally.

Then you must win over multiple interviewers and pass a battery of pre-hire assessment tests. In one test at a hot marketing agency, the interviewer asked Erin to draw a picture, write a haiku, and rearrange a set of word magnets on a computer screen. It took her two hours. The next day she got a wickedly short email that simply read, "We don't think you're a good fit."

Welcome to the real world of job hunting, twenty-first-century style!

Erin was not incompetent, nor did Edouard lack ambition. Neither were they lazy. They were just frustrated job seekers trying to launch their careers, unprepared for the reality of the new world of work.

Both suffered from a problem that affects many new graduates these days:

Failure to Launch Syndrome.

Marketing Yourself: Now Critical

Graduation is a happy day. Once the end of their college years are nigh, it's hard for college students and their parents not to be caught up in the cheers and pomp and circumstance, the bond of sharing a pivotal rite of passage. But, I'm here to tell you that the champagne should stay in the fridge until you master Personal Branding 101.

Unless you're *summa cum lucky*; have the networking connections of a Rockefeller; or are a top student majoring in engineering, computer science, or finance at a top-tier school, chances are you will face periods of frustration, self-doubt, and failure in the days, weeks, and months after that happy graduation day. It can be a long countdown to getting a real job, and you can't ease up until you do.

Large-scale frustration is what sets the millennials and Generation Z apart. The transition from university to a career has long been rocky, and unemployment has generally been significantly higher among people ages twenty to twenty-four than the overall unemployment rate. Finding your first job has always been something of a Catch 22. As the saying goes, you need experience to get a job, and your need a job to get experience.

But in today's economy, what's always been a dilemma has become a crisis.

It's not that the new generation isn't working hard to find a job, but very few are accounting for the reality of today's job market. You will compete with other new grads and more-experienced job seekers willing to accept entry-level salaries. And you can be squeezed out by financially strapped baby boomers who are retiring later.

After all, a young job seeker, even one who's had some good internships, can't compete that well with a candidate with years of experience and extensive contacts. No wonder so many college seniors and new grads feel anxious about their future.

What's a newly minted BA to do?

It used to be about, "Can you do the job?"
Now it's about, "Can you make a better impression
than the other 200 people who can do the job?"

What's truly different today is the quality of the competition and the sheer volume of it. The fact is the economy in most countries is not growing fast enough to handle the number of entry-level employees (top STEM graduates excepted). Millennials, young adults now in their twenties, are the best-educated generation, yet they also have higher unemployment rates than we've seen in recent decades. They make up about 40 percent of the unemployed in the US. Even when they find a job, the picture isn't always pretty. Many new grads are in jobs that don't require a college degree; others settle for jobs outside their area of study.

It's always been beneficial to distinguish yourself, but now it's absolutely necessary. Personal branding rules in the new world of work, and you can rule, too. You must be better prepared, possess marketing savvy, and conduct a smarter job search. But you can do it.

Even in a robust job market, you must brand and market yourself to avoid being furloughed into temp work or a subpar job. Besides, futurists predict that soon switching jobs every few years or so will become the norm, so we'll all have to be in permanent beta mode when adapting and marketing ourselves in changing conditions.

It's Not Your Parents' Job Market

You don't have to be a Phi Beta Kappa graduate to know that the world of work has changed. The career paths of previous generations were linear, simple, and predictable. Globalization, technology, and a lingering recession have changed the old world of employment. Already, an estimated 40 percent of the labor force in the US is composed of "contingent" workers—contractors, freelancers, and the self-employed. Some companies are even reclassifying workers as franchisees or owners of LLCs to cut costs. In short, you have to pay franchise fees for work.

Entire industries can transform or contract at lightning speed, and government statistics are released too infrequently to reflect current employment reality. Then there's the threat of technology and automation. In the future, robots can come for your job. Almost half of US jobs and one-third of jobs in the UK are at risk of being automated, according to a study by Oxford University. So when choosing a career path, we must figure out either what jobs computers could never do or what roles we will absolutely insist be done by a human, even if computers could do them.

We're moving from a world of employment to a world of "employability." There's no longer any single corporate ladder assuring a long career at one company, but instead a "jungle gym" of various jobs and skills you'll market in your lifetime.

It's not your parents' job market by a long shot, and not just in terms of less opportunity. What new grads are looking for in a first job is vastly different from what their boomer parents or Gen X sought. The majority of young people starting out today—some 57 percent—want to do something they find enjoyable, or they want to make a difference in society. (Bravo!) When their boomer parents were asked what was most important when they were looking for their first job, the majority—64 percent—said making as much money as possible or learning new skills.

People in their twenties—the millennials—tend to work for themselves. They have a passion for being in charge of their own destiny. They're driven by an internal ethos and motivated by intrinsic values, not only extrinsic rewards. Yet, if you have loftier, meaningful goals like most young people today, you better have a plan for achieving them.

Memorize This: Work Is Not Like School

The reality is that everything that made you successful in school works rather poorly in the career world. It's not school rules anymore.

School is about doing well on assignments and tests. It's about having impressive grades and objective measures of your performance—the final counts for 40 percent of your grade. It's mainly about solo work. Working with others is cheating.

> Employers are looking for a fusion
> of theoretical and applied learning
> between hard skills and soft skills.

Work requires a whole different set of skills, both to get a job and then to flourish in your career. Work is about *hard power* skills such as real-world experience, vocational knowledge, hands-on learning, practical professional ability, certificates, and aptitudes, along with your academic credentials. It's also about *soft power*, or personal branding skills such as persuasiveness, communications agility, relationship building, self-promotion, leadership, and strategic networking. You must cultivate both to succeed today. This book will show you how.

Fancy Degree. But Can You Get a Job?

A generation ago, a university degree was a ticket to the upper middle class and secured the holder a better job. Today, a diploma doesn't guarantee quality of employment—the main reason degrees are supposed to be valuable. In a land where everyone is encouraged to get a sheepskin, it doesn't brand its owner as highly employable the way it used to. The growth of skilled jobs has lagged behind the rapid increase of graduates in the US, UK, and many other parts of the world. That's why so many new graduates are working in jobs that don't even require a college degree.

> There's an expression for new grads who have a job
> that doesn't require a college degree—*underemployed*.
> In recent years, *over 40 percent* of new grads in the US
> and *over 58 percent* in the UK were underemployed.

While more than 40 percent of grads in the US are overqualified, it's even worse in the UK, where underemployment, which includes people who aren't working full-time and want to work more hours, stands at 58.8 percent according to the CIPD (Chartered Institute of Personnel and Development), a number exceeded only in Greece and Estonia in the EU.

What's more, new grads working in jobs that don't require a degree have no unique advantage over their nondegree colleagues. There is no special track for college graduates.

Underemployed young professionals are missing out on an important rite of passage—independence after graduation. Due to poorly paid jobs and college debt, new household formation is at a forty-year low in the US. Many young people can't afford to live on their own, so they are back at home in their high school bedrooms or camped out in the basement. Young adults are more likely to live with their parents today than they were in the depths of the Great Recession. Indeed, one in five adults eighteen to thirty-four in the US are living in poverty. Of course, it's a comfortable kind of poverty if they are an underemployed or unemployed degree holder living in their parents' basement, but it's still not the outcome they paid for at college.

It's unsurprising that students and recent grads (and their parents) are starting to question the value of a degree, given the cost of higher education and the fact that some degrees are fairly worthless in the job market today. Peter Thiel, the billionaire investor and cofounder of PayPal, is so skeptical of the practical value of a college degree that he launched a fellowship program specifically for college students to drop out and start their own businesses.

Changing the Jobs and Skills Mismatch

There's a widening gap between grads who struggle and those who succeed. Some economists believe that this is the new normal, not just a temporary bump. They propose that the gap will widen between new grads who possess in-demand majors and skills and those who don't.

Indeed, many unemployed or underemployed new graduates are enrolling in *coding boot camps* so they can compete for the abundant jobs in the technology industry or in technology-related careers in just about every industry.

Unlike academe, in the coding boot camps, the emphasis is on crash courses tailored to the specific skills industry is looking for and rapidly training students for a well-paying job. The number of computer science graduates from the coding schools is estimated to be about one-third of the total number of computer science graduates from American universities in 2015.

The code schools get it. They know what skills are in demand and teach them so the boot camp grads are highly employable. Unlike academia, where the model in most universities is to *educate and drop*, many code camps have corporate relationships so they can *train and place* students in high-paying jobs. The job placement rate at Galvanize, one of the largest coding camps, is 98 percent. To quote its CEO, Jim Deters, "Graduation here is you get a job."

Don't get me wrong about the liberal arts. A liberal arts education can be valuable for many careers. It teaches you how to think about the problems and issues you will face in the real world. It gives you perspective, analytical and problem-solving skills, and creative and communications strengths—which are all important in just about any career you can contemplate.

Nevertheless, if you are a student, be smart. Seek out internships and take electives like statistics, programming, or business to give your liberal arts education some "teeth." Students and young professionals alike should seek out skills and certifications that will provide more practical credentials in marketing yourself in the career world. As a new grad who struggled to market her degree in communications after graduation told me, "Every liberal arts major should be required to minor in business or take some technical courses to give your background a different gravitas."

The Revenge of the Liberal Arts Major

We've all been programmed to think that a tech education is the key to success. You'll be a dinosaur in the near future if you don't learn to code, is how the thinking goes. Certainly, learning to code can be a route to success, as the coding boot camp phenomenon shows.

Well, I have good news for you if you're not technically inclined to take up coding. Times are changing, and that way of thinking isn't necessarily so. You don't have to throw your liberal arts diploma in the rubbish bin after all.

A reversal of fortune is taking place as tech companies, particularly fast-growth tech start-ups, are realizing that it's not enough to be technically brilliant: you need brilliant business processes, too.

Some things can't be programmed. Creativity can't be programmed. Client relationships can't be programmed. Business-to-business sales can't be programmed. Tech leaders are realizing that real value will come more and more from people who can sell and humanize technology, not the hard-core technologists. That's why tech companies are zooming in on liberal arts majors, people who use and embrace technology but aren't technical. They are looking for employees with the business skills that technical people lack.

Lo and behold, big tech companies and start-ups alike are looking beyond STEM graduates and realizing that liberal arts majors make them stronger. People who study the humanities and social sciences are important as *social alchemists* who add the human touch to technology, a critical skill for any application to take hold on a large scale. Often the software created by die-hard techies functions poorly without the assistance of nontechie partners who make it more intuitive and user friendly.

Liberal arts and business majors are critical for sales, business development, and marketing. Their value lies in their nontechnical ability to connect with people—not "end users," as techies tend to call customers.

What a relief. Not all of us possess the quant skills or desire to be engineers or computer programmers. It's estimated that only around 30 percent of the jobs in tech companies involve sitting in front of a computer screen and programming all day long. Like any business, tech companies need talent in organic, people-oriented fields like sales, management, marketing. human resources, and the like.

A white-hot area in the technology job market is the recruitment of talented salespeople. The Bureau of Labor Statistics projects that 1.1 million Americans will enter the workforce in sales in 2022, while only 279,500 will enter the ranks as software engineers. It may seem shocking given the current market for software engineers, but the reality is that software development is getting more automated, too. Mobile apps can increasingly be built more quickly with fewer people.

How can you take advantage of this trend if, say, you're a classics major? What's your pitch? Here's the elevator pitch that Ava, a classics major, used to sell herself for a sales job at a growing technology company:

> A successful salesperson needs a philosopher's touch. Studying classics taught me three important things. I learned how to make a logical argument and follow it all the way down so I'm persuasive and relentless. I learned about preconceptions, how people sometimes believe something is true until someone else comes along and logically debunks it and convinces them it isn't true. I learned how to communicate clearly and the importance of touching the mind and the heart in convincing others to your point of view. I can leverage these three aptitudes to help your company win in the marketplace.

Make It STEAM Not STEM (the A Is for Arts)

In future workplaces, a balance of math and social skills will be increasingly valued. One study that analyzed government data on career incomes of more than a thousand people found that those with balanced strengths earn about 10 percent more than those who are strong in only one area.

Even math whizzes did no better than communicators who are poor with numbers.

Even having a STEM degree is no guarantee that you'll be *career ready* or even have a STEM career. While STEM graduates have relatively low unemployment, a large percentage—74 percent—are not employed in STEM jobs, according to the US Census Bureau. In addition, men continue to be overrepresented in STEM, especially in computer and engineering occupations. About 86 percent of engineers and 74 percent of computer professionals are men.

But you will have an easy ride on the career express if you're a strong in technology *and* savvy about personal branding, like Gwendolyn Campbell. Gwen was ranked first in her class in her university's engineering school and was also captain of the university equestrian team. An internship after her junior year led to a dazzling six-figure job offer in operations at a major global investment bank. But Gwen turned it down. What's more, she received another enticing offer and turned that one down, too.

Gwen was picky. (And as an engineering major who knew how to brand and market herself, she could afford to be.) Gwen had a dream. She imagined a nobler purpose for her career. She wanted to contribute to something significant in the world. And with her love of horses and riding, she didn't want to work in a big city. She moved to a major hub for technology start-ups in a semirural area and marketed herself directly to tech companies with a mission in line with her values. She found one, a tech start-up that makes a breakthrough product, a wristband for people with autism and ADHD.

There was no job posting on the company website, but Gwen reached out to the founder anyway with an engaging pitch letter. Turns out, her timing was impeccable. The founder was just about to make an offer to another job candidate but was intrigued by Gwen's pitch and resume. He called her in for an interview on a Wednesday and offered her the job on Friday. The company is also in horse country, so Gwen will be able to indulge her passion for riding. As the song goes, "Nice work if you can get it, and you can get it if you try."

What is Personal Branding?

Branding for people is about finding your brand idea—your *unique selling proposition* (USP). You want to represent something special—the unique combination of talents and skills that sets you apart from others, the X factor that makes you different.

Branding for people is about "packaging" your personal brand and using strategies and principles from the commercial world to enhance your identity. As the storyteller of your own life, you must create compelling narratives to empower your success. Branding also means developing a marketing plan and determining the tactics needed to get from A to B (and through all the other letters of the alphabet, depending on your goals). And it means engaging your target audience without seeming self-promotional or obnoxious.

Perceiving yourself as a brand has enormous advantages. Being good, by itself, doesn't guarantee success. We all know talented people who are underemployed, underpaid, or even unemployed.

Job Candidate: A person with a skill set that is interchangeable with the skill sets of other people

Brand You: Standing for something that offers a special promise of value that sets you apart

Personal branding also requires that you target a market. A market is any group of people that you must engage with to reach your goals, such as hiring managers, recruiters, professors, professional colleagues, and mentors. When deciding how to appeal to your market, don't think of what *you* want to say or do. Flip it. Think in terms of the reaction you want from the target audience and what you must do to get that reaction.

The commercial world of brands also shows you how to build visibility for yourself, and now with social media, all of us can build strong brands online. Visibility is important for brands, and it's important for you, too. Whether it's fair or foul, a strong online brand translates into a superior person in most people's minds.

Personal branding has always been important for anyone who wants to achieve career success, do good in the world, or make a lasting mark by whatever measure. But it is never more important than when you are a college student selecting your career path, or a new graduate or young professional launching your career. Career selection during college and job hunting after graduation are the most challenging assignments you'll ever undertake. That's where personal branding comes in.

Brand You: Your Best Self

You are what you make of yourself. You need to identify the best version of you and communicate that in person and online. Each of us is unique, with knowledge, aptitudes, relationships, and experiences that are powerful assets. Anything you have ever done or thought about can be an asset. We all have assets and opportunities, but they are worthless unless we recognize them and take action.

What do you want your brand to stand for?

Your ability to maximize the asset that is *you* is the single most important ingredient in your success. But I am also talking about becoming who you were meant to be. Achieving success includes becoming who you truly are. The trick to effective career marketing is to devise a strategy that will meet professional and life goals but also remains true to yourself—one that brings more of you into the equation.

While it may initially appear dehumanizing, it can be helpful to look at yourself as a "product" in a competitive framework. Branding is the process of differentiating that product—you—from the competition before taking action.

The cardinal rule of branding is, "Be different." Copying is imitation. When you copy others, the result is inauthentic. You should build your professional identity around who you are and who you can be, the unique strengths and abilities you'll bring to a professional situation. Brands try to own a word or phrase in the minds of consumers that captures their distinct idea. If done successfully, when people think of "X," they'll think of the brand; and when they think of the brand, they'll think of "X." It can be helpful to link yourself to a word or phrase that relates to your own particular value. For example, one new graduate in HR and organizational design wanted to be known for accountability. He used it as a theme in his resume and elevator pitch to stand out from other candidates.

Any way you slice it, brands win over products hands down. A branded item is viewed as better than its generic counterpart. Brands are perceived as higher in quality. They are in demand. They sell for a premium price.

Generic products compete only on price, by offering a very low price. (And if you're reading this book, I doubt that you want to compete that way.)

Personal branding can be subtle or aggressive, modern or old-fashioned, engaging or self-centered—but if you don't participate, today's job market

will leave you behind. Career success, like branding, is a game of perceptions. If people think you would be a talented new hire, you will get the job
offer. If they doubt you'd be a good fit, you won't have the opportunity to
show them otherwise. You must determine the way prospective employers
will think and feel about you, and personal branding can help do just that.

The Future of Work

Some career experts believe that the corporate world is beginning a dramatic shift to the "Hollywood model," a short-term, project-based business
structure that is very flexible and adaptable. To get an idea of the future
of work, simply look at the business of how films are made. A team is
assembled, works together as long as needed to complete the task, and then
disbands. All the various people involved are free agents.

Contrast that with the traditional corporate model and its long-term
business structure and permanent employees in open-ended jobs. We're
already seeing many design firms and technical companies employ the
Hollywood model by putting together short-term teams of various experts
to develop new products or work on big projects. Other companies have
adopted the model by hiring more contract or temporary workers for jobs
that used to be performed by long-term employees.

You can see the advantages for management and business owners.
It's much less costly: they just hire the people they need when they need
them. Then, you're on your own until you find the next gig. This model
shifts the burdens of health insurance, retirement income, and job security to workers, diminishing the risk to employers. And it's very targeted
to each business situation because the best team can be selected for each
particular job.

The Hollywood model can work surprisingly well for people with
in-demand skills and expertise. It favors the adaptable employee who
continually takes the pulse of the marketplace and keeps track of the new
industry players. It favors those who are good at networking and building
mutually beneficial relationships—and, above all, who are good at creating and communicating their value in their elevator pitch, through their
resume, and on social media.

In short, the new world of work favors those who are good at personal
branding.

ATS: The Job Hunting "Iron Curtain"

Today, it's not hard for companies to find job applicants. The supply pipeline is strong. However, job seekers face many tough obstacles, beginning with the "iron curtain" surrounding many companies. It's not easy for candidates to get the opportunity to convince employers that they have the right skills, experience, and personality for the job.

The job-hunting iron curtain is aided by powerful data tools and cheap online software that screens and blocks candidates. Many resumes today get their first read from a machine. That's because large- and medium-sized companies use online automated tracking systems (ATS) to winnow out unsuitable candidates and deal efficiently with the onslaught of online applications. Piles of applications that once took months to evaluate now take only minutes.

Companies also use pre-hire assessment tests to evaluate candidates. Of course, such tests are nothing new, but what's different today is their sophistication and their use for entry-level candidates, not just mid- and management-level hires. They present just one more hurdle for the beginning job applicant to jump. In 2001, 26 percent of large US employers used pre-hire assessments; by 2013, the number had climbed to 57 percent.

But all this automated efficiency has slowed the process as well. In February 2015, employers took 26.8 days on average to hire for open jobs, an all-time high, according to research done at the University of Chicago.

The Modern Job Search

As much as ATS and assessment techniques have changed the job hunt, social media and mobile technology are driving the real change. Social media offers a powerful platform for personal branding, networking, and job hunting. Digital natives, those who have grown up with technology, are uniquely poised to pounce on the modern, social-mobile job hunt. Social media networking is already eclipsing in-person networking, and now job search apps for mobile devices have taken over, too.

Social media is no longer merely social: it is becoming professional. Companies like LinkedIn, Facebook, and Twitter have given young job seekers industrial-grade marketing, PR, and job-hunting tools; and it is easier than ever before to build your brand, manage your job search, and increase your professional network. LinkedIn's sophisticated Alumni Tool plug-in lets you search your university and see the fields and locations alumni have ended up working. By reverse-engineering their career paths, you can start plotting your own journey.

The good news is that all this information is available, right now, on your laptop. The downside is the risk of information overload.

Your job search isn't limited to your laptop. Mobile job-hunting apps from social sites like LinkedIn and job sites like Monster and Simply Hired are exploding in popularity. The LinkedIn app has all the functionality of the main site. You can create your personal brand, connect with professionals, contribute to groups, and follow important people from your beach blanket, bicycle, or bedroom. There's even a job board where you can look at postings on the go from your smart phone.

The new job hunt can take place anywhere and operates 24/7, like it or not. The good news is the flexibility and speed of mobile job hunting. The bad news is there is no downtime. A 2015 Jobvite survey found that over 47 percent of eighteen to twenty-nine-year-old job seekers search for jobs in bed. Yep, searching for jobs on their phone is the first thing most young job candidates do before getting out of bed, or right before going to sleep. How about you?

Say you don't want to make that kind of commitment and you'd like some downtime. (It's not a bad idea to have a life, too.) If you're actively looking for a job (and who isn't these days?), you'd better think twice. Everyone else—your competitors for that plum job—is doing mobile all the time. If you don't frequently check for updates and pounce immediately on new job listings, you could miss out to someone who is tuned in and in the right place at the right time.

Some predict that it won't be long before mobile video interviews eclipse emailing your resume, and finding out about jobs and communicating with recruiters via text may become the new normal. Think of how the all-mobile job hunt will speed things up. You won't have to drive, commute, or fly to any interviews. Just hold up your smart phone and go.

Like any new technology-driven change, the more efficient apps and processes of the future will streamline certain aspects of job hunting, but the stress of being on 24/7 and the risk of information overload will also make it more burdensome.

Debate Club: What's a College Degree Worth?

Colleges are unlikely to give you much information about how much money you can earn after receiving a degree from their institution. Maybe they don't want you to know, or maybe they don't have the information.

Yet, every year, high school seniors and their elite-college-obsessed parents whip themselves up into a frenzy over who got into which school. Likewise, prestigious schools brag about record numbers of applicants and the small percentage who were accepted.

But does it really matter which school you went to?

The answer appears to be, "It depends."

If you look at the American-born CEOs in the Fortune 500 in 2015, only 30 went to elite colleges. The remaining CEOs went to a wide range of nonelite schools.

Recently, the US government released a report outlining the earnings of graduates ten years after graduating at nearly every college and university in America. You probably won't be surprised to learn that students who went to the most elite colleges like Harvard, MIT, Yale, and Stanford earn more than those who went to less elite schools.

But you might be surprised to see just how bleak the situation is for many students ten years out of college, even if they went to a well-regarded school. A college education can be fatal for students who make expensive college choices and don't get a decent return on investment. At hundreds of schools, less than half of graduates were making more than $25,000 per year ten years out from graduation, which is close to what high school graduates earn in a similar time frame. At other schools, even at good colleges and universities, a troubling percentage of graduates had incomes below the poverty level.

> At well-regarded Bennington College in Vermont, over 48 percent of its graduates were earning less than $25,000 a year ten years out; a quarter were making less than $10,600, below the poverty threshold for an individual.

The Department of Education's college numbers show the poor ROI that women receive from a college degree relative to men. At Princeton, for example, men earned $47,700 a year more than women ten years after graduation.

Of course, elite private colleges and universities possess certain advantages. Access to internationally acclaimed professors, cutting-edge curricula, and low student-to-faculty ratios presumably result in a better education and more personal attention. Loyal alums and talented fellow students can provide a valuable career network, and a well-staffed Career Services Office (CSO) can guide students on the transition from college to career. And let's not forget the lovely ivy-covered buildings, libraries, and museums. (There's even an arms race going on at some universities in the US over fancy recreation areas with water rides, spas and massage clinics.)

Above all, you are aligned with a prestigious brand—whether it is Harvard or Cambridge or France's *grandes écoles*—that will provide a beneficial halo at the beginning of your career.

What's Your Degree's Return on Investment (ROI)?

Evaluating higher education in terms of economics—the "corporatization of the modern university"—rubs some people the wrong way. Shouldn't its role be the development of the human being, not how much money you can earn?

The problem is the ever-rising cost of higher education. If attending an expensive university means you'll be taking on a lot of debt, you may want to think twice. In the good old days, college students could use their summer job earnings to pay their tuition.

That was once upon a time. It's not true anymore.

College tuition has gone up a monumental 1,120 percent in the US since 1978. Meanwhile, the cost of food has increased 244 percent during the same period. If you're still paying off your college tuition loans, you probably won't be surprised to hear that student loans have overtaken credit cards as the second-largest source of outstanding debt in the US. (Home mortgages are number one.) Indeed, tuition costs in the US have gone up four times faster than the consumer price index. University tuition is also under scrutiny in the UK due to tuition price hikes for home students and an increase in premium charges for international students.

The high cost of a university degree, along with the vagaries of the job market and a slow-growing economy, has created a student debt collection crisis in the US. The federal student loan balance has more than doubled, from $516 billion to $1.2 trillion since 2007. More than 60 percent of that student debt is held by the bottom quartile of households with a net worth of less than $8,500. And the $1.2 trillion in student debt is just federal student loans. If you count private student loans to students, their parents, and former students, you can add another $150 billion to the number. Indeed, some financial experts predict that we may be facing an education bubble like the real estate bubble, a major factor in the 2008 financial crisis.

Despite its falling return on investment, a college degree can still pay off over time. But you have to look at the lifetime ROI numbers carefully. The $1 million earnings premium of having a college degree cited by the US Census Bureau and the $2.3 million figure promoted by Georgetown University's Center on Education and the Workforce are many times higher than the college premium in the study by the Organization for Economic Cooperation and Development and a separate study done by PayScale. (The OECD study includes many other countries where the ROI on a college degree is much lower than in the US.)

Whichever result you give credence to, there's a big "if" in all of these college ROI numbers. Hidden is the wide range of income disparity between different majors. A poetry major is probably destined to make much less than a computer programmer, yet both pay the same tuition. There's also the crushing effect of college debt, and the lost opportunity cost of additional education can be crippling. On top of that, there is the reality of the new world of work, in which long-term, well-paying positions are harder to come by.

In one study that compared four fictional eighteen-year-olds, Joe the Plumber had sustainable spending on par with Jill the Doctor. The enormous debt and lost opportunity costs of years of education can certainly destroy your finances.

Your choice of field and the internships you do matter more than your college or your grades in getting hired.

A study at Georgetown University highlighted how wildly different your long-term earnings potential can vary depending on your major. Graduates who studied petroleum engineering, for example, earn a median lifetime income of $4.8 million, while graduates in early childhood education have median earnings of $1.4 million. Not all STEM majors are created equal, either. Biology majors have a median annual income of $56,000 between the ages of twenty-five and fifty-nine, about one-third of what physicists earn.

If you're looking for the specific return on your college investment, check out the US Department of Education's College Scorecard (college scorecard.ed.gov) or PayScale's College ROI Report, which has the salary data to rank hundreds of US colleges and universities based on total cost and alumni earnings. You can find the best returns by school type, location, major, and other factors.

Internships and Skill Set = Proof of Performance

Look at what organizations say they're looking for in new graduates. Yes, employers want people with strong critical thinking and communication skills who are team players. But guess what is at the top of their want list for entry-level hires? It's real work experience. Actual job experience is a skill set that cannot be acquired by spending more time in a classroom or earning a degree. It can only be gotten on the job. That's why internships in your field of study are so critical: they give you experience when you have no experience.

> Employers now give nearly twice as much importance to a new graduate's relevant work experience as grades and coursework because they are a better predictor of job success.

Yes, in the new world of work, internships count more than grades in getting hired, according the *Chronicle of Higher Education.*

Employers are looking for candidates who can hit the ground running, do the work, and bring value immediately. Internships make you highly employable because they demonstrate that you are career ready.

Not surprisingly, many grads told me that employers hardly ever ask about their grades. They want to know what you've done, specific job experience and skills that relate to your career path. The days of "no prior work experience required" for entry-level jobs are long gone. So, if you're a student, before you look for a summer job waiting tables or lifeguarding, set your sights on an internship in a career path you want to explore. The earlier you start getting internship experiences with real substance, the more marketable your brand will be.

You'll have more confidence interviewing for a full-time job after graduation if you've had experience in the trenches as an intern. You won't be competing as an X major but as a Y Company–trained intern who's worked on A, B, and C projects. You'll have specific on-the-job skills and real-world experiences, not just theoretical coursework. You'll have the confidence of a veteran, with references and organizations to back you up.

The Promised Land

Internships show you're motivated and can be successful outside the ivory tower. Plus, there's a bonus. The majority of internships lead to the promised land—a full-time job offer.

> Companies offered full-time jobs to the majority of their interns, according to NACE (The National Association of Colleges and Employers).

Even if you're not offered a job where you intern, the real-world work experience will boost you head and shoulders above candidates without experience. By the reckoning of a Gallup-Purdue survey of 30,000 graduates, few schools are offering the necessary number of internship programs. Only 35 percent of students who graduated between 2010 and 2014 reported having an internship or a job related to their field of study. That's just a 4 percent increase from the class of 1990. So, despite companies valuing internships more than grades and typical college coursework, the number of students doing internships has remained stagnant.

Many schools only permit juniors and seniors to take internships. And many students complain that, even if a few are able to land good ones, schools are unable to provide great internships to all their students.

Nothing Stopping You

What's a student to do?

Whether your university has a robust internship program, a middling one, or nothing, as an enterprising personal brander, you can take the initiative as Cole Ungar did.

Cole was fascinated by real estate. "Many buildings stand for over a hundred years, and every building has a story. There's the esthetics—the design and the architecture—and from a career perspective, real estate investment is entrepreneurial, fast-paced and highly competitive."

In selecting colleges, Cole concentrated on schools with a strong business program, particularly in real estate investment. He also looked for schools with robust internship programs located in or near a metropolitan location, so that it would be easy to network and do internships all year round. Talk about smart planning.

Freshman year, Cole met with the folks in Career Services. But unlike most students, he didn't stop there. He also put together a target list of dream real estate companies near his university that he planned to pitch for internships. One real estate executive responded that Cole was a bit young to intern, but asked if he was familiar with Argus software. Since Cole was not, the exec made a proposition: take a course on Argus and come back next year to intern.

That summer, Cole did an internship on social media marketing that he got through his school, but he also took the Argus Valuation DCF online course and got his real estate license to get a broader perspective on real estate.

Guess where he interned the summer after sophomore year?

By the time he graduated, Cole had completed eight internships, including four he had set up himself with real estate investment firms. He had a host of skills and various real estate licenses from the extracurricular courses he took. Real estate companies were impressed that he did all of these things concurrently—coursework, internships, skills certifications, and licenses. Cole's commitment paid off. In a tough job market, he marketed himself directly to his dream list of real estate investment firms with a passionate pitch leveraging his extensive internship experience, certifications and licenses in real estate.

Here's one of Cole's pitch emails:

Dear Mr. Smith,

I hope you're doing well and enjoying the fall weather. I am a senior at Y College, and I am looking to pursue a career in real estate.

From an early age real estate impacted my perception of the world and fostered a mind-set that reality is only bound by the actualization of creativity.

Throughout my time at college I have been fortunate to have had extensive real estate exposure through my many internships.

As my time at college is coming to a close, I am in search of reputable real estate investment and development companies that are both entrepreneurial and competitive as a place to begin my career. X Company fits this mold perfectly with its commitment toward sustainability and innovation exhibited in its recent projects, e.g. Z project.

I realize that you are probably quite busy and don't have much available time, but if possible I'd love the opportunity to speak with you about potential career opportunities at X Company.

I've attached my resume for your review.

I appreciate your consideration and look forward to hearing from you.

Cole Ungar

Cole sent out his job search emails in the fall of his senior year. Because he had a strong pitch along with multiple internships and certifications, he had several job offers lined up in the fall of senior year, months before graduation.

Of course, not everyone has Cole's level of dedication. If you are dedicated and cover these networking and marketing bases yourself, you will be successful.

Usually in life, less is more, but in the job-hunting race, more is better: more internships, more skills, more networking, more experiences, more visibility, and so on. Determining the balance between coursework and these skill-building activities is up to you.

A "C" in Career Readiness

Outside of the sluggish global economy, there's little agreement among hiring managers, new grads, and universities about why graduates are having such a hard time finding jobs. But all these stakeholders agree on one thing: most new grads are unprepared for the job market.

According to a study done by Bentley University, two-thirds of business leaders (64 percent) agree that newly hired recent college graduates who are not well prepared, harm the productivity of their organization's day-to-day business.

Fifty-eight percent of respondents gave recent college graduates a letter grade of "C" or lower on their preparedness for their first jobs.

Students didn't grade themselves any better. Nearly four in ten recent college grads gave themselves a "C" or lower on their level of preparedness for their first job.

Other studies paint an equally sober picture. Only 7 percent of hiring managers said that "nearly all" or "most" candidates have the right mix of skills and traits that companies desire in a new hire, according to a study by DeVry University.

The majority of business decision makers say both hard and soft skills are important, and that new grads are lacking in both. A survey done by the Workforce Solutions Group at St. Louis Community College found that more than 60 percent of hiring managers say new grads lack "communication and interpersonal skills."

Another survey, by the staffing company Adecco, found that 44 percent of hiring managers cited soft skills, such as communication, critical thinking, creativity, and collaboration, as the areas with the biggest gap.

Of course, there's much you can do to make yourself more marketable, such as increasing what I call your *hard power*. Hard power includes the tangible skills and experiences you can put on your resume. You can set up short-term internships and take courses, even short online courses, to improve your skill set. And these are critical things to do and an important part of your career identity and strength as a candidate. Strong brands are always involved in continuous product improvement, and you should be, too.

But this book is also about *soft power*, or personal branding power. The real power lies in harnessing personal branding principles to build positive perceptions for Brand You. You will learn how to apply marketing strategy, analysis, and tactics to positioning your career identity in the best light possible. You'll learn how to maximize your image and visual identity, improve your elevator pitch, and hone your verbal identity. You'll understand how to increase your reputation and visibility through networking in person and online. You'll learn how to develop a resume and marketing materials that stand out. These preparations, combined with other marketing ideas, will attract people to you.

You've Got to Love the Game

What's there to love about launching your career, you might wonder?

Figuring out your career goal and hunting for your first job is no picnic. It's difficult to decide upon the best career option and frustrating when you apply for a job and don't hear back. It's hard not to feel anxious when there are few jobs and lots of talented competition.

And you think everybody else has it figured out but you.

Imagine finding your career path and your first job as an entrepreneurial venture.
The "product" you're launching is Brand You.

But it will be hard to succeed until you change your attitude, take a personal branding perspective, and even start to love the game. You've got to tap into both *the dreamer* and *the realist* inside you, while demanding the best of yourself.

You've got to be an *intrepid explorer* discovering new growth areas in the marketplace. There may be new careers and jobs out there that you were unaware of before, and you must find them.

You've got to be a *chameleon*. You must always consider yourself to be in beta mode, changing as the market needs and opportunities change. The key is to present yourself as a versatile employee able to integrate your skills with what's hot today.

You got to be a *marketing whiz*, your best brand ambassador. You've got to become a personal brand storyteller, connecting the dots between who you are now, what you can do, and where you want to go.

You've got to be your own *personal inspirer* and self-motivator. Realize that the process of launching Brand You can be hard, frustrating, and even unfair at times, but it can be exhilarating, too. You can do it and succeed if you show up every day and implement a multilayered action plan.

You've got to be a *master networker*, a magnet for business friends and personal contacts. Networking is the key to success. It's always important, but never more so than at the beginning when you have a shallow network.

You've got to be *technology and social media savvy*, able to market yourself, network, and hunt for jobs using social media and mobile apps.

Above all, you've got to be *tenacious*. Fortune favors the people who keep on going. When one door is locked, you have to keep looking until you find a door that's open (or that you can open with a little effort).

You Are Your Own Best Advocate

Now, maybe for the first time in your life, it's up to you to do what it takes to find and get a great career. You can be one of the fortunate ones: you know who you are, your career path is certain, and you're in a field that has a shortfall of talent, like computer science or engineering. Congratulations if you are among this lucky breed. This book may not be for you unless you are interested in knowing the best possible ways to market yourself.

But if you're like most students and new grads, you aren't exactly sure about who you are and which career path is right for you. Or you could be in a field that's crowded with applicants and you need to stand out. You could be facing a difficult economy or job market where you live, or an economy that's changing rapidly, making it difficult to take advantage of your knowledge and skills. Often universities are slow to adapt to a changing environment quickly enough for students to take advantage of the new needs of the marketplace. Whatever the reason, you need to get better at networking, online branding, and pitching yourself. If you are in these categories, you need to work smart and brand yourself in order to avoid a long, fruitless slog that will test your ability to keep going on.

You'll find that getting your first job requires careful, calculated branding, both to enter the playing field and to stay in the game.

Success also requires a dose of that great universal force we call luck, that serendipitous combination of time, actions, and people and their infinite possibilities.

But luck is not something that you can count on. (Though the more things you do, the more luck will come your way.) I believe that successful job seekers are not lucky at all. They just show up more than other people.

> You can't rely on your school or other people,
> so you have to rely on yourself.
> And that's not sad; it's powerful.

Some new graduates and young professionals dislike the idea of personal branding. They find it inauthentic, manipulative, or even downright phony. They prefer to believe that getting a job should be about your academic credentials, not how well you market yourself or how well networked you are.

Do you?

How do you see the consummate personal brander? Someone who is a relentless self-promoter selling himself like a used car? That's as far removed from authentic personal branding as stumbling is from dancing.

Like good product branding, good personal branding is always built on authenticity—on who you are and who you can be. In its deepest sense, personal branding is about self-actualization.

Take Action—Now

Personal branding is for people who are smart and talented but not good at branding themselves effectively. It's for people who have come to realize that they must take control of both their identity and their career. You can't rely on—or blame—your university, other people, or luck.

The only person you really have control over is yourself. The only one who can develop a strong career plan that's best for you is yourself. The relationship you have with yourself is your most important relationship. The more proactive and self-reliant you are, the more opportunities will come your way. You'll have a surge in self-esteem as one benefit of finding your own solutions, not to mention that your actions will be like sprinkling Miracle-Gro on your career. You need to own your value, the real, tangible value that you—and only you—offer, and use the principles of branding to stand out and get what you deserve.

Personal branding is a strategic and creative process, one that flourishes when you approach it with a sense of fun and exploration and withers when you are too analytical or try too hard. Let's begin the journey to graduate to a great career and launch Brand You.

Chapter 1 Exercises

1. What is the job market like in your industry, specialty, and geographic location? Write down whatever is on your mind.

2. What actions have you taken so far to find a job? What else are you planning to do?

3. What informational interviews can you set up?

4. What internships can you set up to check out different career options?

5. How can you improve your skill set to become more marketable? Do you have both math and social skills? How can you beef them up?

6. Three years from now, imagine that you are in the perfect job. If you could live your dream, what are you doing? Describe it in detail.

7. Are you career-ready? Rate yourself on having the right mix of hard power skills through internships, relevant job experience and coursework, and having strong soft power abilities such as communication, networking and relationship skills. What can you do to improve your strengths in each category?

CHAPTER 2

What's Your Career Destiny?

Everyone is looking for a purpose in life. We wonder why we're here. College, especially, is a time when we ponder the big existential questions. Who am I? How do I make meaning in the world? What can I offer? And on a practical level, what career is the best fit for my talents and interests? What are organizations looking for in a new hire?

Some may know the answers to these questions and have their career path carefully plotted out, but most of us don't, at least not without a lot of soul searching, investigation, and trial and error.

You may feel that everyone has their career plan figured out but you. They don't.

It's easy to feel anxious. Now, probably for the first time, you'll be deviating from the world of school to face a whole world of possibilities. You have to figure out what you want to do. You have to choose a major, then a career path, and then you have to find a job.

Many students find choosing a career path the most difficult transition of their lives. It's easy to feel overwhelmed by the options and unsure of what field is right for you.

The Hardest Question: What's Your Career Identity?

It should be comforting to know that successful people rarely lead orderly, linear lives. Misfires are rampant. Many people are terrible at picking careers, especially the first time out. Only about 5 percent get it right the first time, according to one economist's estimate. You might not, either. Nearly 80 percent of workers in their twenties and more than half of all adults said they wanted to change careers, according to one study.

Many of us make career choices haphazardly. We see the exciting lives of lawyers, doctors, politicians, or crime investigators on television and buy into the hype. But in the real world, few people live the fictional fantasy. The truth is usually more mundane, even undesirable. Look at the discrepancy between the TV image of the law profession and the reality. The majority of US lawyers regret their career choice and wouldn't recommend others to take up law. Four in ten lawyers in the UK wouldn't either.

> "Destiny" is a dramatic word, but the first step in launching your career is examining yourself and identifying your career destiny—the one you want to create for yourself.

Your major isn't a life sentence; it's only a starting point. For many people, where they end up isn't a direct result of their major. Your career is a marathon, not a sprint, and you may only discover your destiny after much trial and error. But now with the prevalence of internships, it's easier to speed things up and get a taste of different jobs while you are a student.

Remember that your first job is not your last. Don't think you have to find the perfect first job; it probably doesn't exist. There are many jobs that could serve as a launching pad to your career destiny. Open yourself to the possibilities.

Job Number One at College: Figuring Out Your Career Destiny

Don't assume you will figure all this out without too much effort however, or that everything will fall into place at graduation. One of life's biggest challenges is discovering what you want to be when you grow up and the path you'll take to get there.

Make this process of self-discovery a key purpose of your university years. Your goal is to determine what you can offer the world. Have you separated your goals from other people's vision of your future? Have you faced up to the distractions you're hearing from your parents, friends, and society? Many define success in terms of the size of their paycheck, and if that's important to you, make it part of your decision making.

On a more granular level, you need to identify the industries, jobs, and career paths that match your strengths and preferences. Are there suitable opportunities in the marketplace? Don't blithely assume that "it will all work out."

We're often forced to choose a career at a young age and can feel stuck with the decision. You owe it to yourself to rethink your direction if you're having second thoughts. Do you really know how you feel about your career choice? Are you afraid of what your family or friends will think if you make an about-face? If there were no penalties, would you select a different career path? Life is too short to settle.

Choosing Your Career Path

The end result of your self-assessment should be a definite list of possible career paths. Usually there's no dramatic epiphany, but a series of experiences that lead you in one direction over another. A career path is a group of jobs within a professional arena that uses similar skills. For example, if your strengths are interpersonal and teamwork skills along with problem-solving and analytical skills, you might target a career in marketing as Erin decided to do.

> A career path is a group of jobs within a career arena that use similar skills. You can chart a course from entry-level on up.

Marketing, the conduit between product development and sales, is a broad field that comprises many different career paths. Think of marketing as a big warehouse that includes aspects of advertising, brand management, market research, media planning, public relations, social media, sales, marketing analytics, digital marketing, and the like. It's the job of marketers in all of these specialties to create, enhance, and grow brands.

In advertising alone, there are career paths for creative directors, account executives, account coordinators, media directors, media planners, commercial producers, planners, digital advertising experts, ad salespeople, and market researchers. You could work in a large company as part of the marketing brand management team, in an ad agency, or in a digital agency. Each career path has a progression of jobs from entry-level to more senior roles.

If you're interested in marketing, there are a number of possible majors. The most obvious is to major in business, marketing, communications, or even advertising. But many liberal arts majors go into marketing successfully as well. (I was one.)

Erin had majored in psychology because she was interested in what makes people tick, but she wasn't interested in clinical work or going to medical school and becoming a psychiatrist. No, she wanted to parlay her interest in the *human mind-set* (psychology of people) into an interest in the *consumer mind-set* (how customers make buying decisions).

The most obvious career path for Erin was in market research or account planning, areas that focus on consumers: why they choose one brand over another and how they are affected by advertising messages. But there were broader areas in marketing where she could fit in as well. Erin was also interested in trends and forecasting the new hot thing. The more she researched, the more excited she became about pursuing a marketing career path.

When Erin searched "trending skills in marketing," she found a list of the growth jobs in marketing, many of which require an aptitude for technology. She made a note of that. It's smart to acquire at least one of these new skill sets; if you master two or more, you will stand out.

Crowdsearching Career Paths on LinkedIn

There is no special formula or whizzy algorithm that will give you your calling, but social media sites like LinkedIn and career counselors are trying very hard to crack the code. And when they do, as a digital native, you will no doubt embrace the app that helps you select your career path.

In the meantime, you can use LinkedIn's new tools expressly for young adults to explore career paths and jobs (linkedin.com/edu). The social media giant has been collecting information on its over 396 million members: where they went to college, their major, job history, skills acquired, and other data points. Now, they're making it easy for you to crowdsearch and research possible career tracks.

You can crunch the variables and reverse engineer the results to plot your own career path. LinkedIn's tools make it easy to connect the dots on how successful people rose to the top of their careers and their sequence of jobs along the way. Presumably, you can too if you follow their career plan.

You can explore what kind of education and jobs people had before becoming a car designer for BMW, working in product development at Apple, or becoming finance minister in France. You can discover where people who majored in sociology at your university ended up or what schools people attended before getting a job in financial services in London.

Look for themes and overlapping pathways that people took from the time they graduated from school to getting that wonderful job. What job experiences, skills, and accomplishments are highlighted in their profiles? All this crowdsourcing on LinkedIn will help you make decisions about how to "package" yourself. What experiences and professional groups might be the best pathway? What jobs and internships should you explore to make yourself a more attractive job candidate?

Self-Discovery Is Never Easy

While LinkedIn's tools can overwhelm with data overload, many people's initial career decisions are based on incomplete data, as new grad Jessica discovered. Jessica went to a private liberal arts college, majored in sociology and political science, and worked as a news reporter for the campus newspaper. Her vision for her brand: intrepid international news reporter.

Caught up in the college bubble and focusing on her grades, Jessica waited until after graduation before applying for a three-month internship with a TV station in a large metropolitan city, an opportunity that she discovered on Mediabistro.com, a website that specializes in media jobs and internships. She went through a mass interview with over 100 other finalists in the room before getting one of the coveted positions.

Yet after her short internship, Jessica scratched international journalist off her list of desirable careers. Why? She saw firsthand the long hours—including evenings and weekends—that most journalists have to work, especially if they're covering breaking news.

Jessica had focused on the substance of the job without thinking much about the lifestyle of a journalist. "I don't have a personal life. This is my life," one journalist told her. "I hate not being home at 7:00 p.m. and not having a choice about working weekends." Other journalists said they were worried about losing their jobs since many networks, cable news, and newspapers were adopting a model of employing poorly paid freelancers. Suddenly, her career dream of being a global roving reporter didn't seem as inviting.

Jessica had another career idea: to do something meaningful in the nonprofit arena. She signed up for a yearlong paid internship working with homeless children. She ended up scratching that career path before her internship was up, too.

What was wrong here?

Jessica stuck it out to complete her commitment but was disillusioned by the low pay and the lack of opportunity. Most nonprofits were scrappy organizations with anemic budgets and few full-time openings. When they did hire, they looked for candidates with a JD or a master's degree. Jessica would have to invest more time and money, and already she was worried about the return on her college investment. As interested as she was in making meaning in the world, she wasn't sure there was much of a future for her in nonprofits.

The Honeymoon Is Over

Neither of these careers was true to Jessica's authentic self. They were not in sync with who she was professionally or how she wanted to live personally.

Like many of her classmates, she moved back in her high school bedroom to figure out a new career path in a world where so many jobs are freelance, part-time or temp-to-permanent positions.

What should Jessica have done differently?

The tough economy certainly made her job search more difficult. Jessica had done two internships, but maybe she could have done them earlier or sought more informational interviews. Now, more than ever, you can glimpse the inside working of careers by following people in the field on Twitter. That way, Jessica could have put her career aspirations in a real-world context to determine whether her perceptions matched reality. She may have been able to discover early on that her dream careers were more nightmare than dream given her preferences and values.

Jessica even thought that taking a gap year before college would have given her time to explore possibilities and think about what was important to her in a career. Then, when she went away to college, she would have been more focused and had greater self-awareness as an undergraduate.

Much was gained, too. Jessica discovered what was critical to her (challenge, meaning, and balance) and what wasn't. In her career journey, Jessica discovered a better way to use her journalistic writing skills and social consciousness by creating social media content and blog posts for promising start-ups whose mission and culture she admired.

Today, her pitch for her brand is, "Desire to make a difference. Passionate about writing."

Your Passion vs. Your Career Path

Sure, we've all heard the advice: "Follow your passion." It's great when you hit the jackpot and find a career that melds your strengths and passions, and where there is demand in the marketplace.

But if your goal is to get a job at the end of the rainbow, you must distinguish between your major, your passions, your strengths, and your career path.

Your strengths are more important than your passions. Studies show that the best career choices tend to be grounded in things you're good at, more so than your interests and passions. Ideally, you want to find a convergence of your strengths and your values with a career path that is in demand.

> Interests can come and go.
> Your strengths are your core, your hard-wired assets.
> The source of your career power.

If you're a philosophy major, chances are your passion is not something you can make a living at unless you plan to teach. Your passion may be Greek philosophy, and you can major in it, but you should realize that no organization is looking for a resident "philosopher."

Like many liberal arts majors, you will need to figure out your career path. Don't let your major define you. Your career path could be in business or hospital administration or whatever. And if you are starting to think with a branding mind-set, you'll take some courses and do some internships that relate to your career interests so that you have a good pitch and story to tell.

Some Passions Are Better as a Lifestyle

Sometimes your passion is best left as part of your lifestyle and not your career. My teenage son's passion is slopestyle skiing, and like many of his friends, he dreams of being a pro skier or working in the ski industry.

But you have to be careful. Is it realistic? Is he really good enough to get sponsorship? Most of the jobs in the ski industry wouldn't support a skiing lifestyle.

Finding your career path requires self-awareness and knowledge of your strengths and cognitive abilities. But it also requires a clearheaded look at the reality of the marketplace. You need to find the intersection of your strengths and opportunity. Otherwise, you'll leave your career future to chance.

Before You Decide: Widen Your Options

Once in school, it's easy to busy yourself with activities and studies. Graduation and the real world always seem so far away—until they aren't. The best decisions come about when you begin with a wide set of options and take time to explore. Put together a career notebook and write down whatever jobs might match your strengths and interests.

Don't limit yourself to what you know or confine yourself to a narrow niche before exploring the possibilities. There are thousands of possible careers, so do research to start to understand what they are. Talk to people. Set up informational interviews and internships so you can see the career from close up.

Look at where the jobs are. Computer programmers, data analysts, physician's assistants, software developers, and petroleum engineers are in high demand and expected to be among the best-paying jobs over the next decade. If you're good in math and science, why not explore some of them? You might be surprised and find your preconceived notions are myths. For example, many people think the majority of jobs at tech companies require programming skills. Not true: 70 percent don't, according to one study.

After all, every tech company has marketers, salespeople, strategists, HR professionals, and the like who must understand IT in a broad sense but don't have to know coding languages.

There's so much you can do to figure out your career path while you're still a student. Take career assessment tests, seek informational interviews, explore internships, or research options online. You want to find out as early as possible if Brand You and your career choice are in sync—or on a collision course.

The Road Less Traveled

How do you increase your chance of success when there are so many competitors pursuing the same opportunity?

It's simple.

Follow the playbook used by big brands. If your category is crowded, look to new markets for growth. A brand like Pepsi created new markets through its line extensions of the brand (Diet Pepsi and Pepsi MAX) and new beverage categories and brands (Gatorade, Naked Juice, AMP Energy, Izze, etc.).

Likewise, if you find yourself competing with many talented people in a popular, crowded field, maybe it's time for you to break away and find a new market, too, as David Mullett did.

An art history major, David taught himself how to use a computer for video editing and launched a career producing music videos. His idea was to learn the craft of film and develop a personal style. Because he was fascinated by the English film style, David enrolled in a master's degree program at the prestigious Royal College of Art in London. There he learned a more conceptual approach than American film education offers, which is often more focused on technique. It was a great opportunity to experiment with his style and approach while expanding his global network.

Film was an exciting category, but David felt it was too crowded and too competitive, with many talented directors scraping for interesting projects. While studying film, he became aware of the new technology of virtual reality (VR): three-dimensional, computer-generated immersive video experiences that can be interacted with in a seemingly real way.

Creatively, he felt VR suited his training and talent. But there was another appeal. David sensed there would be more opportunities because it was a new field just getting off the ground and there were few people who could actually create VR. The patterns and dominant individuals had not been established yet.

A friend told him about the first virtual reality conference in Silicon Valley, and David found the nascent VR community friendly, helpful, and eager to meet up and do projects together. As he got more involved in the community, he put together a team. After writing an article on VR, David and his group developed two demo reels, one animated and one live action, to show how VR can create exciting, transformative brand experiences.

Before long, David had a new identity as a director of breakthrough virtual reality content. Finding a new market for his talents, one that was growing fast but not yet crowded with talent, allowed him to make his mark.

Informational Interviews: The Trojan Horse

A good way to check for career fit is an informational interview. Much less time-consuming than internships, this is a short conversational meeting over the phone or in person to find out more about a career path or job function. It is not a meeting to pester someone about helping you to find a job.

In addition to the knowledge you'll get from people in the trenches, an informational interview is a smart tactical move that gets you inside companies much more easily than if you say, "I'm looking for a job or an internship." After all, you're only asking for fifteen minutes or so to learn more about the company and industry, so company executives and employees are more likely to agree. Do not send them your resume via email or give one to your interviewer unless you are asked for it.

Most people like to help out students and new graduates and recall their own days just starting out. If you hit it off, your company contact might help you meet other people or put in a good word to the HR manager.

If given the option of speaking over the telephone or meeting in person, always opt for the in-person interview. Face-to-face meetings give you the opportunity to bond and get help for your job search. One upcoming graduate, Stella, went for an informational interview and was told about a new job opening that had just been approved. Right then and there, she was escorted to the hiring manager and got the job. None of this would have happened if Stella had taken the easier route of speaking over the phone.

Make your informational interviews short and fun for the company contact. You want to appear knowledgeable about the company and industry, but you don't want to bombard your contact with super smart questions such as, "What is your strategy in Asia?" That makes it feel like work for them. Prepare a more casual and conversational lineup of questions, such as the following:

- What career advice do you have for someone just starting out?
- What aspects of your college experience best prepared you for your career?
- How did you choose your career? Get your first job?
- How did you navigate your career path and make career decisions along the way?
- What should I be aware of about this job or industry?
- How would you describe the company culture?

Internships: Your Test Markets

Go for full immersion with an internship. It is a great way to explore a career in depth before committing to a career path and your life's mission. Brand managers do *test markets* in smaller towns to try out new products and advertising campaigns. That way they can *fail fast* and go back to the drawing board before investing too much time, money, and energy.

You should test out your possible career paths, too. There's no better way to decide if a career is right for you than by experiencing it firsthand in a short-term internship. You could discover that you've been caught up in a reality distortion field and the actual job is nothing like what you expected. Better to learn this early so you can rethink your career destiny or even change majors before it's too late.

Not all internships are created equal. Some will give you real on-the-job-experience; others might just be grunt work. The reason you want an internship is to test out the career and get real job skills, so make sure to ask smart questions before you make the commitment. Will the experience give you a good understanding of the organization and potential careers? Will you be involved in teamwork projects? How does the internship role compare with entry-level jobs at the company?

When compiling a list of potential internships, include companies near your university for internships during the school year and a broader list of dream companies for summer internships. Include both large and small companies in your search to see which align best with your preferences and personality.

Some internship programs at large companies are highly sought after. These companies may offer structured entry-level career development programs as a pipeline into the field. Internships at smaller companies tend to be more free-form, and sometimes you can even create your own internship experience.

Remember to always try to trade up: turn informational interviews into internships and internships into job offers. To do so, you must excitedly and accurately perform what is asked of you.

Finding an Internship: Let Me Count the Ways

As an enterprising internship hunter, look beyond the internships offered at your university's Career Services Office, which is what most students rely on for internship placement. These opportunities may end up being less relevant and useful than the ones you find for yourself. Cole, our enterprising real estate analyst, did four internships through his CSO, including one for a bicycle company and another for a custom dress shirt company. The CSO internships were both great for networking with alumni and connecting to the community, but the internships he found himself were more closely targeted to the real estate investment area, his chosen career path, and the reason he got multiple job offers.

Here are some of the best ways to locate an internship:

- **Check out your university's CSO to see what internships they offer.**

  Your CSO is intended to serve as internship central for students, particularly juniors and seniors. Make an appointment to get advice, learn about the companies they have relationships with, and explore their connections. CSOs at large universities generally have the biggest range of opportunities. Often a major percentage of university internships, particularly at smaller colleges, are at companies and small start-ups where they have an alumni connection.

- **Create your own list of target companies and pitch them directly.**

  Often large companies have an "internship coordinator" or an internship portal on their websites. At smaller companies, it generally pays to go to the top. For companies both large and small, it can be smart to seek out the head of the functional area you're pursuing. For all of your target companies, send out a compelling pitch email outlining your interest in an internship.

- **Reach out to alumni.**

  Check your university's alumni directory and LinkedIn to see if you can connect to alumni who work at your target companies or are in job functions of interest to you. See if they will put in a good word to the internship coordinator or hiring manager.

- **Tell your family and friends.**

  Tell all your friends and acquaintances that you are looking for an internship. Often the best opportunities come from people you know connecting you with one of their contacts.

- **Go online for internship opportunities.**

  There is a cornucopia of resources online for discovering internships. Here are important tactics to master:

  1. Check out company websites and look under the "careers" or "jobs" sections. Larger companies often have an internship tab.

  2. Google "Internships at X Company," "Paid internships in X industry," or "X internships in [local area]" to find job postings that meet your specific requirements.

  3. Look on websites, that are completely dedicated to internships, such as internships.com and internmatch.com.

  4. Search broad job boards, such as LinkedIn, Glassdoor, and Simply Hired, that have lots of internship listings along with job listings.

  5. Explore niche job boards, such as FindSpark for creative internships, Mediabistro for media internships, and VentureLoop for venture-backed start-ups. Google "Best [industry or job function] job boards" to find niche boards in your focus areas.

  6. Look at idealist.org and globalexperiences.com for nonprofit internship opportunities.

Never underestimate the power of writing a compelling pitch email for an internship that is conversational and not robotic, that is targeted and not just a generic pitch. Something like this:

Dear Ms. Smith,

Currently I am a sophomore majoring in finance at X University, planning to pursue a career in investment analysis and portfolio management, and I feel I would be a good match for your summer internship program.

I have long admired Z Company. Your financial management team and its equity and fixed income funds have been top performers over the last ten years. Your value style of investing is of particular interest, and I've been impressed with the innovative investment products that you've created for investors.

My resume is attached and provides details of my skills, work history, and academic performance. I feel confident that I will be able to add value to the team as an intern.

Sincerely,

Tom Jones

The Lure of Making the World Better

Sometimes your career direction is shaped by a transformative life experience. Alexa Herzog's family moved frequently during her childhood, so she saw firsthand huge wealth disparity when living in Mexico City and other places. That experience gave her a mission to do something about injustice, particularly income injustice.

In college she majored in social policy, and junior year she got an internship through her school with a nonprofit attorney in Chicago who focused on the legal system's treatment of people with mental health issues.

Her relationship with this attorney led to a yearlong internship with a nonprofit that had just received a grant involving the new Affordable Care Act (ACA), and she became an early expert in the intricacies of the new health-care program. She had found her niche. Alexa became a health-care advocate. It was not quite her original intention to fight income injustice, but career paths often meander until you find your role.

Writing a successful grant proposal is also often critical to getting jobs in the nonprofit arena. As her internship was coming to an end, Alexa worked with the fellowship professional at her university's Career Services Office, who advised her on how to write an application for the Urban Fellows program. Her application package consisted of a resume, three letters of reference, and a personal recommendation on a critical policy issue that she was passionate about. Alexa chose the need for mental health reform in prisons like New York City's notorious jail complex on Rikers Island, and soon she was off on her new adventure as an urban fellow.

Who Am I? Tests

Assessment tests such as the Myers-Briggs Type Indicator (MBTI), the Strong Interest Inventory, Johnson O'Connor assessment test, and StrengthsFinder can help you understand your inborn career strengths and steer your career in the right direction. Some versions are available free or for a fee online. Often the fee-based tests come with one-on-one career coaching by a certified practitioner to help you interpret your career profile. Many university Career Services Offices provide assessment testing followed by individual coaching for undergraduates. If your university does, sign up now.

The MBTI, which has its roots in Carl Jung's theory of psychological types, categorizes people into sixteen different types based on four pairs of opposites: Extraversion (E) and Introversion (I); Sensing (S) and Intuition (I); Thinking (T) and Feeling (F); and Judging (J) and Perceiving (P).

The Strong Interest Inventory, one of the oldest and most reliable career tests, is based on six general occupational themes: Realistic, Investigative, Artistic, Social, Enterprising, and Conventional (RIASEC).

StrengthsFinder, introduced in the international best seller *Now, Discover Your Strengths*, by Marcus Buckingham and Donald O. Clifton, helps you find your top five talents. There are other tests that offer comprehensive career testing and ways of examining yourself holistically. Consider not only your skills and strengths, but also your style, personality, and what motivates you.

If you're like many people, you'll have an "Aha!" moment after taking these tests and feel, That's me!

Take a Selfie with Friends

The market research done by marketers on consumers is often spot on, uncovering insights the brand "experts" missed. Likewise, you can find a breakthrough in your brand idea and career path through "market research" with friends, mentors, coworkers, or family about your strengths and career direction. Often we're too close and can't see ourselves as clearly as others can.

This doesn't mean that your friends and others are allowed to determine your identity or choose your career. Only you can define Brand You. But it is helpful to gather additional perceptions and insights that you can use together with assessment tests and your self-evaluation.

The best way to undertake personal career research is informally, over coffee or lunch. Don't share the topic beforehand; the comments and suggestions should be fresh and unfiltered. You can begin the conversation by telling the interviewee that you are doing a personal branding exercise exploring your strengths and possible career paths, and you want to get their thoughts. Here are some questions to ask them:

"MARKET RESEARCH" QUESTIONS TO ASK FRIENDS

- When you think of personal strengths and things that I am really good at, what comes to mind? Why do I stand out in that area?
- If you imagine a career or job I'd be really good at, what comes to mind?
- If you visualize me at the peak of my career success, what would I be doing?
- If you were to think of a job that would not suit me and I should avoid, what comes to mind?
- If I were a character on TV or in the movies, who would it be? Why do you say that?
- If I were a well-known world leader in business, government, nonprofits, or the professions, who would it be?
- What skill set or professional strength should I develop more?

Listen to what the other person says, but don't disagree; simply write down what they share. You can probe with, "Why do you think that?" or, "Can you give me an example?" That way you're more likely to hear something useful.

You need to discover how others perceive you and whether they see the same strengths that you want to be known for. Find out what careers and jobs they think would be a good fit for you, and why. You might be surprised at how good their ideas are. You also need to uncover your *blind spots*, the ways you come across that you aren't even aware of (and we all have them).

The SWOT Analysis

Marketers often use a handy tool called the SWOT analysis, a snapshot of a given brand's strengths, weaknesses, opportunities, and threats. It's also valuable when considering careers because it forces you to match your strengths to opportunities in the job market and to be on the lookout for threats to your career path. Try plotting your strengths, weaknesses, opportunities, and threats on a SWOT matrix.

SWOT Matrix	
Strengths	Weaknesses
Opportunities	Threats

Strengths and Weaknesses

"Strengths" and "weaknesses," the first two areas, deal with you.

Think of strengths as assets that could be links to your career choice and future success. Assets are areas you can build on, and practically anything could be an asset. Start with skills, experiences, and accomplishments. What do you find fun to do? What advantages do you have that others don't? What do you do better than anyone else? Do you have any valuable strategic connections, such as mentors or family friends who are recruiters or work in the field you are targeting?

Then expand your list of strengths to include personality traits. Expand it further to include anyone you have known or even met, and anything that you have explored or been interested in. The hidden assets or self-taught skills that come up through probing often hold the key leading to a breakthrough in finding your career direction.

Look for careers that match your strengths. For example, ask yourself: If you could have any job in the world, what would it be? At the end of your life, what do you want to be known for? Write down all your strengths and assets in the Strengths box in the matrix.

Weaknesses, areas where you are not on solid ground, should be avoided. However, some weaknesses, such as poor relationship, teamwork, communication, and networking skills, should be targeted for development and improvement, as they will be integral to your career success.

What tasks do you hate doing? What do friends and family criticize you for? What are the weak points in your skill set or education that people bring up in interviews? What bad habits hold you back? Write down your weaknesses in the top right box.

Opportunities and Threats

The "opportunities" and "threats" sections in the SWOT analysis deal with things outside your control, such as the economy, that could affect your career. What outside circumstances might dramatically change your career prospects? Is a given profession in a growth phase or downward spiral?

Whatever career you're considering, search for "trending skills in X" to find out what new skills are growing in demand. Figure out how you can learn some of those skills, whether online or through a workshop or course.

The world is dynamic, always full of movement and change. The business news regularly reports on threats to the economy, individual industries, and companies along with new opportunities. Change always creates new opportunities and new threats. What trends do you see in your target industry, and how can you take advantage of them?

Recognize opportunities and threats on a more personal level. What networking events and conferences could be important for you to attend? Professional conferences often have special sessions (and pricing) for students and new graduates, which can be invaluable in launching your career, building your career network, and providing insight into various career paths. Are there shortcomings in your skills and background that keep coming up in interviews? Could any of your weak points lead to threats?

For example, start anticipating the job market in the fields you are exploring. Some areas will offer tons of growth and financial rewards, while others will be tough slogging. In the 1990s, Wall Street and high technology were the hot spots, and many people rode those waves to fame and fortune. Today, high tech is still thriving; financial services less so. You need to find the best wave to ride for your future.

S + C + V + D = O

Try to find the sweet spot: a career opportunity (O) that plays to your strengths (S), particularly strengths that are unusual, where you have credentials (C) through internships, job experience, coursework, and certificates. It's also important to consider your values (V) and the kind of culture you'd thrive in, especially where there is demand (D)—actual opportunities in the marketplace. When all are aligned, you have found the perfect job for you at this juncture in your life.

When our French MBA, Edouard, did his self-assessment, he decided that one of his key strengths that set him apart was that he was a *creative* MBA: he had *the mind of a businessman* but the *soul of a creative person*. Since he had studied for a year in the US, he was fluent in both English and French and comfortable in both the EU and American cultures, so he wanted to work at a multinational company where his background would be a plus. In terms of values, Edouard preferred a dynamic environment where innovation and creative thinking were prized. (His MBA thesis had been on innovation in India.)

But how did Edouard fit in? What was the best role for him? After conducting "market research" with friends and colleagues, along with informational interviews, he devised a career path in business development, where he could use his drive, ambition, and relationship skills to grow sales and revenues. But he didn't want to work in business development for your typical corporation; he targeted innovation think tanks, creative and digital marketing agencies, and start-ups that aligned well with his personal values and creative and business DNA.

Be a T-Shaped Person

To prepare yourself for just about anything the future brings, become a "T-shaped" student or professional, not an "I-shaped" one. Think of the "T" as firmly rooted with a deep foundation, yet possessing expansive abilities. Meanwhile the "I" is narrow and limited.

The vertical stroke of the "T" represents a *depth* of skill or knowledge in a specific discipline. This could be business, science, engineering, coding, marketing, psychology, medicine, art history, what have you.

> The T-shaped job applicant:
> The vertical stroke represents *depth* in a specific discipline.
> The horizontal stroke represents *breadth* across disciplines.

The defining element of the T-shaped person is the horizontal stroke, which represents breadth across disciplines and the ability to perform different job functions. T-shaped people recognize the importance of soft power skills like leadership and collaborating with diverse groups, not just academic strength in their area of expertise.

In contrast, the I-shaped person focuses on their academic silo, and one particular knowledge and skill set becomes the sole object of their life's work. Expertise in your discipline can get you off to a great start career-wise, but you will be unable to move up to more prominent roles without broader soft and crossover skills.

In the intertwined world of today, it's not enough to be good at one thing; you must develop broad strengths that transcend all disciplines.

"Packaging" Your Brand with the Right Stuff

Today's challenging marketplace is like an arms race, and new entrants are compelled to acquire experiences, skills, and credentials that will make their brand stand out. What "ingredients" might enhance the perception of your brand? Even a degree from a prestigious school might not be enough unless you have a technical minor or take some vocationally focused classes. Look for ways to be uniquely qualified. So if you're a liberal arts major, think about a minor in computer science or business. Or if you have a vocational major, think of what "soft power" courses could help you stand out.

Consider the continuous *product improvement* and *product enhancement* efforts undertaken by major brands. You must add the right skills and competencies to the mix in order to stay competitive on a global level. We live in a world where there are thousands of certifications for just about every conceivable skill and competency. How do you know which ones will add value? Seek out information online about which certificates are best, and when going on informational interviews, ask your company contact what skills are most in demand. Joining a club or professional organization and chairing a committee is another way to enhance your brand marketability. For example, if you are exploring a career in finance, volunteer to be club treasurer.

On an internship at a major fashion retailer, Erin, our aspiring marketer, learned how to use Microsoft Excel pivot tables to analyze sales and performance results. "I could have learned this on my own if I knew that it was an important skill for entry-level jobs in marketing and merchandising," she told me. That credential on her resume was important in landing a great first job.

In most things, less is more.
In job hunting, more is better.

Many career paths are skill and certificate driven, probably none more than IT. In addition to regular and online certifications, there are a host of IT certifications offered by software and hardware producers. For programming internships and jobs, employers look for coding languages like Java, SQL, Python, C++, or JavaScript.

Certifications can enhance your prospects in many careers, consider pursuing the Professional in Human Resources certification or one of the Project Management Institute certificates. Many MBA programs don't offer manufacturing-specific courses, so you can enhance your marketability with certifications in supply chain and operations management through the professional association, APICS.

Certificates signal value and show motivation. Remember Cole, our enterprising real estate analyst? By the time he graduated, he had certifications in Discounted Cash Flow, Argus Validation DCF, Compatible Valuation, and Bloomberg Essentials, among other credentials. Certificates can be the tiebreaker in a close job competition and, depending on your path, grease the transition from college to career.

To Double-Major or Not

There's been a dramatic 85 percent uptick in the number of students graduating with double majors over the last ten years, according to the US Department of Education. It's partly driven by a bad economy, partly driven by the belief that more is better.

For some career paths, a double major can increase your marketability. If you're a double major in applied mathematics and business, you have strong credentials for a career as a risk analyst, a decision science analyst, or in a related field. If you have a degree in public health and sociology or economics, you should stand out from the crowd of other candidates seeking an entry-level job as a health policy analyst.

But often, double majors add little value. For example, one new grad did a double major in communications and photography. It was a classic case of "one for me and one for Mom." (You probably have figured out who was who.)

Certain negatives also come with a double major. The cost of an extra year's tuition and foregone earnings can be exorbitant. You might confuse potential employers who are unsure if you're an apple or an orange unless there is a clear synergy between the two majors. And taking all those extra courses can reduce the time you have to indulge in internships and other activities that can burnish your resume more than a double major.

Unnecessary Baggage

In your quest for self-knowledge and career direction, you also will want to reexamine any family and personal messages that you are carrying around. Some of the beliefs in your family creed are assets that will form the bedrock of your identity and future success. Others may be baggage that's better stowed away or thrown out.

Maybe your father is a respected lawyer or your mother is a doctor, and you feel compelled to follow in his or her footsteps. Maybe they have limited ideas of what careers would be best for a woman. Maybe you feel that because you didn't go to a name university, you can't compete for top jobs.

My parents gave me many positive messages, for which I will always be grateful. Having grown up in a difficult economy, job security was paramount to them, and they urged me to take the civil service exam and work in government as they did. But if you're reading this book, you know that we each are unique and have to build our careers based on our strengths and desires. I knew that most government jobs would not have been right for me and never regretted my decision.

Often the most destructive messages are personal ones that you created yourself or assimilated from family baggage. We each have to replace negative credos with positive messages. When applying for jobs, it's easy to give yourself negative messages such as, "I bet everyone else is better qualified than me," but you'll be more confident if you replace them with thoughts such as, "I can bring real value to this company."

Finding your career path is your chance to live your dream. Our strengths and desires are powerful motivators, and far too powerful to ignore.

We have all spent too much time doing what others expect of us. Finding your brand is about determining your career path and then following your own heart.

Chapter 2 Exercises

1. Do this self-evaluation by writing down whatever first comes to mind:
   - What is unusual or special about me?
   - What specific qualities or abilities make me different from or even better than others?
   - What words or phrases do I want people to associate with me?
   - What skill set, ability, or professional strength should I develop more?
2. Now do one-to-one "market research" with friends and professional colleagues. Tell them you are working on a personal branding project and wanted them to provide input. Tell them to say whatever first comes to mind:

- I am trying to differentiate my brand. If I were to ask you, "What is unusual or special about me?" what comes to mind?
- What specific qualities or abilities are different from or even better than others?
- When you think of me, what words or phrases come to mind?
- If you imagine a career or job I'd be really good at, what comes to mind?
- If you visualize me at the peak of my career success, what would I be doing?
- If you were to think of a job that would not suit me and I should avoid, what comes to mind?
- If I were a character on TV or in the movies, who would it be? Why do you say that?
- What skill sets, abilities, or professional strengths should I develop more?

3. Based on your own analysis and market research you've done with friends and colleagues, fill in the matrix in the SWOT analysis of your strengths, weaknesses, opportunities, and threats in the marketplace.

4. Explore one of the popular career assessment tests like Myers-Briggs or StrengthsFinder available online.

5. Are there specific certifications and competencies that can improve your marketability in your chosen career? How can you acquire them?

6. Who are the supportive people in your life giving you positive messages about job hunting? How can you increase their influence?

7. Is anyone giving you negative messages about the job market? How can you decrease their influence?

CHAPTER 3

Pitching Yourself Like a Pro

If you can tell employers why you are better, different, or unique, you will get them interested. But if you can tell them how you can solve their problem, the job offer will likely be yours. You might have your career path selected, but you won't get a job until you can convince someone that you're the perfect fit. That's where the pitch outlining your *unique selling proposition* (USP) comes in.

A pitch should convey the core idea you want people to remember about you. It's your hook, the foundation of your career story.

A pitch's purpose is not to educate. It's to sell.

Its purpose is not to teach. It's to excite.

Your pitch is not about what you want to get out of working at the company. It details how you will solve a problem or relieve pain.

A pitch should be catchy or interesting enough to grab the hiring manager's attention. With practice and refinement, yours will be memorable, persuasive, and good enough to get you the job. After all, you're selling your best idea, Brand You.

> A pitch is a punchy, succinct, and convincing summary of the value you will bring to a job.

Learning to pitch well is especially important for new graduates. Since you don't have a strong track record yet, you will have to use a little artifice and thought. But don't think you can't develop an effective pitch as a new grad. You can, and it will pay off.

After all, if you can't articulate your value clearly and succinctly, how will you stand out? How will you get hired? You need to narrow your focus and bring the sizzle.

Your pitch should answer the questions "What?" and, "For whom?" There are different versions of the pitch. (1) The *elevator pitch*, a short, punchy summary of your personal value, should be thirty to sixty seconds in length, about as long as a brief elevator ride. Use this in interviews and networking events. (2) Your LinkedIn profile, particularly the headline and summary, is a *virtual version* of your pitch. (3) Your resume's profile summary and your cover letters are *printed versions* of your pitch.

Establish Your USP (Unique Selling Proposition)

In a job interview, the first ten seconds and the first ten words are the most important. Dramatize the opening of your elevator speech with a line or catchy phrase that telegraphs your value.

Your key pitch sentence should convey your unique selling proposition (USP). What are the marketable qualities or talents unique to you? How are you different? How does your USP tie in with your larger purpose—the meaning you want to make in the world? In the branding world, the USP is the basis of a brand's tagline or catchphrase. It's the theme tying everything together that conveys what is different, authentic, relevant, and meaningful about the brand. You want to do the same.

This sentence—the essence of your personal brand value—should be simple enough to fit on the back of a business card or cocktail napkin. If it can't be stated briefly and clearly, you probably have a muddled, complicated pitch. Go back to the drawing board and workshop it until it's perfect.

Your USP should dramatize a benefit and solve a problem. And it should be distinct enough to intrigue people and make them curious about you.

The pitch sentence, or USP, should meet these criteria:

- **Be different:** The cardinal rule of branding is to be different. You don't want to be like every Tom, Dick, and Harry. You're different, and your USP must capture your special sauce. (Ritz-Carlton Hotel's *We Are Ladies and Gentlemen Serving Ladies and Gentlemen*)
- **Ring true:** Build your USP around what you're good at, what you're passionate about, the value you bring, and even your style. Ask yourself, "What emotion am I selling?" (Apple's *Think Different*)
- **Relieve pain:** Your brand-positioning sentence should solve a problem, a pain point, or a need in the marketplace. It must connect with current

issues in your career arena. If you're not relevant to the market, you don't have a lot of value. (Volvo's *For Life*)

- **Make a difference:** The best pitches have a larger purpose and aim to transform the world in some way. Your purpose is *why* you do something. You're not looking for a job. You want to make a difference. (Nike's *Just Do It*)

After you've kicked off your interview with your USP, give examples and tell stories about how you can benefit the organization.

Don't Be Afraid to Be Different

In college, it may pay to fit in and go with the flow, to follow the group. But in the real world, what may seem safe (being like everyone else) is often risky (you won't stand out).

When competing with others for a job, it pays to have a different pitch that draws attention to yourself. Sticking out from the herd feels wildly uncomfortable the first time you do it. But sticking out in a good way gives people a reason to choose you.

To find out your differentiator, ask yourself what strengths, skills, and aptitudes make you different, even better than others. Complete the following sentence:

Unlike others who are interested in my career path, I . . .

Brands often try to own a word that conveys the essence of their USP, such as FedEx and "overnight" and Volvo and "safety." What's the word you want to own?

My First Job Pitch

I graduated in a terrible job market. I heard the same scary messages as everyone else and, having taken out student loans, I was anxious. A college degree and an interesting job would be my ticket to success.

I was determined not to go back to live with my parents, but job prospects didn't look good. As an undergraduate, my career plan was to be a journalist, so I had enrolled in Northwestern University's Medill School of Journalism. But early in my junior year, I had my first personal branding crisis and began doubting that journalism was the right career path for me.

So I started sampling other possible majors and career paths. I took a sociology course and did a summer internship at a social services agency in Chicago. No, that wasn't me, either, I realized by the end of the summer. I finally decided to major in art history—Asian art history, to be precise. It was not a promising career path, as my parents reminded me more than once.

Finally, late in my senior year, I dropped by the university's Career Services Office. It was my first visit. "You should have come earlier," they told me. "We don't know you."

So, yes, I did most everything wrong, but I did get lucky. (You can make missteps and get lucky, too). I hatched a plan to target four art museums with strong Asian art collections, two on the West Coast and two on the East Coast. (I was done with cold midwestern winters.) I used my best journalism skills to write a compelling cover letter and resume and waited for a response.

Three of the museums sent me form letters saying they would keep my resume on file. But one person, Henry Trubner, the Asian art curator at the Seattle Art Museum, wrote an encouraging reply. He might have an opening in his department since he was putting together an extensive catalog of the museum's Asian art collection and needed help researching and writing about the collection.

The USP Pitch

Here was my chance!

In my response letter to Henry, I pitched myself as *"an art historian who writes—an Asian-art-loving scribe."*

The letter went on to explain my USP, special expertise in both Asian art and writing. I described my journalism studies and offered to send writing samples. I tied my USP to a larger purpose: as a budding Asian art historian, I was anxious to make the Seattle Art Museum's prestigious Asian art collection more accessible to a larger audience.

What made the pitch successful?

My pitch was a USP, a unique selling proposition that not many people could make (or so I thought). After all, how many Asian art majors were there who had studied journalism?

It was the right pitch at the right time. It promised to relieve one of the hiring manager's pain points: the difficulty of preparing a major book on the museum's collection. I branded myself in a memorable sentence as an *Asian-art-loving scribe* who was dying for this opportunity to contribute to a world-class museum. I tried to connect emotionally with the museum's desire to make its collection available to a wider audience. My USP ultimately met my four key criteria. It was different, authentic, relevant, and meaningful.

> If you pitch well, you will stand out.
> If you keep pitching, you will succeed.

Luck played a role, sure, but I had the moxie to reach out directly to the hiring manager with a compelling pitch letter. (There were no job postings about the opening.)

Truthfully, I was lucky my first time out of the gate. I had stumbled upon an opportunity that was perfect for me at the time, and I was perfect for the museum. I had competitors from the nearby University of Washington's Asian art department, but no one had as compelling a pitch as I had. The reality was that I had just taken a few courses in Asian art, but I fulfilled a need and was enthusiastic. I never got that lucky again and have had to work hard for every other job offer. But I've always tried to give every job opportunity my best pitch, and you must too.

A Pitch Must Be Relevant

Probably no job change was as dramatic as mine when I decided to leave the world of Asian art and come to New York City to find work in advertising and branding. I flew into the city with a handful of contacts from college friends and the names of three media executives from my university. There was no online alumni directory—no Internet either, if you can picture such a far-off time. I had copied my contacts' names from 3x5-inch index cards in my university's career center.

It was not easy to uncover transferable skills between my prior experience and advertising. When I first arrived, my pitch was basically, "I've been working in a museum in the Asian art department and helped put a book together on the collection, and now I want to break into advertising."

The pitch was a dud. No one in advertising cared about my background in Asian art or what I wanted. Because I had only worked in the nonprofit world, ad execs didn't see how I could fit into a frenetically paced agency, even for an entry-level job.

I found myself branded, but not in the way that I wanted. I was seen as an academic, undesirable, too slow and plodding for the branding and advertising world.

So I dramatically revised my elevator pitch and my resume. I removed the overly academic and irrelevant aspects of my background, such as the museum catalog. I had translated a Japanese art book with a colleague, but that would go unmentioned as well. Excising major accomplishments was not easy; I was proud of my work on the two books, but they had to go. I decided instead to come up with a compelling pitch that would connect with ad agency folks.

A strong career identity requires curation. You must jettison any elements that might take people in the wrong direction. Instead, emphasize the parts of yourself that connect the dots to where you want to go and reveal how you can add value to the job you are seeking.

To make the switch convincing, I had to show ad executives that I was relevant. I came up with a new pitch: *I am a marketer for difficult products.* It was a USP pitch, too. It hit a pain point since every ad agency has certain products that are difficult to market, and consequently, no one wants to work on them.

In interviews, I likened marketing Asian art shows in a Western culture to marketing a difficult product. It took a certain ingenuity to find the right hook, and I had been successful at it. I told my potential employers to give me the difficult assignments to work on since I could find a way to make them sizzle.

My new pitch, "marketer for difficult products," was relevant, authentic, and different. (I had never met anyone who used that pitch.) And it got me my first job in advertising in New York City.

Tie Your USP to a Higher Purpose

It's very powerful to tie your brand to a higher purpose, as top brands do. (Take, for example, Apple's *Think Different* or Nike's *Just Do It.*) If asked,

"Why did you choose your career?" you need a more meaningful answer than that it was the first job offer you got.

Erin's pitch was: *Aspiring marketer with strong marketing analytics and the ability to capture the pulse of the consumer mind-set.* With this, she captured what differentiated her from other beginning marketers. She took her internship experience in marketing analytics and aligned it with her higher purpose: to understand the "consumer mind-set." This was supported by her background as a psychology major.

Edouard, our creative French MBA, needed to develop a pitch for going after business development jobs at ad agencies, digital agencies, and innovation firms. One person in his network told him that business development jobs were the "most dangerous jobs in advertising." Not exactly encouraging news for a first-time job seeker, but Edouard accepted the challenge. He soon learned the reason for the high turnover: few could bridge the gap between the account management and the creative sides of these businesses. Edouard knew he could. He was a creative businessperson, not your, number-crunching, green-eyeshade-wearing numbers guy. So Edouard captured his USP with this pitch line: *The creative MBA: the mind of a businessman and the soul of a creative person.* In short, he was an MBA with creative genes in his DNA.

Cole, our enterprising real estate analyst, wanted to emphasize two things that were different about his candidacy in his pitch: *Aspiring real estate analyst with lifelong love of real estate and extensive exposure through my many internships.* David, our virtual reality pioneer, pitched himself with the following: *Innovator of breakthrough virtual reality content that creates transformative brand experiences.*

Gwen, our equestrian engineer, wanted to work for a company involved in doing good, but she also wanted to move away from urban congestion to a semirural location near a tech hub.

She certainly had a novel USP pitch. In essence: *Top engineering graduate who left all behind to follow a dream of helping others.* In her pitch, Gwen recounts how she left two plum job offers, her family, her friends, and her home, packing up all her belongings that would fit in her car in order to pursue a more meaningful career and lifestyle goals. Her actions speak to her drive, determination, and passion to use her engineering degree to help others. It was a winning pitch that got her a job offer at a start-up creating innovative products for people with autism and ADHD.

As a job candidate, Gwen had the perfect balance between hard power (her engineering credentials) and soft power (her personal marketing). Her success also demonstrates the power of a great story. She was a woman who graduated first in her class in engineering school. She was captain of the equestrian team. She had a humanitarian mission. She was willing to leave family and friends behind in pursuit of a higher purpose. That's quite a story!

What's Your Line?

Here are some USP pitch lines that other college students, new grads, and young professionals have used to sell themselves for a first job:

- New human resources graduate trained and experienced in transformational organization efficiency design and change management
- Innovative computer programmer with a talent for creating breakthrough gaming apps
- Accountant, CPA, with tax and audit experience and internships at two of the Big Four accounting firms
- Aspiring financial analyst: analytical and creative, hardworking and driven, internship experience at X, Y, and Z Companies

What's your pitch line?

The Elevator Pitch

Once you have your USP pitch line, you're ready to develop your thirty-to-sixty second *elevator pitch*. (It's called an "elevator" pitch because it should last about as long as it takes to go a few floors on an elevator.) If you're asked broad questions such as, "Tell me about yourself?" or, "Why should I hire you?" in interviews, that's your cue to launch into your elevator pitch. The elevator pitch is also the foundation of your cover letter, LinkedIn profile, and the like.

We are influenced by beginnings and endings. The best elevator pitches begin with a memorable positioning sentence that communicates your career identity and the value you'd offer in a work situation. Then give examples, such as a compelling story about a project or internship that relates to your brand idea and the job at hand. It's smart to end with a question to get a conversation going.

Here's Erin's elevator pitch for an entry-level marketing job:

> You might say I'm a consumer mind reader. At X University, my focus area was psychology because of my fascination with the consumer mind-set and why people choose one product over another. I'm also fascinated by how trends and viral campaigns develop and grow, and how to predict what will be the next new thing.
>
> I spent last summer as an intern at Company D, where I did market research on how to reposition a media company in the new digital media era. The summer before, I interned with a very smart, dynamic team doing market research on a hot sauce that's more savory than anything on the market. Sales of ketchup and mustard are flat, but hot sauce is hot. One of our products that tested well was a hot sauce that had a tangy sweetness. Its tagline was, "Finally, a no-tears hot sauce."
>
> My internships helped me find my calling. I learned how to get insights from consumers, spot trends, and develop new products. On a more practical level, I learned how to put together sales projections, competitive analyses, and other analytical reports, so I'm confident I can hit the ground running. That's why I'm so interested in the position at XYZ Company. Can you tell me more about the marketing assistant's role?

Practice your elevator pitch until you can internalize what you plan to say. Tape yourself beforehand so that you can critique your performance. (See Chapters 6 and 7 for ideas on how to ace the interview and make a strong self-presentation.)

Don't Apologize for Your Major—Flaunt It

Embrace your major in your pitch. Don't disown it. Notice that Erin doesn't hide or downplay her psychology major, but uses it to give her background a different spin. You chose your major for a reason. You'll appear weak and a poor decision maker if you disparage your major, your college, or an internship experience in your pitch or in interviews.

Like Erin, tie in your major to the job you are looking for so it's a positive. For example, if you were an English major, talk about how it taught you to write and talk clearly and persuasively—great for sales, customer care, PR, and other careers. If it was sociology, discuss how it taught you to handle projects in diverse organizations and collaborate successfully in diverse teams—perfect for business, project management, nonprofit, and social entrepreneurship careers.

If you have a strong technical background in computer science or engineering, talk about how it gives you an edge not only in technical projects but in algorithmic thinking, solving complex problems, and making good decisions. If you're a liberal arts major with a broad array of courses, point out that being well-rounded gives you a broad perspective when problem-solving and innovating.

Here's how one new graduate pitched his background:

> I majored in information technology with a minor in communications. I know that technology leadership today is more than writing brilliant code; it is imperative for technology leaders to humanize technology. I feel that my communications courses will help me do that and also prepare me for working well with clients. I've been active all four years as a reporter for the campus newspaper and have done two internships at leading tech companies. I have researched your company and know that you have the product range and innovation strength of a large technology company with the personal touch of a small company. That combination is why I'm seeking you out as a great place to launch my career. I'm particularly interested in your rotational program. Can you tell me more about it?

Focus Your Career Identity

Don't try to be a jack-of-all-trades, I-can-do-anything job applicant, aka a "slash" person. When you say you're a computer programmer/chef/Pilates instructor, people at college mixers might be amused, but no hiring manager will be.

Companies won't know what to make of you. Slash identities work best if they are in related fields, such as social entrepreneur/consumer activist, or coder/app developer. If you're unsure if you want a job in marketing or sales, develop slightly different pitches and resumes so each has a clear focus. Remember the T-shape concept—emphasize depth in one key area and breadth in a group of related areas.

As a rule, the more focused the brand, the better. Swiss army knife–type brands generally end up in the rubbish bin. Likewise, "I can do anything" or, "You can train me" is not compelling. You must stand for something. Organizations with job openings are looking to fill a slot in one area, and they need someone who can jump in right away.

In creating your pitch, you should think *Outside-In*, as marketers do. First imagine your target audience: the hiring managers and HR people of a specific organization (Outside). Try to figure out what they want; step into their shoes and see the world through their eyes. What's on their minds? What has happened there recently? What are their pain points?

Then figure out your message (Inside). Your pitch must telegraph your career story and the value that you can bring to their company. What positioning message will appeal to the hiring managers you are targeting? How can you cure a pain point the company must face? What problems there can you solve?

Search online to get ideas. Maybe company sales are up—or down. Maybe the company is expanding globally—or contracting. Maybe it has just merged with another company—or spun off a division. Each of these situations generates problems that you can help solve.

Remember, when someone says in an interview, "Tell me about yourself," they are really asking, "What can you do for us?" Even in a networking situation, when someone asks, "What do you do?" she is really wondering, "Do I want to get to know this person?" A compelling elevator pitch needs to answer the real question behind the question.

Ramping Up Your Pitch

You'll need to tweak your pitch as your job interests change. After I was at my first ad agency job for four years, I longed to work at a hot Madison Avenue agency with big network TV accounts. That's where all the action was. John, a copywriter friend, told me about a job opening on a big account at his ad agency.

I was salivating. The ad agency was a creative shop known for its award-winning commercials for everything from cars to airlines, packaged goods to tourism, beverages to cigarettes. I was most interested in its "flagship" account, the one with the most award-winning, important commercials—the account that led its new business pitches and built its reputation.

My friend John tried to warn me against interviewing. The previous account person had left after six months, and everyone at the agency felt that the client was impossibly demanding. I begged John to get me an interview anyway. I saw it as my opportunity to break into the big time when I didn't have much big-client-media-budget experience. I'd figure out how to handle the client later.

In the interview, the hiring manager's first question was, "Why are you here? I see you don't have much TV or big agency experience." But I was prepared. I had tweaked my former pitch line, "marketer for difficult products," to incorporate the agency's pain point—the difficult client I had just learned about from John. (Of course, I didn't tell the interviewer all that I knew.)

My pitch: "My specialty is working with difficult products *and with difficult clients.*" This piqued his interest, and I proceeded to give him examples of my adeptness at working with various constituencies and achieving consensus. That pitch got me the job. (By the way, I figured out how to get along with the difficult client, and she left after a year anyway.)

I used the same pitch when I moved from Madison Avenue to Wall Street. There was a job at a major investment firm that I wanted very badly: SVP, director of advertising, in charge of global advertising. The recruiter told me that the company was only interested in MBA candidates and that I wasn't qualified. But I didn't give up. I kept networking, and through a friend of a friend, I snagged an interview.

My first interview was at 6:00 p.m. with the senior executive vice president, Mr. Big. When I arrived for the interview, I was already frazzled. I had just gotten back from a last-minute business trip to Boston and barely made it. A bad snowstorm had closed Logan Airport. Even train service was canceled. I partnered with some other stranded New Yorkers, and four of us rented a car and drove back to New York through the blizzard. I was determined to make the interview.

I arrived at 5:45, panting and disoriented. Mr. Big's assistant told me that he was working on an important deal and was running late. I could see various people running in and out of his large corner office. After about two hours, the assistant told me that Mr. Big was ready to see me.

By this time, I was parched, famished, and exhausted. As I walked down the wood-paneled halls decorated with pastoral nineteenth-century paintings, I could see my job prospects withering like the dead leaves on the lawn of one of the landscapes.

Mr. Big, standing by a large conference table in his office, barked orders to a small group of bankers who then sprinted out of the room. It seemed like a three-ring circus. This was the big time. I wanted the job even more.

Then Mr. Big looked me straight in the eyes and said, "What makes you think you can handle the investment bankers of our company?"

Luckily, I had my USP pitch. "My specialty is working on difficult products and with difficult people. At my last ad agency, I worked successfully with all types of clients, including politicians and government officials who have big egos, too. I feel confident I can handle the investment bankers at your firm." Then I went on to describe specific challenges that my team and I had solved, and the intimidating interview soon turned into a pleasant conversation.

What's the Best Way to Pitch Brand You?

When developing your USP and elevator pitch, look for inspiration in the commercial world of brands. Below are a few popular positioning strategies marketers use in pitching products. See if any of them spark a clear direction for Brand You.

- **Leadership positioning:** What roles and activities have you been involved with that demonstrate leadership? Can you build your USP and elevator pitch around your ability to rally others or achieve big results?

- **Maverick or opposite positioning:** Unlike others pursuing your career path, you might be doing something different. Entrepreneurs and creative people are often mavericks by choice, personality, and style. The positioning is simplicity itself: everything the status quo stands for, you stand for the opposite. Being an outlier was a key component of Edouard's positioning as "the mind of a businessman and the soul of a creative."

- **Attribute positioning:** What is the one word or phrase that you want people to remember about you? (E.g., productivity, organizational skills, innovation.) How can you build your career identity and pitch around your attribute?

- **Expert positioning:** Your unique selling proposition can come from knowledge of an area that's new and in demand. Alexa, a recent graduate in public policy, secured a one-year internship as a consultant on the Affordable Care Act (ACA). By the end of her internship, she had a valuable pitch for her next job as an expert on the ACA, a USP that not many people could make at the time since the legislation was so new. Erin also uses this kind of pitch to stress her expertise on the consumer mind-set and marketing analytics.

- **Heritage positioning:** Do you have special credentials because of your background, training or country of origin? An internship program at a top company can mark you as among the best and the brightest. Graduating from a top coding "boot camp" could be your brand differentiator.

- **Cause positioning:** Is there a cause or issue that you are passionate about and want to dedicate your career to? For many young people, doing something meaningful and significant is much more important than the standard definition of success.

- **Innovator positioning:** Do you have a special sauce that makes you come up with novel solutions? Do you have ideas for products, services, or market niches? It could be developing apps, innovative computer code, or a new product that solves a problem.

The Visual Pitch

Your pitch will really get noticed if you can express it in a catchy or memorable way. That's why the advertising world is filled with visual metaphors and analogies that lock in a USP with a visual handle. It can be memorable to link yourself to a famous image or personality. For example, a female market researcher specializes in getting female consumers to open up about products and compares herself to a celebrity known for her empathy. Her USP: "My clients call me *the Oprah of Madison Avenue.*"

Once you associate her with that USP, it's hard to forget it. Her catch-phrase is visual, memorable, and has a benefit—namely, she gets women consumers to talk about the brands they use and what motivates them.

One new grad is interested in gaming and the convergence of technology and entertainment. His USP: *Versatile business graduate adept in the converging worlds of Hollywood and Silicon Valley.* He stresses his expertise in the technology and entertainment industries, but notice that he makes his brand more visual and interesting by referencing Hollywood and Silicon Valley. So it's altogether a more memorable handle.

Edouard makes his verbal pitch—his words—stand out by putting together a very visual PowerPoint presentation for each company he interviews with. (See Chapter 8 for a sample.) Even when the company was not a good fit, interviewers often told him how impressed they were with the ambition of his presentations.

Wordplay Makes a Catchy Pitch

Advertising creatives use literary devices like rhyme, alliteration, and repetition to make their taglines and catchphrases stick in the minds of others.

Literary devices can work for you, too. Consider this USP developed by Jack, a new design grad: *Enterprising engineering major with a passion for making the old new and the new old.*

His brand sentence combines alliteration (enterprising engineer) and the crisscross literary device called *chiasmus* with the reversal of the words "old" and "new." A famous example of chiasmus is John F. Kennedy's line: "Ask not what your country can do for you—ask what you can do for your country."

Tug at Old School Ties

For many alumni, their college years were the best (and most emotionally charged) time of their lives. Whether through nostalgia or a special emotional attachment to their university, alumni want to help out students and new graduates. Reaching out to them can be a great resource in finding internships, jobs, and funding for creative projects, as new graduate Ben Prawer discovered.

One of the careers Ben wanted to explore was working as a talent agent in the entertainment business. He made it his mission to email every alum at his university in the entertainment business for advice.

Here's a sample of one of his email pitches:

Subject line: Informational Interview Request

Ms. Smith,

I hope this finds you well. I am currently a junior majoring in business at Z University and saw on the directory that you work for Y Entertainment Company. Recently I have been seriously considering becoming a talent agent. I was hoping you could spare a few minutes to talk with me a bit about your company and the industry, as I would love to learn more about how to get involved.

Thank you so much. Looking forward to hearing from you.

Best,

Ben Prawer

University/Major/Year

Email signature

Ben found that many alums were eager to help an upcoming grad, and about one in five responded to his email, a very strong hit rate. He wanted each call to be fun and casual, more like a conversation between friends than a formal meeting. He researched each person before the meeting so that he would have ideas about how to kick off the conversation.

Ben always made sure to listen more than talk and did not question his position as the less informed and experienced person. Alumni like giving advice, but not to cocky students who talk only about themselves. Ben hoped that over the course of the conversation, they would feel enough of a connection to ask him to send his resume. He never asked the alum if he could send his resume—never ever. He wanted them to request it.

Through his prolific alumni networking, Ben got help in writing a proposal and getting selected for a summer internship at a major entertainment company in Los Angeles, the most coveted internship program in the industry. Interns were encouraged to mingle with the other agents, speakers were brought in regularly to teach them about various aspects of the business, and the HR department offered help with resumes.

The summer before senior year, Ben and a fellow student came up with the idea of making a full-length documentary about a classmate, Ty, who had tragically died. The directing duo was inspired by a list that Ty had compiled of special things to do in his hometown of San Francisco. The documentary about living life to the fullest was also a great way to learn the entertainment industry from the ground up—from concept through script through funding and distribution.

To get funding, Ben launched a Kickstarter campaign and came up with other creative ideas to raise money. He discovered that there were tons of university alumni in the travel industry and wondered if they could help with the travel and location expenses. Maybe the college bond could help in financing the film, too.

In composing his pitch email, Ben used a nonthreatening subject line such as "Informational Interview Request" rather than the more direct "Seeking Funding for New Documentary," which would probably not be opened. In the first paragraph, he kicks off with the university tie-in: identifying themselves as two students making a documentary about the tragic death of a fellow student. Then he launches into a short description of the project and piques the reader's interest by providing only a few compelling details (What's on Ty's list? What will his friends discover?)

Ben makes his "ask" in paragraph two. Notice he doesn't ask for funding directly (an easy proposition for the recipient to reject), but for "advice on how to navigate" and who to go to for travel support. The third paragraph is a short call to action. Here is one of his email pitch letters to alumni in the travel industry:

Subject Line: Informational Interview Request

Dear Mr. Jones,

I am an X University student making a documentary about a former classmate, Tyler Lorenzi, who died tragically in a sailing accident last spring. My directing partner, also an X University student, and I discovered a list that Ty had written of awesome things to do in his hometown of San Francisco. Now we are planning to send four of Ty's best friends to San Francisco as they use this list to learn more about who Ty was and explore living life to the fullest.

I am reaching out to you because I am in need of some advice on how to navigate Company Y, as a company that might be interested in providing travel support for the documentary. Would you be open to chatting with me about the different opportunities that may be available to us? I know you are very busy, so any time and advice you can offer will be greatly appreciated. If you know of someone who might be more fit to address our specific needs, I would be very grateful if you could refer me to them.

Thanks so much, and I am looking forward to hearing back. If you want to learn more about the film, you can look at our website: www.TysList-TheMovie.com

All the best,

Ben Prawer

University, Major, Year

Signature Line

One response was from a senior vice president at a major online travel site who was surprised to learn that so many other people from the university worked at the company, too. The SVP suggested a phone call with the VP of travel and head of PR: "Tell them about the film and your wish list of what you need from a travel perspective."

It was a win-win. The travel site got a great cross-promotional marketing campaign, and the two budding filmmakers got all travel and hotel expenses covered for the entire crew and on-camera talent to shoot the documentary on location in San Francisco.

Right after graduation, Ben tapped the alumni database to land a role at a start-up, again through a fellow alum, which gave him the flexibility to finish his documentary while working there. Boy, did that college tuition pay off! There really is something about old school ties. Ben had a high success rate because he made a direct appeal to the natural bond felt by fellow alumni and then turned those contacts into a powerful professional network.

How compelling is your elevator pitch? Can you sell yourself in thirty seconds or less? If you're having difficulty figuring it out, start by taping sheets of paper or index cards to the wall, each with different ideas based on the work you did earlier using the SWOT analysis and focus groups with friends. Write down skills, accomplishments, and work experiences. Then slowly weed out the nonessentials until you get a focused idea for your winning pitch, one that is different, authentic, and relevant.

There are so many things in life you can't control—the economy and the unemployment rate, for example—but you can control how you come across in your elevator pitch, resume, and social media profiles. You'll find that the more you pitch yourself, the better you get at it.

Chapter 3 Exercises

1. Who are you? What are the core principles you stand for? What's different about your career identity?

2. What's your unique selling proposition (USP) in a sentence? What core idea do you want people to remember about you? Is there a catchier way to phrase your brand sentence?

3. Put different ideas together to express your brand:

    I'm a cross between _____ and _____.

    I'm like _____ meets _____.

4. Explore some of the brand positioning strategies mentioned in this chapter. How can you use them to make your brand distinct?

    -   **Leadership positioning:** What roles and activities have you been involved with that demonstrate leadership?

    -   **Maverick or opposite positioning:** How are you different from the pack?

    -   **Attribute positioning:** What is the one word or phrase that you want people to remember about you?

    -   **Expert positioning:** In what subject are you particularly knowledgeable?

    -   **Heritage positioning:** You have special credentials because of your background or training in _____.

- **Cause positioning:** Is there a cause or issue that you are passionate about and want to dedicate your career to?

- **Innovator positioning:** Do you have a special sauce that makes you come up with new ideas and solutions?

5. You have a job interview at one of your dream companies. The hiring manager walks in and asks, "Why should we hire you?" What's your elevator pitch?

6. Videotape yourself giving your elevator speech. How could it be made stronger? How can you create a stronger USP and career story?

7. Ask two or three friends to watch the video and listen to their comments. If you agree, incorporate them into your pitch.

CHAPTER 4

The Winning 70–30 Job Hunt Plan

What's your game plan for finding a job?

For many new grads and young professionals, the answer is a no-brainer. Surf the Internet for openings, fill out as many online applications as possible, and wait for a response.

Cruising the job boards and filling out lots of outline applications seems like a good strategy. These are actual jobs, right?

The Online Job Hunting Loop of Despair

In most cases, the job specs are based on boilerplate from the previous job description. Then the hiring manager and the HR department powwow over what additional specs to add. Often, before long, you have a job spec with six to ten bullets or more. Not many people could have all of those skills even after a decade in the workplace, and particularly not a new grad with limited to no experience.

Yet, somehow, you've got to make yourself into the perfect candidate. And you need to conquer the automated *applicant tracking system* (ATS), the "iron curtain" that most medium- and large-sized companies use to process job applications, which makes them difficult to penetrate.

Most online application systems don't work, at least from the job applicant's perspective. Job hunting is becoming more high tech, impersonal, and transactional. If you're not a perfect match for the ATS screener, most likely your resume will be lost in the black hole of the corporate database.

But for companies, ATS systems help weed out the hundreds of applications that make no sense for the job opening.

The online application strategy can take up a lot of your time. As you're cruising job boards and filling out online applications, you'll feel that you're working hard, really hard, day and night. But the experience will likely crush your spirit as most of your online job applications are vaporized, never to be heard from again. Online ads only work when you're a perfect match and all the planets align. That doesn't happen very often. After all, the ATS robot can only make sure every box is checked. There's no nuance.

Another trend affecting job candidates is the use of predictive analytics to determine your on-the-job performance. Companies are starting to crunch everything they know about you, including what they find on the Internet. Then there are the assessment tests, online games, and other technology tools that are becoming standard. The job-hunting world is becoming increasingly high tech.

The Hidden Job Market

The problem with the online applications strategy is that it is a one-dimensional process for finding a job and is rather ineffective if you consider the bigger picture.

The majority of jobs—and the best jobs—are found in what's called the *hidden job market*. These openings never even make it to the job boards, and they are filled by people the employer didn't find through an advertisement or job posting. Applicants come in the "back door" through one of these routes:

- **Referral:** The job candidate was referred or introduced by someone who works at the company.
- **Direct pitch:** The job candidate wrote a letter/email/social media message to the hiring manager or recruiter that was so engaging they were invited in for an interview.
- **Internal hire:** They already work at the company.
- **Personal marketing:** A recruiter or hiring manager found the candidate online through social media like LinkedIn or through networking.

Getting in the back door takes more time than filling out online applications in the *public market*, the market of advertised jobs, but it's worth it. The size of the hidden market is hard to pin down exactly because it's hidden. Using data from the Bureau of Labor Statistics and recruiting reports, many career experts estimate that the majority of jobs are found through the hidden job market.

When you spam every online ad you see in the *public market*,
you're missing out on the *hidden job market*—
the majority of jobs that are unadvertised.

Given the pitfalls of online applications and that so many of the best jobs are taken in the hidden market, it makes no sense to put all your eggs in one basket—the public market of Internet job postings. You also should be aware of the *phantom job market*, job posts that aren't real because the company has already lined up who they plan to hire. It could be an internal person or someone who was referred to the hiring manager. So why is the company running an ad when it's a fake? Often it's for legal reasons or company policy.

When you're putting all your focus on online ads, most likely you're submitting a *robo-resume*, an impersonal, generic resume that is general enough to send for all job listings. Your resume, unfortunately, reads like everyone else's. If it is not targeted for a specific job or company, it will be pretty ineffective.

When you come in the back door through networking and personal marketing, you get to circumvent the robot world. You get a chance to sell yourself in person. Maybe you don't have every spec in the job description, but if the interviewer likes you or you've been referred, you're in.

You can sell your potential and your personality in the hidden job market. If the interviewer questions your lack of certain skills or work experience, you can counter with an example of something comparable that you've done. In the public job market, there's no chance to sell your potential and personality unless you make it through the ATS computerized minefield.

That's why you should change the way you're searching for a job so you can capture both worlds: the hidden market and the public job market.

The 70–30 Rule for Job Hunting

The vast majority—some 70 percent—of jobs come through networking, according to the US Bureau of Labor Statistics. So put the majority of your time and effort (70 percent) on what works, namely networking and marketing, and less of your time (30 percent) filling out online applications on job boards and social media sites. This dual strategy is the best way to get in front of the maximum number of recruiters and hiring managers for the most appealing jobs.

Here's how your agenda should look:

The 70–30 Job Hunt

70 Percent of Your Time: Networking, Branding, and Marketing

- Analyzing your strengths and the needs of the marketplace to develop a clear job focus and career path
- Refining your elevator pitch and your unique selling proposition (USP) for informational and formal interviews
- Building a strong online career identity and network on LinkedIn and other social media
- Improving your "packaging" by seeking relevant internships, experience, and credentials (hard power) and improving your self-presentation and interviewing skills (soft power)
- Establishing a target list of companies and hiring managers and trying to arrange meetings through networking or sending direct pitch letters; following them on LinkedIn, Twitter, and Facebook
- Letting everyone know what types of industries and careers you want to explore
- Crafting a strong resume, pitch letter, and marketing materials
- Attending networking and professional association events and building your network, particularly your strategic network of influential people
- Tapping the university Career Services Office for help, advice, and introductions
- Utilizing your university's alumni database and reaching out to those who work at your target companies or in areas of interest

- Preparing for interview questions and important meetings
- Recording and keeping track of all networking and marketing activities

30 Percent of Your Time: Online Applications Activities

- Exploring which job boards and social media sites are best for searching for online job postings
- Setting up job alerts on key job boards and company websites
- Applying for relevant online job postings with a customized resume that reflects the job's keywords
- Following up your online application with direct outreach to the hiring manager

Make all this part of your daily ritual. For every six hours you spend on marketing and networking activities, spend two hours on online applications. That way you're covering all the bases but spending the majority of your time on what works.

Each Career Is Unique

Sometimes the reality of the job market gets in the way of even the best career plans. That's when the 70–30 job hunt and thinking like an entrepreneur launching Brand You can really pay off, as Tiffany discovered.

In analyzing her passions and strengths as an undergraduate, Tiffany came up with two possible (and very different) career paths: early childhood education, since she loved working with small children, or working in the entertainment industry, based on her love of pop culture and music.

While an undergraduate, Tiffany set up internships to explore each career path. She did an internship at a pre-K program near her university one day a week and then did a summer internship at a marketing company that specialized in entertainment clients. Given the notoriously competitive world of entertainment, education seemed a safer bet, so Tiffany went on to get a master's degree in early childhood education.

With her master's degree in hand, Tiffany was ready to launch her career as a preschool teacher. She applied online at each school district's website and went to events where she interviewed with different teachers and principals.

Try as she might to get a full-time teaching job, gradually Tiffany smelled a whiff of failure. What Tiffany thought would be a safer career choice turned out to be risky. School budgets were tight, and most districts were not hiring. Only a handful of the other students in her master's in education program found jobs, so she wasn't alone.

Luckily she had a Plan B, and if you're thinking like a brand, you will too. She put together a target list of entertainment companies and followed their websites. She also reached out to people who could connect her with others in the business. (It's all about who you know.)

In creative industries, it's smart to come up with creative ways to shine such as making videos and slide presentations, setting up Twitter and Instagram accounts, or blogging on a relevant topic. A resume matters, but not as much as your personality, drive, and ability to connect with the company culture, Tiffany discovered. In her resume and elevator pitch, Tiffany downplayed her education background and highlighted her entertainment internship and musical activities with her band.

A Good Pitch and an Effervescent Personality

Tiffany prospected on online websites like LinkedIn, Twitter, EntertainmentCareers.net, and Mandy.com. On LinkedIn, she looked for employees at target companies with whom she had a mutual connection and asked them to introduce her or pass along her resume. She applied online at company websites, making sure to add keywords from the job posting to her resume. She also followed smaller entertainment companies on Twitter and reached out by tweeting them about opportunities.

She attended networking events, free ones and those with a nominal fee. Through a sorority friend, Tiffany was referred to an internship at a company that put together marketing projects for the entertainment industry. She also found out about a one-day networking event through FindSpark, a job board and social network that specializes in creative jobs for first-time job seekers. Rather than just take notes and network with other attendees, Tiffany went up to panelists after each session to comment on their remarks and hand out her resume. Then she followed up.

Now, you might not think that someone with a newly minted master's degree in early childhood education would be able to land a job at a major entertainment powerhouse, but infectiously effervescent and versatile Tiffany did. One of the panelists she contacted hired her for an entry-level opening in operations at his company, a large global brand.

How did Tiffany pull this off?

She did everything right. Tiffany put together a target list of companies. She told all of her contacts that she was looking in the entertainment field. She put together a good pitch and networked everywhere, even in elevators on the way to job interviews. She did two entertainment-related internships. She searched online job posts. She went to industry events and networked in the hallways and with key panelists. She wrote direct pitch letters customized to each company and position. She set up informational interviews. She followed up with little thank-you emails and handwritten notes. It was the 70–30 job hunt in action. And it paid off with a great entry-level job at one of her dream entertainment companies.

Launching Brand You

A brand launch is a big deal, and the launch of Brand You should be, too. To best "package" and market yourself, put together a special launch campaign the way marketers do:

- **Brand strategy:** Marketers define what the brand stands for and communicate its USP, the clear differentiating idea that sets the brand apart in the marketplace. They define the ideal customers of the brand and how best to reach them.

- **Developing a brand strategy for Brand You:** You must position your brand and uncover your USP, your own special value that makes you stand out. You must define your "customers," the companies and hiring mangers you want to reach. For large companies, locate the HR person who specifically recruits for entry-level positions as well as the hiring manager who makes the final decision. In smaller companies, there may not be a dedicated HR recruiter; focus instead on the head of HR or senior managers.

- **Test markets:** Before marketers do a national rollout, they often test the brand in key smaller markets to gauge consumer reaction and fine-tune the product and its messaging.

- **Doing test markets for Brand You:** You should test your brand's message (pitch letter, resume, elevator pitch) and image before you take your show on the road, too. Test out your markets by setting up informational interviews or conducting mock interviews with friends or professionals in your Career Services Office.

- **Advertising, PR, Internet, social media, direct mail, events:** Product launches often include a concentrated *heavy-up media plan*, a high concentration of advertising in an intense media blitz over a short period of time. Heavy-up plans often include television, print, Internet, and social campaigns all running at once so that the launch is hard to miss. Every promotional vehicle—from TV spots to live events to direct mail—is designed and coordinated to bring maximum brand exposure to the target audience.

- **Advertising and promotion for Brand You:** For your own media campaign, create strong and representative profiles on LinkedIn, Facebook, Twitter, and other social media. Your direct mail campaign should include sending pitch letters to sell yourself and uncover opportunities, and your events strategy can be going to industry and school events that can help you increase your professional network. Part of your promotion strategy should be an active networking program to increase your contacts and visibility.

- **Partnerships and alliances:** One way to accelerate a brand's visibility and propel rapid growth is to set up mutually beneficial partnerships and alliances.

- **Partnerships for Brand You:** You can create a "brain trust" or personal board of directors who can advise you on your career journey. You should also see if you can put together a small band of friends—people like you who are just starting out—who help each other and share ideas and advice.

Brand You Marketing

Launching Brand You and implementing the 70–30 job hunt has a lot of moving parts, so you'll need to get organized. You'll never go anywhere unless you have a system for planning and keeping track of all your job search and marketing efforts. Treat your search like a full-time job and put in the time, too.

First of all, you'll need a central notebook to keep all your notes together and a calendar to keep track of your appointments, interviews, and phone calls. You'll need a digital and/or physical filing system for keeping information about your target companies, as well as every job application. Put together folders for career paths, pitch letters, resumes, internships, informational interviews, and the like.

You'll also need a system for tracking what you've done and next steps, such as an Excel spreadsheet or contact management software. Key items to keep track of are the dates that resumes and pitch letters were sent, the dates of interviews, and the dates of sending thank-you notes and making follow-up calls. (Always keep a backup system, either a separate hard drive or Google Docs, Dropbox, the Cloud—whatever works for you.)

What's Your Dream Company?

Rather than start with online job listings, reverse it! Instead start making a Top Twenty list of target companies, your dream places to work.

So how do you put this initial list together?

Choosing the industry you're interested in is only half the assignment. What type of work environment would suit you best? A dynamic start-up can be very exciting, and involve wide-ranging job responsibilities, but it can be high risk if the company fails to take off or loses funding. If you're looking to kick off your career at a major company, you'll have more stability and a brand name under your belt but probably a more confined role. There are small and medium-sized companies that will give you more responsibility without the risk of a start-up. You may be interested in working at a nonprofit where you can do good in the world.

An important thing to look for is cultural fit. Culture-driven companies put their people first. Thanks to websites like Glassdoor, LinkedIn, and Indeed, we can find out who these companies are and how current employees rank their employer's brand. *Fortune* publishes its "Best Companies," and Glassdoor and LinkedIn have similar rankings. Check out the company's mission statement. Are its values in sync with yours?

You may want to live in a specific location and just focus on companies in that area, like top engineering grad and equestrian Gwendolyn

Campbell. She turned down two big-city job offers to find work that was meaningful to her, indulge her passion for riding, and enjoy the lifestyle she wanted.

Confident, proactive Gwen moved to a tech hub right after graduation, before she even had a job. But she immediately started job hunting and networking. Her equestrian team captain put her in touch with a contact who suggested various companies in the area that employed engineers. The list was a mix of small and large companies that produced many different products. Gwen researched each company and applied to the ones with open positions online—the public job market.

But Gwen also tried to uncover jobs in the hidden job market, those that were not posted online. Gwen stumbled on a company that makes an innovative product, wristbands that help children with autism and ADHD. There was a quote on the website from the founder about how the company believes in "people before profit." Gwen liked what she read and emailed the founder, writing that she was a new graduate with an engineering degree looking for a position at an innovative start-up. He emailed her back: "You have quite interesting timing. I was just about to hire a new person, but since your resume shows such relevant experience, I'd like to bring you in for an interview."

The email came on Wednesday, she interviewed on Thursday, and they offered her the job on Friday. The founder told her that part of the reason he hired her was her passion for bringing good to the world, which resonated with his personal and company values.

Start to finish, Gwen pulled off her job hunt in seven weeks. Of course, she had a lot going for her with her engineering degree and core competencies, but she took a risk in passing up a six-figure job and moving to a new part of the country where she had few contacts. Gwen's vision and career plan didn't consist of taking what was first offered to her. Her ideal job was unadvertised and could have been found only through networking or direct pitching. But Gwen marketed herself well and created her own happy ending.

Once you put together your list of dream companies, here is your to-do list for each:

- **Build a list of key HR and hiring managers:** It will take a bit of sleuthing online to get the names of key hiring managers and HR people at each of your companies. For smaller start-ups, reach out directly to the founder or CEO as Gwen did. If their email addresses are not listed online, then Google: "Verify email" and you'll get a list of online resources to verify email addresses. Now you're ready to send a pitch email or letter to each.

- **Try to get an "in" at each company:** Using referrals through networking is the number-one way to get a job. Look for connections through LinkedIn's Higher Education tools to reach alumni in target industries. Also check whether any of your LinkedIn connections are connected to people who work there. The next step is to set up an informational interview and build relationships with different contacts.

- **Set up Google Alerts for your target companies and job alerts on job boards:** The news alerts will give you topics to talk about in interviews. It's important to pounce on new job opportunities since applications are less likely to be opened after the first three days.

- **Adopt rolling admissions:** Companies hire throughout the year when they need someone, yet most students launch their job campaigns in the spring or summer after graduation. Everyone is breaking out of the box at the same time, so it's easy to feel frustrated and lost in the onslaught. Be smart: start looking early and continuously.

Let *Everyone* Know

Now that you have a list of target companies and hiring managers, it's time for a mass email campaign. It may seem obvious, but make sure everyone knows about your job search. People you already know are your best source of job leads because they each have their own circle of acquaintances. This means your relatives, your parents' friends, your friends (and their parents), and people you've met in jobs and internships. It's a major advantage to be referred by someone who works an organization, and this should be your focus.

> The number-one way to get a job is to have someone inside the company endorse you.

One HR director told me that an employee recently called her about a job candidate. The employee had just met the job candidate over coffee in a short informational interview for about fifteen minutes. She liked the candidate and called the HR director to say so. And that call was enough to sway the HR director in favor of that particular candidate.

See if any of your LinkedIn contacts have connections at your target companies, in related industries, or in similar job functions. Reach out to everyone: your college crowd, your professors, your relatives and family friends, your high school teachers, even your tennis coach. You never know who will provide the missing link in your job puzzle.

Here's a sample email that Erin sent to a family member:

Dear Uncle Victor,

Graduation is just around the corner. As you can imagine, it's exciting but a bit scary, too. Right now I'm focusing on using my studies in psychology to find a job as a marketing assistant at a large company where my knowledge of the consumer mind-set, analytical skills, and ability to assess trends will be an asset.

Since you've had a successful career, I would love to talk to you about it and get your thoughts on specific people I can talk with who could provide advice about launching my career. I'll give you a call to set up a time to talk.

Love,

Erin

Master the Art of "the Ask" to Alums

Asking for a favor can make you feel needy or pushy or vulnerable. Most of us are afraid of rejection. But if you don't ask, the answer is always "no."

Most people want to help. After your family contacts, your richest cache of job contacts is in your college alumni database. Best of all, many alums are interested in getting to know upcoming graduates and want to help. If your school doesn't have a good alumni database, use LinkedIn's or its tools for new grads, or do an advanced search with your university name as a keyword. Also join your school's alumni group on LinkedIn. Target alums who work in your field of interest or who work at your target companies. Reach out with a brief email explaining who you are, your mutual school affiliation, and your interest in meeting them for a short informational interview over the phone or in person. Be sure to include your university and graduation date in your email signature line to emphasize that you're just starting out.

Here's the basic template Erin used in pitch letters to alumni:

Dear Mr. Smith,

I am a psychology major graduating this spring from Z University. I am very interested in a marketing career where I can bring value with my strengths in analysis, consumer insight, and problem solving. I would love to meet with you to discuss breaking into marketing. I did an internship last summer at Y Company, which convinced me that it is an exciting option for me.

I know you are very busy, but I would love to hear your thoughts about a career in marketing. Could you suggest some times that work with your schedule?

Sincerely,

Erin Jones

(University, Major, Year)

If you don't hear from Mr. Smith in two weeks, send another email:

Dear Mr. Smith,

I wanted to reach out and follow up on my note requesting an informational interview with you. I am graduating soon from Z University. I know that you are very busy, but I am hoping that we can schedule a short, fifteen-minute meeting. I am very focused on a career in marketing and would love to get your thoughts about it. Could you suggest a time that works with your schedule?

Sincerely,

Erin Jones

If Mr. Smith still doesn't respond in an additional two to three weeks, you can try sending one more email. If this does not get a response, it's clear that Mr. Smith does not belong on your prospect list. But, no worries: in general, you'll find that you get a hit rate with alumni of 20 percent or better, an extraordinary rate of return in direct marketing.

If a professor from your university suggests you contact an alum, make sure you emphasize the connections in the email subject line and body of your message:

> Subject Line: Professor Miller suggested I contact you
>
> Dear Ms. Smith,
>
> I am a student at Z University majoring in psychology but with a career focus on marketing. Professor Miller thought you might be willing to offer me advice since you were also a psychology major and broke into marketing. I'm particularly interested in how you chose to focus on pharmaceutical marketing and how you got your first job. May I take you out for a coffee near your office or set up a time to talk on the phone for fifteen minutes or so?
>
> Thank you in advance for considering my request. I hope that we will have time to meet or chat.
>
> Best, Erin Jones
>
> (University, Major, Year)

The Power of Strangers

In reality, an important job contact can come from anywhere, so that's why you should tell everyone—and I mean everyone. When I was first trying to break into advertising in New York, I had no contacts. This was pre-Internet, so you couldn't search online alumni databases at your university or on LinkedIn. So it was infinitely more difficult to build contacts. I just had a few names of media executives copied from the index card file at my school's Career Services Office. There were no names of advertising executives in its files.

A couple of weeks into my job search, I went to a talk on entrepreneurship for women at Catalyst, a women's research organization in New York

City. I was attracted to the event because the speaker was a creative director at an ad agency. She had some fascinating advertising stories, but her most riveting story was about being fired the week before.

At the end of the talk, I stayed around to network with the other women and told them that, funnily enough, I was looking for a job in advertising. One woman said that her father was a partner at an ad agency and offered to call and set up a meeting. When I met Bob a few days later, he introduced me to his other partners at Trout & Ries Advertising. There were no openings, but Lady Luck was with me. Three days later, I got a call from Bob telling me that a junior person had jumped ship and now there was a job opening.

It was the perfect agency to start my advertising career. It was small enough to get to know everyone and learn how the advertising business works and big enough to offer opportunities for rapid advancement. All of this came about because I told a complete stranger about my desired career path and she made an introduction.

Asking for an Introduction

An important ask to master is asking for an introduction or recommendation. Make sure your ask is clear and leaves the recipient with a graceful out so that one of their options is to say, "No, I don't know him well enough to feel comfortable making the introduction."

Here's a sample email:

Dear John,

I hope this finds you well. I am applying for a marketing assistant position at ABC Company, a favorite company I've been following for some years now because of their leadership as a global fashion brand. I saw that your friend, Peter Smith, works at ABC Company. He spearheaded the launch of their new women's line four years ago, which has become one of the most successful fashion brands ever. Needless to say, I am very excited about the opportunity there.

I was wondering if you would feel comfortable introducing us. I'd love to meet him to discuss the company's expansion plans and my background, particularly my internship last summer at one of ABC's vendors that gave me good experience in project management and launch promotions. I'm very excited about the marketing assistant position there.

Many thanks in advance.

Best,

Erin

Notice that Erin indicates that she's been following the company for some time, so it isn't just the current job that's got her attention. She gives a specific example of why she's so interested and the fact that she's had related experience through her internship.

By the way, be a person who introduces people to each other as well, not only someone asking for favors. It's the best way to nurture your network.

Master networkers take email relationship building to a whole new level. When you have your list of companies, research key employees' bios and write an email requesting an informational interview.

Pay particular attention to the company's mission statement. In your email to hiring managers, talk about company initiatives that you admire, citing both a current one and an accomplishment from a few years earlier if possible. See if you can bring up something specific about the hiring manager and how you admire her role and the way she has navigated her career. Your goal is to develop a relationship that grows over time. Save the emails in a folder on your computer, so when you recontact her six months later, she can see the thread of previous conversations and remember her dialogue with you.

Make Career Services Your Second Home

Don't avoid the Career Services Office because it's in the basement of the math building. Get comfy with the folks in Career Services as soon as possible. Many universities offer personal one-to-one coaching and a cornucopia of services to make the transition from college to career a happy experience.

Get acquainted early (spring of freshman year or fall of sophomore year) and go often. It's a resource most students regret not taking advantage of. Some CSOs are better than others, but don't write yours off if you have one bad experience. See if you can locate a career advisor who can advise and open doors for you.

People in career services have seen it all and are up to date on what companies are hiring and what's in demand. You'd be crazy not to tap this resource. They serve as a career marketplace and can make valuable introductions to companies and hiring managers, particularly alumni predisposed to help new graduates of their alma mater. The CSO can help you improve your pitch letter or even apply for grants and internships. They can connect you with alumni in your field of interest and help set up job shadowing and informational interviews. They can introduce you to internships and give you in-depth advice about career paths that could be a good fit. Some universities even let you carry on a relationship with Career Services after graduation.

Here are some of the services you can expect from your CSO:

- Career marketplace of companies and jobs
- Resume writing, online profile, and cover letter help
- Fellowship applications
- Assessment testing
- Mock interview training—in person, via Skype, or by telephone
- Personal career counseling
- Workshops and talks with career experts
- Internships, job shadowing, and informational interview experiences
- Alumni database
- Career fairs and company recruiting events

Many CSOs keep students aware of upcoming career fairs, talks, and advice via email alerts and social media feeds. Getting involved with your university CSO pays—and not only in good career advice. According to a National Association of Colleges and Employers (NACE) study, students who visited Career Services during their senior year and applied for jobs, had an offer rate that was higher than respondents who did not utilize Career Services.

Internships = Job Offers

Unpaid internships have come under attack in recent years as a new type of indentured servitude. Reacting to lawsuits and bad PR, some companies have dropped their internship programs; others that once had unpaid programs now offer paid internships.

Paid internships have a clear advantage beyond being paid for your labor: You're more likely to get a job offer. Sixty-three percent of paid interns receive a job offer compared to 37 percent of unpaid interns, according to NACE's study of for-profit companies. Many companies use internships as a major part of their entry-level talent pipeline. Sometimes the internship program is the only avenue into a large company. On the other hand, unpaid internships through your CSO can give you academic credits toward your degree.

Internship experiences can vary greatly, ranging from, "It was wonderful—the best job ever," to, "OMG, main assignments were making coffee every morning and filing reports." The differences in what you experience as an intern can come from the size of the company.

What's the best way to go—big or small?

Big companies give you a recognizable brand name to add to your resume and can make you more marketable when you graduate. Often, big companies have well-defined, highly competitive internship programs. On the downside, large companies can be impersonal and bureaucratic, and you might feel lost or marginalized if there isn't a structured program. You might get caught in a narrow silo with little interaction with others outside the department.

Small companies often make up for their lack of brand recognition by giving you more responsibility, autonomy, and visibility. While interning at two small companies, Lisa relished the opportunity to interact with all the departments, access she didn't have when she did her first internship at a larger company. She was able to do meaningful work that gave her stronger entries on her resume and see firsthand how everything fit together.

Strategically, try for a mixture of small and big company internships. The big-company internship programs can open more doors when you're looking for a full-time job because of their instant brand recognition. On the other hand, it's often the small companies where you learn the most.

Whatever the request for a work assignment, your answer should always be, "Yes!" (Unless it's illegal or makes you uncomfortable.) And that's a

"Yes!" with an exclamation point, not a put-upon look. A great attitude is one of your most marketable traits as a junior-level person. People will love your willingness to take it all on no matter what assignment is thrown your way. Taking on the grunt work will pay off. You'll be rewarded with plum assignments when they come up, and perhaps a job offer.

When you do an internship, you may not be a "real" employee yet, but that doesn't mean you can adopt a casual attitude. Follow the lead of your colleagues in the way you dress and act. Be friendly and ask, "How can I help?" The more you look and act like a member of the tribe, the more likely you are to receive a job offer or references for your job hunt.

In addition to pitching hiring managers at your target companies directly, there is a cornucopia of places online to find out about internships. Larger companies often have an internship coordinator. Most companies have a tab for Careers or Jobs and list internships there. Some have a special tab for Internships. If you can't find information on the company's website, try Googling "Internships at X Company" to find job boards where the company's internships are posted. There are also websites dedicated solely to internships, such as Internships.com and InternMatch.com.

Are College Job Fairs and Recruiting Events Worth It?

College career and job fairs are a staple at most universities, with 90 percent of colleges hosting them and about 64 percent of companies saying they recruit on campus. But how effective are they for getting a job?

In the age of the Internet, college job fairs are not as relevant as they once were. You can feel like you're at a cattle call with all the long lines at the big company booths and lightning-fast interviews. Most companies must pay to have a booth at a college job fair, so it's a revenue stream that deans don't want to give up, even if they don't work so well from a student or company perspective.

To make the college job fair worth your time, you have to come in with a plan. Universities publish in advance which companies are coming—figure out which ones are appealing and research them online. Check the company website, what they are talking about on Twitter, and their fan page on Facebook. If you run across a company booth that looks interesting, research them quickly on your smartphone so you don't waste time asking basic questions.

You want to use your time selling yourself and getting contacts. Since you've outlined your target companies beforehand, you should have customized resumes for the different companies and fields you are exploring. Be enthusiastic as you give your elevator pitch. Most companies rate students on a series of measures including personal appearance, confidence, and leadership, so make sure to dress like you're on an interview and give your best pitch. At the end, ask for next steps and the interviewer's business card. Follow up. It's important to let them know that you did what they suggested and try to build upon the relationship. You never know where things will lead. There might not be a job right now, but companies are always adding new jobs, and you want to be the one they remember.

Get Professional

Don't think that joining a professional organization is only for when you're established in your career. One of the smartest things you can do to supercharge your job hunt is to get involved.

Most fields have a professional association (or two or three) that holds annual conferences and regional meetings with presentations, guest speakers, and networking opportunities tailored to your career of interest. Its members are your future bosses, professional colleagues, and mentors. It's one of the best ways to explore the array of jobs in your chosen career path and determine if any are right for you.

Like your college network, you'll find that members of your professional association are willing to help people just starting out. Ask them how they got started in their careers and hired in their current job. Ask them questions that you can take action on, such as, "What college courses best prepared you for your career?" and, "How did you navigate from an entry-level job to where you are now?"

You'll get the inside scoop on what's going on through the association's website and newsletter. Along with access to webinars and events, you'll learn what career areas are trending up and down. Many associations have job boards, mentorship programs, and internship opportunities. And you'll learn about the industry culture. Is it a good fit for your personality and preferences?

Associations often have reduced fees for students and young professionals, as well as special pricing for events. If not, reach out and pitch yourself for a scholarship or try to volunteer in exchange for attendance. Many professional associations have special sessions for college students at their annual meetings along with job fairs, so a lot can be accomplished by attending. Industry affiliations are a valuable credential for your resume, and you can often receive accreditation for participating in their training workshops at regional and national events.

Get Smart Online—The Other 30 Percent

If you have adopted a personal branding mind-set and are following the 70–30 rule, you won't be spending your entire day on job boards. You will spend just 30 percent of your time on online applications, applying only for jobs where you have a legitimate chance based on the specs and keywords used in the post. If you don't have a good match, you'll need to network your way into an interview.

As a personal brander, you're not going to do online applications the way everybody else does, either. There is a way to make Internet job applications more effective. First, select the best job boards, social media, and company sites for your areas of interest. Here are good websites that can be your jumping-off points:

TOP ELEVEN WEBSITES FOR JOB HUNTING

1. **LinkedIn.com:** Your profile is your resume and the site contains one of the best job boards. The site's ability to search for and connect you with target contacts makes it a very powerful platform for networking your way into a job. Has a mobile app with all the functionality of the website, so you can save jobs of interest, follow companies, and get updates on the go.

2. **Indeed.com:** Over 180 million visitors a month. One of the best aggregators, bringing together thousands of company websites and job boards. Can set up searches directly to your inbox. By attaching your resume to your account, you can apply for jobs on the app efficiently.

3. **Simplyhired.com:** Aggregator of thousands of websites with good information on regional job markets. Mobile app gives a bigger view of the job market by aggregating job offers from company websites, job search engines, and online newspapers.

4. **Glassdoor.com:** Good resource for researching companies of interest with more than eight million corporate reviews, including interview questions and tips, salary reports, and more.

5. **Careerbuilder.com:** Has versions in major countries around the world. Can store up to five resumes and create up to five personal search agents.

6. **Monster.com:** The granddaddy and one of the largest job boards. Lists full-time, part-time, and hourly jobs in most careers. Lots of advice articles. Has a smartphone app that brings you the last job postings from the website and lets you apply on the go.

7. **Idealist.org:** A very good source for nonprofit and volunteer opportunities.

8. **Hiddenjobs.com:** Great source for the hidden job market— open jobs that aren't advertised. Good research tool.

9. **LinkUp.com:** The web contains many fake or scam job listings. LinkUp's listings are pulled from company websites, so the jobs are current and real.

10. **Craigslist.com:** Its strength is job openings in your town and with small and medium-sized companies. All jobs are posted by employers, and there's no aggregating.

11. **Snagajob.com:** Here the focus is on part-time and seasonal jobs, which can be a good source for part-time work while you are looking for your dream job.

In addition to these mega job-hunting websites, there are thousands of job boards that cater to every industry and niche, such as Dice and Switch for technology and engineering jobs and Mediabistro for media and journalism jobs. Professional associations can be a rich source of job openings.

Many have their own job boards and post positions on their LinkedIn groups and Facebook pages.

There are also job sites specifically focused on college students and new grads such as CollegeGrad.com, CollegeRecruiter.com, AfterCollege.com, Bright.com, and Experience.com. Many job boards also have sections for student jobs such as LinkedIn.com/studentjobs. There are also good local and regional job boards like FloridaJobs.com. Talk to your CSO, mentors, and friends to get their take on which job boards, big and niche, are best for your career focus. You can also ask friends and the people you meet in informational interviews which career sites are best.

For many job websites, you can search for a particular job title or entry-level jobs. You can set up email blasts and mobile alerts and apps to notify you of specific job titles as they are added. This is important because a company might shut you out if you respond too late and they already have a good pool of prospects.

The Trifecta: The Best Way to Do Online Applications

When you are applying for jobs online, my advice to job seekers is to implement what I call *the online application trifecta*. You'll stand out and have a better chance of getting the job if you follow these three steps:

The Online Application Trifecta

1. **Pepper your online application and resume with keywords from the job posting.** Make sure to sprinkle the exact keywords from the job post throughout your application, resume, and pitch letter. If they emphasize certain skills and experiences, you should, too, assuming you have the credentials. You can use web services such as Wordle, Resonate, and TagCrowd, which target the most frequently used words in the job listing to help you do that. Check out the company website for any deeper connections you can make by using keywords in the company's mission statement, philanthropic interests, or company activities in your application.

2. **Redouble your effort to connect with someone who works at the company.** Increase your efforts to find an internal contact at the company. Check out LinkedIn to see if any of your first-degree contacts

are connected with someone there. You can also send an email alert to all your friends and check out LinkedIn and your alumni database to see if someone works there. Try to set up a short coffee or phone call, even if it's the day before your interview. Your goal is to learn more about the company and its culture and to emphasize your interest in working there. If you hit it off, the person may offer to put in a good word. At the very least, you can mention in the interview that you met with so-and-so.

3. **Follow up with direct outreach to the hiring manager.** Show initiative by doing a little research on LinkedIn and the company website to find out the name of the hiring manager or HR manager. You will have a serious advantage if your online application is followed by a well-written three-paragraph pitch letter. The way you approach them is important, and you have options to choose from:

- **InMail:** Send a short pitch via LinkedIn InMail to the hiring manager or HR manager.
- **Email:** Send a short email pitch emphasizing your interest in the job with your resume attached.
- **Snail mail:** You'll stand out with a handwritten note: The note should say something such as, "Very interested and confident I can add value to your team."

There's no rule that says you can't reach out with a direct pitch letter to the hiring manager and HR director. You will increase your success rate dramatically, particularly if you send it through regular mail with a short handwritten note. It will make you stand out.

Job Hunting on Steroids

Social media is not only for peer-to-peer interactive dialog; it is a platform for companies to post jobs and recruit candidates. Many social sites offer powerful tools for candidates to hook up with companies and jobs.

Now, with mobile apps, you can keep yourself in play 24/7 as you go about your life. The advantages of the mobile job hunt are propelling a migration from the web to mobile devices. It offers immediacy, ease, and simplicity. What could be better than to have targeted job opportunities delivered right to your phone?

> Online job applications received in the first three days are the ones that are opened.
> After that, the chance of your application being opened drops by 50 percent.

Mobile apps are streamlining the online application process. Rather than complicated forms and procedures, mobile job apps are simple and immediate. If an interesting job gets posted, you can jump on it.

Most of the apps let you search for new jobs and filter your results based on your needs. Here are five mobile apps to use in your job hunt: LinkedIn, LinkUp, Simply Hired, Indeed, and Monster.

Job-Hunting Strategy

Job hunting is an important skill to learn. If you're a millennial, born between 1981 and 1997, it's estimated that you'll change jobs every three years. The next group, Generation Z, will likely change jobs as often or even more. It pays to master personal branding principles like networking, marketing, and smart job-hunting tactics because chances are you'll constantly be on the market.

The 70–30 job hunt is designed to maximize your chances of getting the job of your dreams, whether on the hidden or the open job market. Your goal is always to raise the ante: to turn email pitches into informational interviews, to turn informational interviews into job interviews, and to turn job interviews into job offers.

Like many things in life, finding a job is a numbers game. Realize that the more interviews you have and the more rejections you get out of the way, the more likely you will get an acceptable job offer. On average, it takes ten to fifteen interviews that end in rejection before you get a job offer (this is pretty typical in today's job market).

Smart job hunters realize that you have to get those rejections out of the way before you can celebrate a winning job offer. Rejections aren't all bad since they bring you closer to your goal!

Many factors of job hunting are beyond your control—the economy, the quality of the competition, who knows who. But with the right mindset and the 70–30 process, you'll always land on your feet.

Chapter 4 Exercises

1. Write down your initial target list of ten companies and set up a Google Alert for each one. Research the names of potential hiring managers and HR professionals at each company and set up Google Alerts for them as well.

2. Expand the list to include those companies' competitors and vendors and smaller companies. Set up Google Alerts for each one and for special people working there.

3. Set up Google Alerts for the broad industries you are interested in and stay up-to-date.

4. List the companies you have an "in" at to set up an informational interview. How can you network to build connections at your other dream companies?

5. Develop a big list of family, friends, former coworkers, bosses, coaches, and the like for your mass launch email announcing what career path you are exploring.

6. Set up a meeting with your Career Services Office to get help in your job search. Have them critique your resume, suggest alumni you should contact, and make introductions to companies.

7. Look at the alumni database at your university for people who work in your target companies and in similar roles. Reach out to them for advice and informational interviews.

8. Ask at least five people, "What is your best job search tip?" Write down the best tips in your notebook and how you plan to implement them.

9. See if you can get a family friend or acquaintance who is a professional recruiter to take you under her wing to help you in job hunting. Recruiters don't handle first-time job seekers, but they can be invaluable as mentors in your job search.

CHAPTER 5

Leaving Your Mark with Memorable Marketing Materials

Your resume is often the first impression you make with a potential employer. Just like the first impression you make in person, this happens very quickly and has lasting consequences.

When you're a new grad with limited experience, you may feel that you have little to say as you stare at a blank computer screen, much less create a resume that makes an impression. You do and you can. You can put together a strong resume and a host of other marketing materials. It will just take some effort to translate what you've done into marketable skills.

But there's a twist today. Most likely your resume won't be seen by a human first. You've got to beat the resume-reading robot, the ATS (applicant tracking system), that most large and medium-sized organizations use to deal with the sheer volume of applications submitted for each job.

This is where many young job seekers can get frustrated. If you don't understand how the corporate recruiting process works, particularly the ATS robot, you are likely to get caught up in a cycle of madly filling out applications, sending in resumes, and never hearing back.

I'll tell you why.

ATS Is Not Kind to New Grads

New graduates and young professionals are at a disadvantage in the ATS game. Typically, organizations screen your application first based on keywords such as specific skills and experience. Your application will be discarded if you're missing critical keywords or don't answer every section of the application. It's hard to check all the boxes when you're just starting out, which is precisely what the computer measures. You must try to copy all the keywords that apply to your experience or go back to the drawing board and figure out how to position your activities so that the keywords are included.

Your resume will face a lot of competition. Depending on the job advertised, hundreds of resumes are received for each job listing. According to one study, 75 percent of applications never make it through the ATS, about twenty-five resumes are seen by the hiring manager, and only four to six are invited for an interview.

> If you don't have a good keyword match
> with the online posting, forget about applying.

It's critical that you emphasize the ATS keywords for each application. Look at the job description and use the same exact words and skills throughout your resume, cover letter, and application for everything where you fit the bill. If certain words and skills are emphasized in the job description, it's very likely they will be in the ATS screen, too.

You can use services like Wordle, Resonate, and TagCrowd to target the most frequently used words in the job listing so that you can emphasize them in your resume. It's important to use both the acronym and complete title for skills and certifications. For example: "Had yearlong internship as consultant on the Affordable Care Act (ACA)."

The emphasis on work experience and skills means that you need to get as many internship experiences as possible and pick up relevant skills in your career discipline. If you lack most of the abilities listed in the job profile, don't bother applying. You will be better off using that time to network.

How the ATS Robot "Reads" Resumes

Your resume will be discarded if you format it incorrectly. Keep it to one page, but don't cram a page and a half of text onto a single page—then your resume will have all the esthetic appeal of a phone book. You want a clean design with clear-cut sections. A good format for the resume of a young professional includes the following:

- Profile
- Skills/Accomplishments
- Education
- Experience

Use a simple modern font like Arial or a traditional font like Times New Roman. (Don't use more than two different fonts on your resume.) Avoid graphics, images, tables, fields, shading, underlining, and PDF formats; these can stump the ATS and send your resume into the black hole, the corporate repository for discarded resumes. Since the ATS will be thrown off if you use unusual section titles, use standard section names such as Profile, Work Experience, and so on.

In writing your work and internship history, present the information for each job in the same way and in reverse chronological order. Some ATS software even looks at how closely your work experience matches the job requirements, so try to match the wording in the job description if you can.

Make sure you have fresh eyes to give your resume a final spelling and grammar check. A high percentage of resumes have typos and grammatical errors, and the ATS will throw them right out.

You'd be smart to do a final resume test with an HR or CSO professional. Make sure that your resume communicates your intended positioning and that anyone who looks at it for ten seconds or so can find everything they need. One final word of warning: An unprofessional email address will get your resume thrown out 76 percent of the time.

Don't Spam Your Resume

Most resumes are a laundry list of skills, jobs, and academic credentials with no focus or customization to the advertised job. They're what I call *robo-resumes*: generic and boring, with no personality. Some career experts estimate that 90 percent of candidates use one standard resume for every job application. Wary hiring managers see these one-size-fits-all resumes as evidence you're applying for jobs en masse.

There's no branding in a robo-resume. To create a winning application, you must craft a customized resume and pitch letter for each company. Your research on the company and career path will help you identify the qualifications and all-important keywords needed for a resume that is strong, not puny; interesting, not dull; and relevant, not generic.

Six-Second Resume Review?

Count yourself lucky if your application and resume pass through the robotic scrutiny and into human hands. Only about 25 percent do. Of course, if you're applying to smaller companies and start-ups, your resume will likely bypass the ATS phase entirely and go straight to the recruiter and hiring manager.

While employers may swear they spend five to ten minutes reviewing each resume, it appears that is a huge exaggeration. *Six seconds* is more accurate, according to eye-tracking research.

For four of those six seconds, the recruiter is looking at four key areas: job titles, companies where you worked, start and end dates, and education. That leaves just two seconds for everything else on your resume, including scanning for keywords that show you are qualified for the job.

> In the typical six-second initial resume review,
> recruiters focus on relevant experience, skills, and education.

In this quick six-second scan, the recruiter or hiring manager is trying to quickly determine whether you are a fit or not. Your application must grab their attention from the get-go to prove you're a fit in order to get in the "yes" pile for a more extensive review. Omit visuals from your resume because recruiters will focus on them and ignore the content, according to eye-tracking research. Including job-specific and company-specific keywords throughout your resume is critical. Also, based on your research, see if you can use relevant industry lingo in your resume to show you are a member of the tribe.

Your Resume Is an Ad for Brand You

How can you impress recruiters and hiring managers?

Stop thinking that your resume must be a boring CV that looks and reads like everyone else's. Think of your resume as a print ad for you, the product. That means it should be interesting, focused, and attractive, like an ad.

Link the various aspects of your background together to provide a unified career identity. Above all, remember that your resume is a branding document, not a career history. Highlight compelling accomplishments and abilities with action words and metrics, but there's no need to describe your role or include everything you've ever done.

Sell yourself "above the fold"—the top half of your resume is the most important part.

The top part of an ad or newspaper ("above the fold") is the most important since it is the most read. Hirers scan the top first and may go no further if you fail to capture their attention.

Skip the objective statement: "New graduate seeking entry-level job . . ." Nobody cares what you want. Branding resumes begin with a profile or qualifications statement, a couple of crisp sentences that define your value. It must answer what every employer wants to know: "Why should I hire you?"

A strong profile statement is critical for new graduates. You can't put at the top "Top-Producing Sales and Business Development Executive" and follow up with a profile paragraph that tells a David and Goliath story of your sales achievements. You don't have an impressive job title and career history (yet), so you'll need to do a bit more work to define your brand.

A big problem with new-graduate resumes is a lack of focus, and employers often find it hard to identify what you're looking for. Don't rely on your college major to convey your career identity or job focus if you were a liberal arts major or want to do something different. You will need more ingenuity to craft your profile statement than a seasoned pro with a linear job history. But here's a chance to lay out your vision for your career future. What could be better than that?

In fact, if you have a well-written resume profile statement along with relevant skills and accomplishments, you can turn your lack of work history to your advantage and stand apart from other graduates, as our aspiring marketer Erin discovered.

Here is her "above the fold" profile statement and key proof points:

MARKETING ASSISTANT: PSYCHOLOGY GRAD WITH PULSE ON THE CONSUMER MIND-SET

The most successful products in today's marketplace will put the needs of consumers—not technology—first and foremost. My mission is to read the pulse of consumers to develop better products and marketing campaigns.

- Conducted consumer research with 100 prospects and created strategic options for X Media to increase sales by 20 percent
- Helped launch new product promotion that was picked up by twenty-five national magazines with successful tie-in at international film festival
- Developed a marketing strategy for Y product to increase sales by 25 percent for university marketing course, based on market research and competitive analysis

---

Erin tells us a lot in her profile statement and three bulleted accomplishments.

She differentiates her brand with her USP: *Psychology Grad with Pulse on the Consumer Mind-set*. She reveals her point of view on marketing with a provocative statement: "The most successful products will put the needs of consumers—not technology—first and foremost." A thesis or point of view in your profile statement will really make you stand out.

Bullets: Actions, Numbers, and Results

Don't talk about job responsibilities anywhere on your resume. That's wasting valuable real estate on the basic duties that everyone knows. Show employers how you got results and gained important skills in summer jobs, internships, and at school.

How do you make your abilities and skills stand out when you're a new grad with limited job experience? It's a challenge that every first-timer faces. It might take more effort than for an experienced job seeker, but you have more accomplishments than you realize. You just have to take the time as

Erin did. Make a list of everything you've ever done to accomplish something on internships, school projects, volunteer activities, part-time jobs, and the like. Then, follow this formula to create a results bullet:

Action + Numbers = Results

Did [A] + as measured by [N] = with these results [R]

Look back at Erin's three results bullets under her profile summary. The first two were based on marketing internships she had while a student, and the third bullet is based on a school project. Since analytics, Excel proficiency, and teamwork are important in entry-level marketing jobs, Erin emphasizes driving through projects to successful completion, the results (providing a measurement number), and the benefit (how it improved things).

Here are a few other examples of how university students and recent grads have created strong results bullets out of internships and part-time jobs:

- Raised $55,000 in first month calling alumni for university capital campaign, the top student performer all four weeks.
- As a brand ambassador interning at X Company challenged to increase website traffic, wrote ten blog posts that generated over 240 responses and helped boost sales.
- Made fifty outbound telemarketing calls per day at busy at X Company Call Center with a 10 percent sign-up rate.
- Prepared detailed Excel reports and pitches for business development group at fast-growing venture-supported technology company that increased response rate by 15 percent.

Positioning Volunteer Work, Entrepreneurial Activities, and Gaps

If you don't have many internships or jobs, you must capture your volunteer, school, entrepreneurial, and other activities and position them so that they align with in-demand skills and experience.

Companies often program ATS to look for gaps, searching for roles with dates that include the words "present" or "current." So even while you are looking for a job after graduation, you should minimize the gap by doing internships and positioning volunteer and part-time activities as "current."

Here are some ideas on positioning your volunteer activities, coursework, and moneymaking ventures so they will impress hiring managers:

- **Position a group college project like a job assignment.** No reason to let all of that hard schoolwork go to waste. Group projects can be particularly useful:
  - ☐ "Led four-person student team in developing a mobile game app, 'Career Hunter,' using the Java programming language for Android and iOS devices."
- **Highlight how you launched a moneymaking side business.** Did you create a successful business in your college dorm that demonstrated planning, leadership, and innovation? Here's an example:
  - ☐ "Set up successful babysitting business, College Nannies. Directed training program including CPR certification for twenty part-time student nannies and set up efficient online booking service."
- **Quantify how much money you raised for a nonprofit organization.** Show how much money you raised, how you created a plan, and how it was better than previous years, such as:
  - ☐ "Led annual fraternity drive to create holiday care packages for kids at the local hospital, providing fifty-five holiday packages, the most successful fund-raiser to date."
- **Emphasize how you improved something:** Companies are always looking for ways to do something better, faster, cheaper. Did you introduce a new training program to the sports group you are coaching? Did you make an expensive process cheaper and better by putting things online? Here's an example:
  - ☐ "Created successful online event promotion for arts nonprofit using website and social media rather than expensive four-color brochure to promote annual 'Arts Walk' event."
- **Reposition menial jobs so they portray entry-level job skills:** It's easy to discount waitressing, babysitting, retail sales, and other bottom-rung

work. But most of these jobs involve highly important business skills like teamwork, decision making in a fast-paced environment, and the like. Here's one way to make menial big:

☐ "Developed strong problem-solving, teamwork, customer service, and leadership skills working in retail sales at Starbucks and other venues."

Play to the Keywords

Every field has keywords, the skills in demand with that line of work. The more the ATS can check them off on your resume, the better your chances of getting an interview.

It's always smart to emphasize your core competencies and skill set, but in more technical and regulated fields, you'll want to include licenses, programming languages, and hard-core specifics. For example, Cole, who got a real estate analyst job right after college, wrote a summary followed by core competencies near the top of his resume:

CAREER SUMMARY

Professional real estate analyst with entry-level portfolio analysis and management work experience, specializing in asset management, financial modeling, and underwriting.

CORE COMPETENCIES

Argus DCF; Discounted Cash Flows; Comparable Valuation; Microsoft Excel; Bloomberg BESS Certified: Commodity Essentials, Equity Essentials, Fixed Income Essentials, FX Essentials.

Avoid overused phrases such as "value add," "results driven," "team player," "thought leadership," and "go to person." Phrases like "think outside the box" are so overused that they brand you as totally inside the box.

Different Strokes for Different Folks

Sometimes the realities of a dynamic marketplace point you in a new direction. Erin, our aspiring marketer, noticed that big retailers were advertising entry-level jobs and internships in merchandising, a related area that involves selecting products and evaluating sales performance. Erin decided to expand her job search and pursue both career paths: merchandising and marketing. Because there were a lot of merchandising internships online, she snagged a three-month internship at a large global retailer.

But Erin needed a different brand pitch and resume to go after full-time merchandising jobs, and now with her internship, she had a story to tell. She had a hands-on role in compiling trend and competitive analysis reports, which gave her new marketable skills. Here is Erin's new profile statement for her merchandising resume:

MERCHANDISING ASSISTANT WITH STRONG ANALYTIC, MERCHANDISING, AND MARKETING SKILLS

My passion is understanding shoppers and what makes them tick when they are shopping in the store, shopping online, or shopping with their smartphone. As a merchandising intern at ABC Company, I compiled detailed merchandising forecasting reports to ensure that the company has the right product available at the right place at the right time to align merchandising decisions with customer expectations.

- Compiled five Excel reports for accurate demand forecasting for new fall product line
- Learned new Z software platform that decreased report time by 50 percent for store-level and increased department productivity
- Assisted in developing new report to examine transaction history against demographic data that will result in more accurate buying

---

In this version of her resume, Erin focused on what merchandising managers are interested in—how to analyze the numbers to get accurate readings on what products sold in what markets, and how to predict what will sell next season.

She emphasizes her "special heritage," the internship at ABC Company and her newly acquired merchandising analytical skills, specifically the Excel spreadsheets and trend reports. It was just a three-month internship, but Erin had cut her teeth at a top company known for its merchandising analytics. To stand out in a competitive marketplace, her training was a powerful brand credential, and she needed to flaunt it.

The Organic Resume

Your resume is an organic, ongoing process, and you should always add new skills and experiences.

To make her original marketing resume even stronger, Erin added the new merchandising internship experience at ABC Company, but she gave her newly acquired merchandising experience a marketing slant.

MARKETING ASSISTANT WITH DNA IN MERCHANDISING ANALYTICS AND THE CONSUMER MIND-SET

My mission is to read the pulse of consumers, analyze buying decisions, and spot trends. My internships gave me an in-depth experience in preparing marketing and merchandising analytical reports using Excel.

- Helped prepare presentation to the marketing team on merchandising results, outlining what was popular in store vs. mobile and e-commence

- Analyzed data and compiled trend report and customer segmentation study to improve sales results 15 percent

- Prepared key analytic tables on Excel to develop recommendations for key promotions

---

Both of Erin's resumes and interview pitches told a true story, though they were slightly different, emphasizing what was most relevant to each audience. Double-tracking her job search turned out to be a wise strategy. She noticed a merchandising job posting that seemed perfect, although she almost didn't apply because it was an online posting and she had never gotten a response from an online application before. But the entry-level merchandising job was for a major fashion chain, and she thought, "Okay, I'll try the online application route one last time."

Erin made sure that her resume, cover letter, and application had most of the same keywords as the job posting. In fact, she later learned that the ATS screened for experience at the company where Erin had done her merchandising internship. It was the perfect credential and made her application stand out. Turns out, the hiring manager had started his career there, and in the interview he told her it offered the best merchandising training program. Lo and behold, Erin got the job!

Master the Pitch Email

After your resume, the next core marketing piece you need is a compelling pitch email or pitch letter to send to hiring managers or along with your resume in online applications.

Email is the best and most immediate way to pitch people professionally. Regular mail is too slow, and most employers are laser-focused throughout the day on email messages. InMail on LinkedIn can also be a good way to reach professionals. In most cases, you'll want to paste your pitch in the body of the email rather than include it as an attachment, which may go unopened. The best time to send emails is between 9:00 a.m. and noon on weekdays. You can always follow up your email with a snail mail letter to emphasize your interest. If you do the one-two punch, write a slightly different letter from the email message that brings up additional points.

Wordy pitches, lengthy explanations, and a laundry list of skills will not impress hiring managers. They are too busy for that. That's why you must master the engaging, punchy pitch email that focuses on what is important to them:

- **Email subject line:** Keep the subject line short. Identify your "ask" or have an interesting personal angle.
- **Beginning—the hook:** Most email platforms show the subject line and first sentence of the email when people are scrolling through their messages. So you need to kick off with a *strong first sentence hook* to interest the hiring manager enough to read the entire email. Your hook could be something specific about why you are reaching out, a challenge the company is facing or a mutual contact who referred you.

- **Middle—the pitch:** You need to establish two things in the main body of your pitch. *First, show that you are passionate about the organization and have been interested in it for some time.* It's smart to cite a major company initiative or a project from three or four years ago as well as its recent activities. That way you won't come across as some Johnny-come-lately who is only applying because there's a job opening. You want to convey that you are passionate about the company and have been following it for a while. *Second, explain why you'd be perfect for the job and provide a short snapshot of your special sauce.* Tie in your strengths and experience through a proof-of-performance story from one of your internships, school activities, part-time jobs, or coursework.

- **The Closing—call to action:** End with a short call to action requesting a meeting, phone conversation, or informational interview. *Request one action and supply one contact point.* It could be to set up an informational interview or a time to meet. It could be, "To find out more, contact me at . . ." or even, "Are you the right person to talk to about this?"

- **Email signature line:** Your email should have a well-formatted, automatic signature with your name, school, and graduation date. If relevant, link to your LinkedIn profile, and contact information.

Attach your resume if you are pitching the hiring manager or senior executive at one of your dream companies, especially if the company has job postings. If you're requesting an informational interview, don't attach your resume. It will come across as inconsiderate. Let them be the one to request more information. Often you'll find that you get a better response if you don't flag in your first email that you are looking for a job. Everyone will know you want a job anyway; you wouldn't be reaching out unless you did.

Here's a sample pitch letter used by Michael, a business major interested in breaking into sales at a technology company. His core brand idea: *Versatile business graduate adept in the converging worlds of Hollywood and Silicon Valley.* He's writing directly to the head of a small start-up he'd heard speak at a conference. Michael's goal is to request an informational interview and subtly position himself for an opening in the sales department, but he decided to appeal to Mr. Smith's vanity in his subject line and hook paragraph.

Here's his pitch email:

Subject line: YOUR TEDX TALK WAS AWESOME

Dear Mr. Smith,

I caught your talk on the future of technology and the role of your new X App in transforming how we communicate. I was mesmerized. I loved your point that X is the new Twitter. Your new marketing campaign for the X App was terrific, and I see it is taking the world by storm with predicted sales of $5 million year one. Congratulations! Your salespeople must be swamped!

Since I started coding in high school, I've been fascinated by emerging technologies and the converging worlds of Hollywood and Silicon Valley. I've been following your company for some time and was particularly impressed with the launch of the X App four years ago and the pivotal role it has played in app development. As an intern over the last three summers, I worked at dynamic tech start-ups and wore many hats. While I want to break into sales, I'm a salesperson who's equally at home debating technical features as I am working with marketing on launch plans or with customer service on customer problems. I'm graduating in May and am curious how you're handling the sales challenge with the popularity of the X App.

If you have time to chat by phone, my contact details are below.

Best to you and the team,

Michael Jones

Email Subject Lines That Stop the Scroll

What you are trying to do with your email subject line is to stop the scroll. No one will see your expertly crafted pitch if the subject line in the email doesn't intrigue the receiver enough to stop scrolling, open it, and see how wonderful you are.

You've got to master the subject line pitch. There's been a dramatic shift in what works in email subject lines due to the enormous number of email solicitations people get every day. Clever magazine-style headlines don't work well these days. "Do you have the right entry-level talent for your organization?" is likely to be met with a shrug and the thought, "Maybe, if I have time to read later," as the reader continues scrolling.

What works now is a quicker, more direct approach. Keep it short. There is a big drop-off in the email opening rate after three words.

Here are some winning ways to approach subject lines:

- **Appeal to the recipient's ego:** "You" makes most people open emails fast.
  - ☐ I loved your TEDx talk
  - ☐ Your article on X was amazing
- **Be direct and with a clear ask:** Often a no-nonsense, honest approach gets opened.
  - ☐ Request for informational interview
  - ☐ Bob Smith following up on sales assistant position
  - ☐ Technical writer application
  - ☐ I need your feedback
- **Appeal to common ground:** Do you share something in common, such as a mutual contact, university, major, career focus, or professional organization?
  - ☐ Jane Smith suggested that I contact you
  - ☐ Referred by Jane Smith for financial analyst position
  - ☐ X University graduate seeking informational interview
  - ☐ Upcoming law school graduate seeking informational interview
- **Make an emotional appeal:** Show your passion for the company or flaunt the fact that you will be graduating and launching your career soon. The majority of people want to help young professionals just starting out.
  - ☐ Passionate about Z Company—want to learn more
  - ☐ Four reasons I want to work at Z Company
  - ☐ Upcoming X University graduate seeks your advice

Whom Is Nobody: Find Out Who Is Somebody

Never address an email or letter to "To Whom It May Concern." That will attract no one's concern. Research who the hiring manager or HR recruiter is for the job and list their name.

Okay, so that might not be so easy. How do you find out who they are? Many job postings just list a generic email address such as HR@CompanyX. com. Finding the right person requires your best Sherlock instincts:

- **Call the company.** Often you can find out who the hiring manager is from the general operator, particularly at smaller companies. Try to start a conversation and appeal to their charitable instincts by asking, "Can you help me out?" Then ask for the name of the person who heads up such-and-such department. At the very least, you should end up with the contact information for the HR director or recruiter.

- **Research them online.** You can look for their profile in the executive team section of the company website, or do an advanced search on LinkedIn or Google. On LinkedIn, look for someone who knows an employee at the company and ask for an introduction. If you come up with a name, it should be easy to figure out the corporate email address. (Check out Email-format.com for corporate email addresses, or Google "Verify email address.")

- **Seek help from your network.** Here's where it pays to be part of a professional organization where you can reach out to members who work at your target companies and seek help in finding out who's who in the organization.

- **Start at the top.** A good tactic can be to send your pitch letter and resume to the CEO, president, or division head of your target companies both by email and direct mail. Most likely they will have their assistant forward it to the hiring manager. Then it's up to the power of your prose and resume to get a callback.

Your Email Signature: Last Chance to Brand

Your email got opened and read, so you've made a successful first virtual impression. But, don't forget, last impressions are important, too.

Your final chance to brand and impress virtually is with your email signature. As the one constant on every email that you write, it's important to use it to your advantage.

Here are some pointers to keep in mind in crafting your email signature:

- **Make your signature simple and classy.** You may be on ten social media sites, but keep your email signature contacts simple. If you include too many contact avenues, you'll look a little desperate. Besides, brand research shows that the more choices you give someone, the less likely it is that one will be clicked. Key items that must appear are your name, email address, phone number, and a link to your website or LinkedIn profile. Don't include a physical address, alternate phone numbers or excessive links to your social profiles.

- **Design your signature for the small screen.** More and more, professional email is opened on mobile devices, so you have to design your signature with a smartphone screen in mind. That means simplicity and clarity. Use a simple sans serif font with a point size of twelve to fourteen. Make sure that your links are thumbable.

- **Reinforce your brand.** As a personal brander, you'll want to have a branded look for your signature in your choice of layout and design. You can include your major or your USP brand sentence as Edouard, our French business school graduate, did in his signature line reproduced below. If you design a logo or use graphics, don't make the entire signature an image. Companies often block images, and people can't easily copy your contact information from an image. If you use a logo or graphics, it's best to upload the files to your server and use an absolute URL. Make sure that the signature will look nice even when the logo doesn't load.

the creative m.b.a.

Edouard Bellin
M.B.A. International Business & Geopolitics
Phone: 123-456-7890
Email: edouardbellin@gmail.com
LinkedIn: linkedin.com/in/edouardbellin

Be Creative in Competitive Markets

If you're looking for a job in a creative field or are targeting innovative companies or start-ups, you can kiss the traditional black-and-white paper resume good-bye. You'll stand out with a more creative approach, such as a portfolio of your work, or even a comic-book storyboard pitch on why you'd be the perfect candidate.

Showing that you want the job more than your competitors can be the tiebreaker in a close competition. One finalist for a job as art director for a fast-growing global brand created a cartoon strip that told a compelling visual story about why she was right for the job, and it worked. (The hiring manager still talks about what a clever close it was.) Another candidate for a web designer job redesigned the company's website as his *pièce de résistance* to stand out from the other candidates. He got hired, too.

Edouard, the creative MBA, does a graphically and visually interesting slide presentation on why he wants to work at a company and would be great on the job.

He first puts together a target list of dream digital companies and finds out who the hiring manager or HR person is for the job. Then he sends a direct pitch in the form of a short slide presentation with eye-catching graphics and ad prose on why he wants to work there and why they should hire him. Agencies pitch themselves in a creative way, so why shouldn't he?

Conventional? No, but people in creative industries or cutting-edge companies tend to be mavericks. They don't like convention. Even if you're looking for a job in business development, you must show that you fit in with a creative agency culture. Here's one of Edouard's slide pitches that landed him a dream offer [pp. 118–119].

You can track responses by using a link from a URL shortener like bit. ly on your email and privately posting a customized slide presentation for each company on SlideShare (www.slideshare.com).

The Infographic Resume

We live in a visually driven world, and pictures beat out words in conveying more information faster. Infographics are new, hot, and a more ad like way to present your resume. An infographic lets you consolidate material in a creative, visual format so that you can tell your story in a more artistic, visually appealing, and insightful way than on a traditional resume. You can bring your career story to life using time lines, graphics, and pictures along with narrative.

Here are some things to keep in mind if you're thinking about an infographic resume:

- **Use it in addition to, not instead of, your resume.** Don't think of developing an infographic to replace your resume unless you're in a creative or unconventional field. Remember, the bulk of large and medium-sized companies screen candidates using an ATS, and your infographic resume will get thrown out. Think of it as a nifty marketing piece to make your candidacy stand out that you can use as a meeting handout or send in a follow-up email.

- **Think of the infographic resume as an ad that tells your brand story.** You can call attention to the important parts of your story through the use of imagery, placement, colors, design, and narrative. When new graduate Chris Spurlock, a journalism and political science major, posted his infographic resume online, it went viral and led to a job offer by the Huffington Post to be its first infographics editor. He put together an *experience time line* from his teenage years as a staff writer for the local newspaper covering the teen beat to the jobs he held in college. Below his experience time line, he told the story of his skills development and education in a clever way with a bubble chart. The size of the bubbles was based on the number of projects he had completed in each skill category, such as programming languages, Adobe Client Suite, social media, and content management systems. Chris's infographic displays his brand story in a telegraphic, visual way that a traditional resume could never do.

- **Keep it simple: not everything but the kitchen sink.** The whole reason you're doing an infographic is to make your strengths, skills, and experiences more telegraphic and easier to understand, not more difficult. So don't go crazy with color, graphics, arrows, text boxes, and dozens of different elements. When you present too much information, nothing can break through.

The Slide Presentation Job Pitch

Edouard sets up his pitch premise to engage the hiring manager.

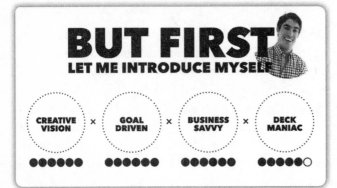

Edouard highlights how he is different and can bring value as a creative MBA who's goal driven, business savvy and has good presentation skills.

The first reason Edouard wants to work at XYZ Company is because the company is in a growth mode and he can help them win new business.

INTERN ON PAPER
FULL-TIME
COMMITMENT

×

TITLES ARE FOR
ORG CHARTS

My real value lies in my work ethic and restless efforts to improve.

Reason two: Edouard establishes that his true value lies in his work ethic.

PROMISING
EXPANSION
PLANS

I bring a dynamic profile with a global vision.

Reason three: He's dynamic and global, like the company.

4
I LOVE DIGITAL &
UNDERSTAND HOW
TO LEVERAGE
NEW TECHNOLOGIES

To learn more, click here.

Reason four, Edouard is a digital native who can help fuel the agency's growth in the digital space. He ends with a call to action: Click here to get in touch.

The Branding Power of Voicemail

Your voicemail greeting might be one of the first impressions employers and recruiters have of your personality and your brand. Although they can't see you, they can hear your voice, which is a very potent branding device. Think of how quickly you can identify a friend just by hearing a word or two, or recognize a celebrity voice-over in a TV commercial or an animated movie. Make sure that your voice is in line with your brand positioning.

You have two opportunities to impress with voicemail: your personal voicemail greeting for callers and the messages you leave to follow up or stay in touch professionally. Take a moment to put yourself in a confident, positive state of mind before you speak. The sound of a smile creates a friendly, upbeat tone that will make a big difference in the way you are perceived.

Above all, keep your voicemail messages short and to the point. There's nothing more annoying than a rambling message, so resist the temptation to go into a lot of detail explaining the whys and wherefores of your call. It's smart to rehearse what you're going to say and exactly how to say it so that your message is powerful without a lot of ums and ahs.

Let's say you're in the waiting period after a series of job interviews and you want to leave a message after business hours in hopes that the hiring manager won't be there. Your goal is simply to leave an upbeat message and to stay on the hiring manager's radar screen for the job. A good message might be something like this:

> Hello, Marty, this is Sara Jones. We met two weeks ago when I interviewed with you and your team for the financial analyst position. I am very excited about joining your team. I saw the story in the *Wall Street Journal* yesterday about the additional business the firm has gained. Congratulations! What an exciting time to be at the company. Given my internships at Z Company and Y Company, I'm confident that I can hit the ground running. I look forward to hearing from you.

For your personal voicemail greeting, keep it friendly but let your callers know what they need to tell you—for example, something simple and straightforward such as, "Hello, this is Sara Jones. I can't take your call right now, but please leave your name, phone number, and the best time to reach you, and I will get back to you shortly." By asking for the best time to call, you can avoid playing phone tag.

Here's My Card

You can't do business as a bona fide job seeker unless you have a card. And you don't need a company-issued business card. There's nothing worse than meeting someone at a professional event who hands you a business card when you have nothing to hand back but a ripped-up piece of paper. Not exactly a professional image.

Here are a few ways to make sure that your business card helps you find a job:

- **Go for a clean, quality design.** Choose a simple, uncluttered message and layout. Don't try to fit your resume on the card. Simplicity does it: your name, a positioning line, and your contact information. If you have an MBA, PhD, or CPA, put that on your card, too.
- **Say who you are and what you're looking for.** Make it easy for new people to remember you by providing a tagline with your job focus and unique selling proposition. Here are a few examples:
  - □ "Business major with a cutting-edge grasp of big data analytics"
  - □ "Marketer focused on the consumer mind-set"
  - □ "Systems analyst: computer science/engineering double major"
- **Don't use free cards or glossy stock.** Some online printing companies offer free business cards. But there's a catch: "Free business cards from X!" will appear on the back of your card. Since the cost of cards is so low online, don't brand yourself as a cheapskate and flub your chance at a great first impression.
- **Have a call to action.** Include a link to your LinkedIn profile with a custom URL (LinkedIn.com/in/YourName). Or include a QR code so that people can scan it and immediately read your profile.

There are also digital business cards you can "hand out" using your mobile phone. Often they take too many steps to make the handoff easy. I'm sure paper cards will eventually be replaced by digital, but for now nothing has replaced the ease of handing someone a physical card.

One-Pagers to Hand Out

A clever way to set yourself apart from the pack is to prepare an *achievements one-pager* that you can hand out at interviews, attach to a follow-up note, or use as an addendum to your resume. It's a must for more established professionals, but it can clinch the sale in your favor as a new graduate, too.

An achievements one-pager lets you showcase the most powerful parts of your career story with more detail, storytelling, and excitement. Consider using an effective format such as Challenge, Action, and Results (CAR).

Set up the problem or assignment in the *challenge* section. In the *action* section, try to capture the struggles and obstacles the hero (you) had to overcome and how you solved the problem. End with concrete *results* and accomplishments. You can even include a short quote from your manager or a colleague at the beginning or end of each case study. There's nothing like a third-party endorsement to make your case.

Preparing an achievements one-pager also ensures that you'll have good stories to tell during interviews.

Another useful document to develop is a *references one-pager.* That way if an interviewer asks you to prepare a list of references before going to the final stage, you can whip out your references one-pager. You will be prepared.

Modesty Is a Virtue, but the Internet Gives You Visibility

Your LinkedIn profile page is a free distribution channel for getting your marketing materials out to hiring managers and recruiters. You can upload images, documents, presentations, and videos to showcase your accomplishments and career story.

I bet you're thinking that you don't have anything to put there at this beginning stage of your career. Wrong! You probably have more marketing materials than you realize. Look for a relevant school paper that you can adapt. Maybe put together a short slide presentation or infographic on top trends in the industry. You can include blog posts on your career journey or upload a video resume or demo. Check around to see how people are using rich media to market themselves on LinkedIn.

The job marketplace for young professionals may be frustrating, but there's one way to improve your odds that most of your competitors ignore. The majority—some 56 percent—of all hiring managers are more impressed by a personal website than any other branding tool, yet only 7 percent of job seekers have one.

Do you?

A personal website shows you're committed and take your career seriously. It gives you visibility. From a branding perspective, visibility is important. That's why companies spend so much money promoting their brands. When you're more visible, people will think you are better than someone with a low profile. "Megan must be better than Morgan because she has such a strong online presence and reputation," is how the thinking goes.

Owning your own Internet real estate, yourname.com, means you will show up right away when someone searches for you. Unlike a LinkedIn profile, where you must follow its format, you are the art director, designer, and copywriter. You have the freedom to express your personality through the site's design and content.

Everything, from the site's color palette to the navigation, makes a statement, which can increase your chances of being called in for an interview. Different sections might detail your personal profile, academic courses, skills and certifications, internships, and the like.

If you're in a field related to technology, social media, communications, or design, a website is a great way to market your portfolio.

Your Narrative Bio: Your Career Story on Paper, Video, or Slides

Celebrities promote themselves using all sorts of media, and you should, too. Producing a short two- or three-minute video bio or slide presentation can be very powerful, particularly if you highlight your point of view on an issue or an interesting project.

A short, narrative-driven bio is also important for well-known people because it gives the press and consumers a quick snapshot of their life and career highlights. The press might not be calling you yet, but you'll find a narrative bio useful for posting on social media sites. Later, if you get involved as a panelist or speaker at industry events, you'll need it.

Bios are written in the third person and give you the opportunity to step back and contemplate your identity and accomplishments. You'll want to craft your professional career story. The mission of a bio is to convey how you got where you are and how you make meaning in the world. You must tie all the pieces together into a coherent core theme, a metanarrative that is the overriding idea of Brand You.

Leave Behind a Brag Book

A more elaborate way to distinguish yourself is to put together a *brag book*. It can take the form of a marketing brochure, attractive binder, or Power-Point, and its purpose is to sell Brand You. Don't bore the interviewer by taking him through the brag book page by page in your meeting. It's best to use as a leave-behind, though you can top-line its contents in your pitch. You can include personal marketing pieces such as:

- Profile statement or narrative bio
- Resume
- Achievements one-pager
- Recommendation letters or one-pager
- Academic highlights or transcript
- Awards and certifications
- Articles and PR materials
- Relevant school papers or projects
- Community service and volunteer activities

Always Be Improving Your Marketing Materials

As a personal-branding-oriented job seeker, you should always be updating and improving your marketing materials, both the graphic presentation and content. Look at other resumes and LinkedIn profiles for ideas on how to strengthen your career story. For example, if you want to show leadership in your career story try to volunteer to lead or co-chair a committee for an organization event. If you've done a lot of work, your role may be recognized and you can link to the organization's website or press release on your marketing materials. It can be an important differentiator. For example, in my first job at an art museum, I was a low-level curatorial assistant hired to help the department head research and write a catalog of the museum's collection. Given my low job status, my role would most likely appear in the Acknowledgments, yet my name is included on the title page as a co-author.

How did that come about?

I asked.

I had done a lot of the grunt work and my boss was receptive, but I doubt that it would have happened unless I asked.

The key to a successful resume and marketing effort is to go for quality over quantity. You can't put together a targeted resume without a little thought or write a compelling profile statement without crafting it. Awesome personal marketing materials take more than just a couple of hours to put together.

You need to invest some time to create marketing materials that sell Brand You well, and tweak them so they're right for each job.

But it will pay off. Your efforts will be rewarded, and you'll be on your way to the interview in no time.

Chapter 5 Exercises

1. **Pre-work:** Give your resume an editorial pass, then ask a couple friends to double-check it for typos. Then have an HR or CSO professional give it a formal critique.

2. **Market research:** Select three people and give them your resume to read for ten seconds. Then ask:
   - What was the overall message?
   - What specific points do you remember?
   - What words or phrases come to mind?
   - How could the layout be improved?
   - What about me is missing?

   Repeat the exercise, this time showing them your resume for thirty seconds.

3. **Actions:** Based on the feedback you received, how will you tweak your resume?

- What keywords do you want to emphasize?
- How can you strengthen the "above the fold" portion of your resume: the headline, profile statement, and support points?

4. Draft your pitch email letter and ask three friends to give you feedback on how to improve it.

5. What other marketing materials do you plan to develop?
   - Business card
   - Signature line for emails
   - Slide presentation pitch
   - Infographic resume
   - Achievements one-pager
   - References one-pager
   - Narrative bio
   - Brag book

CHAPTER 6

Acing the Interview

Trying to look confident, sitting awkwardly on a couch as the interviewer scrutinized his resume, writer John Pollack was still in the I-can't-believe-they-let-me-through-security phase of the interview.

Only a day earlier he had been sitting in his fifth-floor walk-up, "unshaven, unemployed and uncertain about the future."

The call took him by surprise. Yet here he was, sinking into an over-stuffed couch as the interviewer read his resume behind an imposing dark wood desk.

"Your writing is good. I have no doubt you can do the job. But you have a lot of other projects. What is the 'cork boat'?"

The way he asked the question, John realized it was more of a challenge than a question.

The interviewer was referring to the last line on his resume: "Currently building the world's first cork boat."

John explained that building a cork boat was a childhood dream. He was saving a hundred thousand wine bottle corks to build a boat similar to a Viking ship, which he planned to take through French wine country.

As the room went silent, John could feel his dream of being a speech-writer in the White House sinking fast. Then he rallied as an analogy came to mind.

"Sir, building a cork boat is a lot like writing a good speech. In both cases, you have a jumble of small things—corks or words—that don't do much on their own. But if you assemble them carefully and put them in the right order, they'll carry you on the most amazing journey."

The hiring manager couldn't help grinning, impressed with John's clever reply. Obviously the interviewer had seen samples of John's writing and liked them. So he had passed the competency test.

The sentence about the cork boat in his resume made John stand out. No doubt, it intrigued the hiring manager enough to schedule an interview; after all, it was his first question. But John took control of the interview and made a good first impression with a confident delivery and the analogy that linked his hobby to why he'd be good at the writing job. Pollack's performance showed that he was quick on his feet with a quip and helped him to connect quickly with the interviewer. He was offered the job.

The First Ten Seconds May Be It!

Making a good first impression in an interview is critical. What you need to know is that positive or negative impressions are formed very quickly—often in just seconds.

Believe it or not, the decision to hire you may be made by the end of the handshake!

The first ten seconds can make or break you and predict whether you will be hired, according to a study done at the University of Toledo. For nine of the eleven variables they tested, such as ambition, intelligence, and trustworthiness, researchers found that observers who saw just a *ten-second* clip made similar assessments and hiring decisions as interviewers who conducted full-length interviews in person. They even made the same judgments when the sound was turned off!

> The beginning of an interview is the most important part.
> Be ready.

As Laszlo Bock, leader of Google's people function, points out, "Most of what we think of as 'interviewing' is actually the pursuit of confirmation bias." First impressions are powerful. Interviewers actually spend most of an interview trying to confirm the impression they receive in the first ten seconds along with the initial impression given by the candidate's resume and background.

All that preparation, you may be thinking, and you could blow everything in the first ten seconds.

But look at it this way. You can use this as an opportunity to wow interviewers with a strong entrance. What's critical is to focus initially on your *visual identity*, the silent signals that speak so loudly in forming first impressions: your clothes and hairstyle, your posture, your energy and facial expressions.

Yet, most of us do the opposite. We focus almost entirely on *verbal identity*, memorizing responses to all those interview questions or internalizing a carefully crafted elevator pitch. How will you answer difficult questions? What exactly will you say? Preparing a verbal response is good, but it's not enough.

It's a mistake to focus primarily on words if your goal is to make it to the next round. Pay attention to your visual identity as well as your verbal identity. What should you wear? How can you convey energy and confidence through body language and posture? Is your hairstyle appropriate? How will you use your voice and gestures to make a point? How can you come across as confident? Likable? Energetic? A good fit?

Even with your words—your elevator pitch and prepared responses— you should practice your delivery exactly as if you were in an interview setting. How will you say the very first words? What gestures and facial expressions will you use? How can you engage the interviewer in your story?

First Impressions Are Largely Visual Impressions

Despite how often we've been told, "Don't judge a book by its cover," we do just that. First impressions are largely visual, based on looks, clothes, body language, facial expressions, posture, the way you walk into the room, and even how firmly you shake the interviewer's hands.

It's not that what you say doesn't matter; it does. But people naturally draw on nonverbal cues, like the "tells" a poker player relies on. It's as if the nonverbals scream at us so loudly that words can't be heard until we process all these visual messages.

This blink-of-an-eye initial impression, what social scientists call *thin slicing*, is very sticky. It tends not to change or dislodge from the mind once it is made.

Someone's first impression of you is
likely their last impression of you.

How do you make a good impression from the get-go?

Make sure you dress the part so that you look your best and look like you belong. You need to project energy and warmth, so walk in standing tall, shake the interviewer's hand, and look her in the eye. Take the lead by greeting the interviewer with a friendly manner and a natural smile, the kind that uses the muscles around the eyes. (This is known as a Duchenne smile.) Let your eyes reflect your upbeat attitude.

Plan to answer the likely first question, "How are you?" with an enthusiastic response. For example, you could say, "I'm great. I'm really eager to learn more about the job and talk about myself and how I can add value to the role."

As you say your first words, focus on the interviewer as you lean in and extend your hand to shake. You want to use a firm handshake. Too strong will make people wonder if you are controlling; too weak will make them wonder if you are, in fact, weak. (Women take note: Studies show women tend to have a weaker handshake.) Make it three shakes, what experts believe is the perfect handshake.

You want to blow away the interviewer with your enthusiasm, confidence, and openness in the first ten to thirty seconds with your powerful silent language: strong posture, open hand gestures, animated facial expressions, and looking like you belong. People like animated faces and varied vocal patters since they are easier to read and connect with, studies show. Sending the right visual signals will help you come across as warm, energetic, and confident.

Now you need to deepen the rapport.

Click Click: Interview Choreography

Remember, the interview is as much a popularity contest as high school ever was. The hiring manager is wondering, "Do I like this person?" "Will she be a good fit for the company?" "Is he passionate about working here?"

Whether it's meeting someone new at a social gathering or striking up a conversation with a stranger on the street, we all know what if feels like to "click" with someone. We feel instant rapport and recognition, as if we've known them forever.

What researchers haven't realized until recently is that "clicking" is not just for social situations; it plays a big role in getting hired and in career success.

"Clickers," people who connect easily and rapidly with others, are:
* More likely to get hired and promoted
* Closer to the social hot spot of a company

The good news is that clicking is something we can all learn how to do. So how do you click?

Clickers are social chameleons who can tune in to the subtle dance, the *interaction synchronizing*, that takes place in any meeting or interview. Whether consciously or intuitively, they adapt their personalities and behavior to those around them. If about to meet someone new, they might even study pictures and videos online for body language clues about their personality and business style.

Clickers quickly find common ground and synchronize with others because people like it when you ask questions and express interest in them. Clickers pick up subtle clues, like the energy levels and emotions, and mirror them. Often people even start to imitate each other's movements, gestures, and facial expressions.

Yes, it's true, quick social bonding comes from mimicry, but clicking is subtler and more natural than directly copying someone.

While this may seem staged or fake, clickers begin with a genuine attitude and interest in the other person. Superclickers, like top salespeople and networkers, tend to mirror and match other people unconsciously, but you'll have to practice, consciously at first, until it becomes second nature.

To click with another person or group, use similar words and display similar interests, movements, and facial expressions. Try to match the other person's tone of voice, speed of dialogue, types of language, body movements, and even breathing patterns.

What Clickers Do Differently

In an interview situation, clickers think, What is the situation here? What is the hiring manager looking for? and then try to resemble that person.

It's the opposite of the individualist who thinks, How can I be me in this situation?

> In preparing for an interview, ask yourself these two questions:
>   Who does the hiring manager want me to be?
>   How can I be that person?

Before you meet with a hiring manager or HR professional, research them on LinkedIn and the Internet to look for common ground, whether it is going to the same school, being fluent in French, or playing tennis. Scan the room for ways to connect, such as by noticing a book on the bookshelf or vacation photo.

Throughout the interview, look for ways to reach the same tempo and stay in sync with the hiring manager's body language and communication style. Maintain a vibe of goodwill.

If the hiring manager concentrates his eyes on you, do the same. If he is laid back and speaks slowly, take the meeting slowly. If the person gestures and speaks energetically, do the same after pausing for a second or two. If the person is all business, get to the point quickly.

To be effective, you must do your clicking imprecisely and after a short pause, else people might wonder what you're up to! But done well, clicking creates camaraderie, and the interviewer will think, "This person is a good fit."

Strong interviewers are also good at reading silent signals, like the poker player mentioned earlier. This might be difficult if you're a digital native raised with a smartphone in one hand and feel more adept at texting than meeting in person. You could be clueless to subtle body language and important meeting dynamics.

Look for clues about how you are doing. If you notice that the interviewer is mimicking your body language, it can signify that things are going well and that a connection has been made. If the interviewer has crossed arms or crossed legs, this can indicate resistance and lack of receptivity, never a good sign.

If the interviewer's voice goes up and down, that can be a good sign, too. People tend to vary their vocal range when they are interested in someone. Best of all, if you get the interviewer to laugh with you, it means they like you and your candidacy has a great chance of going forward.

Clothes Are Messages

As mentioned in a Huffington Post article, just because Mark Zuckerberg likes to wear a hoodie and flip-flops doesn't mean it will help you impress a hiring manager—unless you're interviewing in Silicon Valley, where a tie is often a job disqualifier.

Clothes say a lot about a person, and it pays to look the part. Items of clothing are messages, and new grads should think about what those messages convey.

Wearing inappropriate clothing is the biggest interview mistake young adults make, according to a survey by Adecco, a human resources consulting company. About 75 percent of the hiring managers complained that people in their twenties fail to wear appropriate interview attire. According to another survey by NACE (National Association of Colleges and Employers), nearly three-quarters of hiring managers said that a candidate's grooming made a strong impact on whether to hire the person.

> The way you dress and present yourself—your "packaging"—is how your professional value is communicated in person.

Casual dress and poor grooming can signal to hiring managers that you wouldn't fit in or may be clueless about the work world. So nix the baseball caps, overblown jewelry, or flip-flops. Don't ruin a professional suit with rubber-soled shoes, a wrinkled shirt, or a ratty overcoat. The whole outfit has to send a consistent message that ties in with your personal brand.

One hiring manager interviewed a new graduate who arrived with a shaved head on one side and a chin-length bob on the other. Her hairstyle might telegraph hipness on the downtown club scene, but on Main Street it can destroy your chances of getting the job before you've even said a word.

As a result of preconceptions about young professionals, hiring managers in the Adecco study said they were three times more likely to hire someone over fifty than to hire someone in their twenties. It's easy to counteract that stereotype with a powerful and appropriate self-presentation.

It's all about perceptions. Inappropriate dress triggers perceptions that older hiring managers already have about young people—that they are entitled, not committed to work, or too individualistic to fit into the company culture. Turn those stereotypes upside down with an impressive self-presentation. It's always appropriate to dress conservatively in a classic manner. For men in most traditional industries, the dark suit will be the foundation of your attire. For women, it's a well-cut suit or sheath dress in a solid color.

Of course, trendy attire is the garb for small high technology companies or creative agencies, and a dark suit might mark you as too buttoned up for the company culture. Many industries have adopted business casual attire, but there is a wide range of interpretation about just what "business casual" means.

If you're not sure about what to wear, call and ask someone in HR: "I have an interview scheduled and wanted to get a sense of the appropriate attire at the company." In most cases, they won't ask your name, but even if they do, you'll score points for being well prepared. If you're still not sure, dress up a notch.

Fake It Until You Are It

An actress friend once told me before an important interview, "It's like auditioning. As much as you want the job, try not to look nervous, desperate, or too eager to make a good impression. Acting confident will increase your value, and acting needy will decrease your worth."

"That's great advice," I said, "But how do you do it?"

"Do what actors do," she said, "Fake it. The part you're playing is the confident you." She advised me to get "in character" by doing research. Study people who project confidence on television or film. What is their body language? How do they speak? Practice being the confident you and staying in character in mock interviews. Visualize projecting confidence, energy, and authority as you prepare. My friend gave me another show business tip: block off time before and after your interview "performance" so that you have time to get in and out of character.

When you "act" confident, people will think you are confident. Stanford's Graduate School of Business even offers a course, "Acting with Power," where students learn acting techniques and concepts such as "owning the space" (this is my room, this is my chair). They also practice body language and speech patterns that convey authority, such as expansive body stances and speaking slowly and concisely. You'll find that the more you "fake" it in interviews following these acting techniques, the more you genuinely feel confident, less nervous, and in control.

Four Types of People You Meet in Interviews

Most likely you'll be asked to interview with four to five people in the job interviewing process. Here are the most common "characters" you should be prepared to "perform" with:

- **The HR Rep:** She's nice, friendly, and fairly powerless in terms of deciding to hire you. But she stands firmly in front of the initial corporate gateway, and you won't make it to the final rounds unless she likes you. Plus, if you win her over, she can be a valuable ally and can give you tips on how to score with the other interviewers. In your answers, emphasize your current skills and desire to learn.

  Favorite question: "What's your vision for your future career?"

  Best answer: "I'm passionate about your company and its products, so I see joining the team as a wonderful opportunity to take on new challenges, develop new skills, and propel the company's growth and my own in the process."

- **The Hiring Manager:** The hiring manager is the key person you have to impress because he often makes the final call on whether to hire you or not. Generally, hiring managers don't like interviewing, recruiting, or training new people. They want continuity and people who work well in teams, so emphasize your desire to build a long-term career at the company and help the team succeed. Most hiring managers are driven (or they wouldn't be heading up a team), so emphasize your workaholic tendencies.

  Favorite question: "Why do you want to work here, and why should I hire you?"

  Best answer: "Though I'm a new MBA, I am a tireless worker with a track record of overachievement both at school and in my internships. I have long been an admirer of your products and am interested in growing with the company and helping your team win in the marketplace. Ultimately, I want to take on more responsibility, particularly with sales strategy."

The Trickster: Proof that ice water can run in people's veins, the trickster relishes ambushing job candidates with questions out of left field. He enjoys "gotcha" moments and disqualifying candidates. Don't give him that satisfaction.

Favorite question: "What would you do if you won $5 million tomorrow?"

Best answer: "I'd come to work as usual. My career and meeting challenges are important to me. I'm sure my lifestyle and career would be very similar, though I'd put half of the money in a foundation so I could support my favorite causes."

Mr. Big: The senior executive who's talented, accomplished, and a bit full of himself. Mr. Big likes to weigh in on new hires. He has impressive credentials from all the right schools. The key to winning him over is stroking his ego and praising the new heights the company has achieved under his leadership. Make sure he knows he is your role model.

Favorite question: "What can you contribute to the company?"

Best answer: "I've read about your career and accomplishments, particularly the innovative new products you've launched like Z Product. My wish is to be able to make a contribution as impressive as yours."

Take Control with the Pivot

Don't feel like a sheep being led to slaughter when you go on an interview. You must take charge of the experience if you want good results. Take a page from the politician's playbook and master the art of the pivot.

Figure out the holes in your background (and we all have them) that the interviewer may try to use to eliminate you from the running. Calculate in advance how to answer those questions and make lemonade out of lemons.

Say you're a new graduate applying for an entry-level job as a sales assistant for a technology company, and you have no direct technology sales experience. You need a way to dispense with the question and pivot to something positive, such as how you can help the company achieve their sales goals.

So, if the interviewer says, "I'm concerned because you don't have any relevant sales internships," you could reply with the following:

> I have been passionately driving sales for four-fifths of my life. I started selling at age five with a neighborhood lemonade stand and honed my sales skills later as the top seller of Girl School cookies for three years running. In high school, I mastered direct customer sales working at fast food retailers like McDonald's. In college, I worked summers at a call center, cutting my teeth on telephone sales. The job was 100 percent commission. If I didn't sell, I didn't eat. That's why I'm confident I can drive sales at X Company . . ."

You Can Predict Most Interview Questions

Most interviews begin with a general question such as, "Tell me about yourself," or, "Why are you interested in this job and working here?" That's your cue to launch into the elevator pitch you worked on in Chapter 3. Don't get lost in too many details. Be specific but brief, highlighting what's different about you and how you can solve a pain point the company is facing. Bring your capabilities to life with stories about specific accomplishments and experiences. End your elevator pitch with a question so that the conversation doesn't stay one-sided.

There are many possible interview questions—just look at all the books and articles written on the topic. In one way or another, most questions are trying to determine (1) Can you do the job? (2) Can you fit into the company culture? and (3) Are you an achiever? Prepare one-to-two-minute answers for each question, but keep stressing why you're a good fit for the job responsibilities and the company culture.

Here is my list of the most commonly asked questions you should be prepared for:

- Tell me about yourself.
- What is your greatest strength?
- What is your greatest weakness?
- Why do you want this job?
- Have you looked at our website?

- Why should we hire you?
- What can you offer us that someone else cannot?
- Tell me about a tough problem you've solved or a challenge that you overcame.
- Tell me about a time when you demonstrated leadership.
- Tell me about a time that demonstrates that you are a team player.
- Tell me about a time when you went above and beyond the requirements to solve a problem.
- What's your dream job?
- How would your friends and classmates describe you?
- Why did you change career paths from your major?
- What three things would you like to improve on?
- What do you like to do outside of work?
- What would you like to accomplish in the first ninety days on the job?
- What was your biggest failure? Biggest success?
- What motivates you?
- What was the last book you read for fun?
- What are your salary requirements?

Questions Should Beget Stories

People don't remember general statements such as, "I have strong people skills." They remember examples, anecdotes, and stories. Answers work best when each has a story attached that demonstrates your point or shows what you can do. The best stories are about how you altered something.

After examining the role and job specs, develop specific stories that demonstrate comparable achievements. Let's say core competencies of the job include organizational skills and the ability to juggle multiple assignments. For a common question such as, "What are you strengths?" you could answer, "I'm good at organizing complex projects. For example, in my internship at X Company . . ." Tell a story with vivid details about organizing the project, specific events that happened, and what was accomplished.

Memorable stories have a structure like a three-act play—with a beginning, middle, and end—or a case study outlining Challenge, Action, and Results (CAR). Look for examples that demonstrate your competence and make your abilities come alive for the interviewer. For each of your selling points, be prepared to tell a story that sets up a challenge or problem—act 1. Then, describe the difficulties surrounding the challenge and the actions you took—act 2. In the final part, explain the outcome and how it benefited the organization—act 3.

Great stories have an emotional element and reflect the human side of things. They're primarily visual; the listener should "see" what happened as if it were a movie. Riveting stories have suspense, a string of difficulties finally broken by a turning point. (In plays, this usually happens at the end of act 2.) Describe the challenging twists and turns you faced before the breakthrough, and voila, success.

The best stories focus not only on your actions but on the outcome. How did being part of the customer team on your internship lead to something being done better, cheaper, faster.

Always be prepared with a leadership story. Erin didn't feel she had one, but she was a resident adviser in her dorm for a semester. This was how she applied the CAR format: "When I first became a resident adviser in my sophomore year, I noticed that a lot of freshmen were homesick. They were nervous about the college experience, having difficulty with time management and other freshman fears. So I set up a monthly meet-up where people could share their coping mechanisms and tips for succeeding in a university environment. It worked so well that other RAs have launched meet-ups, too."

Your stories should be relevant to the job and connect the dots so that the interviewer can see that your skills and abilities are similar to the skills needed for the position. Leave out or de-emphasize aspects of your academic background or experience that are irrelevant, and emphasize what is apropos, even if it is from a very short internship experience. You've got to make the most of what you have.

Get Inspiration from Timeless Story Formats

You can even be inspired by ageless story formats from history and literature in crafting your business stories:

- **The Quest story:** The Quest is about overcoming obstacles to achieve a difficult goal (think *Ulysses*). Achieving the goal seems impossible until you (the hero) figure out a way to overcome the problems (the turning point) and are able to achieve the goal. The dominant emotion is relentless determination to succeed. Most internship projects and job assignments can be turned into a Quest story.

- **The Stranger in a Strange Land story:** The Stranger story is about mastery. This story is about dealing with change and adapting to a new environment that you initially don't understand and even fear. In the end, you understand how to cope and succeed in the strange environment. You understand it so it's not strange anymore. You can use the Stranger story format to talk about accomplishments where you had to master something that was initially foreign and difficult.

- **The Love story:** This story is about being changed (hopefully for the better) by a partnership. Like when two people fall in love, phase one is often infatuation and boundless hope about the future, followed by phase two: disillusionment and concern about whether the partnership can work. In love stories with a happy ending, the pair is made stronger by the partnership. It's a great story format to use when talking about a joint project and the different phases you went through before succeeding.

- **The David and Goliath story:** This story is about using your wits and creativity to defeat a stronger foe. Rather than fight the giant conventionally in one-to-one combat, which he knows he can't win, David fights on his terms with a slingshot. It's a great story format to use when talking about how you used your ingenuity to achieve a goal.

Telling business stories is an important skill to learn. You'll find it invaluable in selling yourself in person and online. People need to make decisions despite being deluged with information. It's a natural human desire to fit complex ideas into a simple, engaging narrative. It's how we understand the world. The power of story has grown stronger in the Internet era with round-the-clock news and social media. Make the ageless power of story work for you.

If you are interviewing with more than one person, come up with two answers or story examples for important questions. If you sense that the first interviewer did not like one of your answers, veer in a new direction with your backup story for the next one.

Awkward Moments

A question people often dread is, "Tell me about your biggest weakness." I'm not a fan of responses such as, "I work too hard and find it difficult to leave a project incomplete," since every hiring manager can see through this ploy. It's best to share a real weakness—for example, a fear of public speaking—and how you overcame it. Bottom line: your weakness should never be a core aptitude needed for the job.

Money questions make many people uncomfortable. For some questions, such as, "What are your salary requirements?" it is generally smart not to give a precise number. At early stages in the interview process, the best answer is usually, "I'd like to talk about that soon, and I'm confident that we can arrive at a number that works for both of us if you decide I'm right for the job." You'll have more negotiating room later by not locking yourself into a salary until they know they want you. If you're pushed to give a number, use a range based on the research you did on typical salaries for the type of job.

Sometimes you might blow a question completely. Rather than ignore it, say something such as, "That was not a good answer. I meant to say . . ." It will show that you're quick to acknowledge and correct mistakes.

Trick or Treat

Some employers pride themselves on ambushing you with trick questions, puzzles, and quizzes. Most trick questions test your thought processes, creative problem-solving skills, and ability to think on your feet no matter what is slung at you.

On one of his interviews, Edouard was told, "We are a small company trying to scale our business. How would you use social media to increase our website page views by one million people in one week?" Now, that's probably a better question for someone who's been working at the company for six months and knows the profile of potential customers in depth—but no matter, Edouard had to answer.

If you get a question like this, take a second and try to come up with a logical rationale for your answer. The worst would be a short, glib answer, such as, "Give me a million dollar budget, and I'll come up with a plan," or, "I don't know." The interviewer wants to see how you think and also if you've done your homework on the company, so come up with a plan. Something like this: "This product targets young adults, so I would focus on Instagram, which has the most engagement with people in their late teens and early twenties. I might develop an Instagram photo contest that . . ." And so on.

Sync with the Company Mission

Good answers show an understanding of the company's philosophy and vision. New grad Cole, while searching for a job as an entry-level real estate analyst, was asked, "If you had $100 million to invest in real estate, what would you do?"

From his research, Cole knew the company specialized in value investing, finding undervalued assets in areas ripe for development. So what was his response? Cole said that he would look for properties in a marginal area of the city where a major redevelopment project had just been announced. He outlined a plan for using the $100 million to buy adjacent properties to the redevelopment area, a classic value investing move.

If you're looking for an entry-level job in finance, be prepared for such questions as, "You're smart, but do you know how to make money?" If you're up for a quantitative job, don't be surprised by a test of your mathematical thinking ability or an off-the-wall question such as, "How many tennis balls can you fit inside a limo?" You might even be given a puzzle to solve. If you're interviewing for a sales job, be prepared for the interviewer to hand you a pen and say, "Sell me this pen."

In some specialties like engineering, the early rounds focus on technical questions. They'll often throw in a behavioral assessment test to make sure that your social skills aren't totally dysfunctional.

To stand out, it's wise to prepare three to five ideas about what the company can do to improve its products and increase sales. That way, you'll be remembered as the "tech guy who has innovative ideas." If nothing else, it will show you can do more than write code. Having a point of view regarding the industry and a sense of the big picture as well as tactical ideas will make you a valuable hire.

Level the Playing Field

As a self-brander, you have your agenda in meetings, too. As soon as you can, take control and ask the interviewer a question. Interview them, and listen more than talk. Often the quality of your questions can be the tie-breaker in a close competition.

Asking questions is a powerful tactic for several reasons. Studies show that the more an interviewer talks, the more likely you will get offered a job. After all, you can't sell anything when you do all the talking.

You show confidence when you ask questions to assess the employer to determine if the job and company are right for you. By working in a series of questions throughout the meeting, it becomes more of a conversation between equals. You immediately level the playing field and turn a one-way speech into a two-way relationship.

Always go into every interview with a handful of quality questions. You can ask questions about how your performance will be evaluated, such as, "What does the person in this position need to do to be considered successful?" or "What challenges will the person in this job face?"

Ask specific questions about the job profile, such as, "How would you describe the ideal candidate?" or, "What can I do as a follow-up to the interview?"

Ask questions that show your desire to make a mark at the company: "What would be viewed as outstanding performance in this role in the first six months?" or "How does this job tie into the organization's long-term plans?" After the interviewer answers, respond with examples of how you met challenges in similar situations.

Ask about the company vision and initiatives: "What are some of the biggest challenges facing the company?" or "Can you tell me a little more about the new manufacturing plants you've set up in Asia and how that's going so far?" Ask about a specific company initiative. Taking the lead by asking questions will also help you with less-than-great interviewers who expect you to keep the conversation going. Be prepared to do so.

The secret to a great interview is to take control by asking quality questions and letting the interviewer talk.

Ask the interviewer personal questions about his career such as, "How did you get involved in this industry?" or, "Why did you choose this company?"

When you take an interactive approach (in a friendly way), you will come across as a person with options. You'll find that your worth will sky-rocket in the mind of the interviewer. On the other hand, if you try to sell yourself too hard or act needy and subservient, your value will plummet.

You want to be evaluating the company, too, so make note of fuzzy answers and red flags. Listen to your instincts.

Listening Flatters the Interviewer

Most people love talking about themselves, and you'll want to give them that opportunity. When you listen rather than talk, you flatter your audience. Listening suggests that you think the other person is smart and worth your time.

When you listen and don't try to sell yourself too hard, the interviewer will often start trying to sell you on the company and the job. What could be better than that!

When an interviewer feels comfortable, she might even share war stories about her company, industry, or personal career journey. When the balance of power between two people is more equal, you are much more likely to be viewed as a member of the tribe.

By creating an interactive dialogue in an interview, you come across as confident, not desperate. You give the impression that you're not just grabbing at the first thing but looking for the right thing.

It's a principle of branding (and human nature) that people want things that are not so easy to get. Give the impression that you are a brand in demand and that things are going well in your job search. You must do this even if this is your only job prospect at the moment and you're going to post the news on Facebook the minute you get a job offer.

Bone Up on Each Company

The job interview is not just about you, your skills, or your career aspirations. It is about what you know about the industry and the company, and how you can help. What's their philosophy and vision? If they appeal to you, how can you wrap yourself in similar values?

The biggest interviewer complaint is that job candidates too frequently ask questions they could have easily found out on the company website. So before you go on an informational interview or job interview:

- **Review the company's website.** Pay particular attention to the Home and About sections. Read recent press releases, which are generally easy to find under the "News" tab or equivalent.

- **Look up the management team and hiring manager.** Research your interviewers so you know who they are and key facts about their backgrounds and accomplishments. Look at their body language in pictures. What might it tell you about their personality and style that you could use to your advantage?

- **Get an outside perspective.** Google the company and use news sources for a more nuanced view of what is going on. If possible, study the company in person by checking out its products or visiting a local store or branch office.

Lights, Camera, Action

More and more companies are using video and web-based technology to screen job candidates. Now, in addition to all the normal preparation for in-person interviews, you also must prepare for being on camera.

The news anchors you see on television every day didn't just wake up on a set and deliver a perfect performance. They worked over time to develop the wide skill set needed for success.

Of course, professionals have advantages. They know they will have good lighting. They know the importance of eye contact and the gestures and body language that read well. They know what to wear and what to avoid wearing. They've got hair and makeup stylists to make sure that they look their best.

For the rest of us, we're on our own. Applying for jobs all over the EU and the US, Edouard perfected the art of the video interview, but Erin had little experience. Now she had a very important job interview, the final meeting with the SVP who was the head of the department. It was make or break time for Erin. Worst of all, Erin just found out at the last minute about the change from an in-person interview to Skype due to an unexpected business trip.

Erin was upset.

"What's so bad about that?" I said.

"Have you ever seen me on Skype?" she groaned.

I totally understood. For most of us, a Skype interview takes careful planning and practice. Here's what to keep in mind:

- **Choose the best device.** Which device are you most comfortable with? Your laptop, smartphone, or tablet? If you're unsure, do some mock interviews to check them out.

- **Choose a simple, quiet setting.** Pose against something simple and static. Avoid sitting in front of a window if there is movement outside. A cluttered desk or bookshelf with family photos and knickknacks can take attention away from you and your message.

- **Set the scene with good lighting.** Plentiful lighting is more important than you realize. Turn on all the lights in the room and bring in additional lights if necessary. Put lights in front of you to brighten your face. Put extra lights behind you for backlighting to avoid a flattened look or dark shadows behind your head. You can test your setup in calls with friends before the Skype interview.

- **Frame your face.** Check your image on the computer, tablet, or smartphone. You want to have your face centered on the screen with a straight sight line between your eyes and the camera. Look directly into the camera, not the screen, as you talk.

- **Look your best.** Wear clothes or suits in solid colors and avoid busy designs and patterns. Don't forget hair and makeup. You want a natural look, but if you're a woman, achieving that will probably take a little more attention to your makeup than usual. Make sure you have some powder on hand to get rid of any shine on your face.

- **Keep your answers to the point.** Video interviews can be less forgiving not only in how you look but in what you say. Speak in a conversational voice and try to have a conversation as you would in an in-person interview. Avoid one-word answers, but it's even worse to go on and on and lose your point. Keep your answers no longer than twenty seconds.

Phone Talk

Telephone interviewing is important to master because the phone is the most common way for the first screening interview to take place. The interviewer wants to determine if you're a good fit and have the needed entry-level skills.

Your voice is a powerful branding device. It can brand you as classy or crude, urban or rural, native born or immigrant, smart or simple, confident or anxious.

As a brander, you'll want a voice that is not only easy to understand but projects confidence, warmth, and personality. And in a telephone interview, your voice and choice of words are what will take you to the next level or not.

You'll project higher energy if you do the interview standing—even walking around the room a bit. If you smile while speaking on the phone, you'll have a friendlier tone that feels positive and confident.

The biggest advantage you have in a phone interview is that you can have your application, resume, and checklists handy and no one will know. You can take notes, too. What's not to like?

If the telephone call comes unexpectedly, say you're running to a meeting, set up a new time to talk, even if it is an hour later. You need to assemble your interview materials and be mentally prepared so that you are at your best.

The purpose of the telephone interview is to determine if you make the first cut. You'll likely be asked such classic questions as, "Tell me about yourself," "What is your greatest weakness?" and, "What are your salary requirements?" The interviewer may ask you to clarify relevant internship or job experience.

Have your written list of stories that illustrate key accomplishments. You'll likely be asked, "Tell me about a time that you lead a group," or, "Tell me about a time that you successfully worked with a team on a project." Your stories can be from internships or anything else you've ever done, even your lemonade stand when you were ten years old.

Practice Makes Perfect

Try to get as many interviews as possible, and rehearse your elevator pitch before each interview.

Most people practice by reviewing their notes on the company and how they would answer interview questions. But that kind of rehearsal is not very productive.

You must practice your delivery as if you were in the actual interview. Do not read your pitch from the page when you practice. You must verbalize it aloud and act out exactly what you plan to do and say, like an actor preparing for a role.

Every successful job seeker has more failures than successes.

Practice walking in and carrying yourself with presence. Feel respect for yourself and what you can bring to the party. Rehearse how you are going to introduce yourself and establish rapport.

As you rehearse, visualize the meeting going well. Focus on conversing and connecting with the interviewer. As you practice, throw in a power pose or two: standing tall, leaning in, and making expansive gestures.

Interviewing Fine Points

In a nutshell, you'll be evaluated on a series of criteria: your skill set (Can you do the job?), your first impression (fair or not), the quality of your questions and answers, and whether you're a good fit for the culture. Here are some final thoughts on how to ace the interview:

- **Arrive early.** Aim to show up thirty minutes early. Better to cool your heels in the lobby than to get stuck in traffic or held up at the security desk. It's hard to recover from a late arrival.

- **Use what you learn in the first interview to adapt your pitch.** The first interview is usually with the HR rep. Use this opportunity to get insight into the hot buttons of the other interviewers and what the higher-ups are looking for. Then cast yourself in that persona as the solution to the company's problem.

- **Admit your mistakes on the spot.** If you answer a question badly, don't ignore it. Otherwise, it will simmer in the back of your mind for the rest of the interview. Just say, "That was a bad answer. Here's what I meant to say." It shows that you are quick to correct a problem.

- **Bring your resume and marketing materials.** Don't forget to bring your resume, even if you've emailed it more than once. The interviewer is busy and may not have it handy. Not having a resume on hand can sometimes be a job disqualifier. Also carry (a) your business card—you may be asked for it and will look unprepared if you don't have one; (b) a one-page list of references—so you can whip it out near the end when they ask about contacting your references; and (c) an achievements one-pager listing key accomplishments relevant to the job at hand. Extra points if you have a graphically and visually interesting leave-behind such as a short slide deck, an infographic resume, or brag book.

- **Go for the close.** Passion and assertiveness count for a lot. So if you're really interested, make sure the interviewer knows you want the job. Ask about the next steps. You'd be surprised how many people don't ask for the job.

- **Stand out in a group interview.** Some managers believe there is nothing like a competition to see how potential hires perform under pressure in a business situation.

Generally, a small group of job candidates are given a group presentation exercise. What they are testing is your leadership and teamwork abilities. So you need to demonstrate that you work well with a group so make suggestions and interact with the group, but also try to have a breakout moment where you show your passion and insight.

As you interview, often you'll feel that employers have unrealistic expectations. You're just interviewing for an entry-level job, yet you're expected to have mid-level skills and experience. You'll feel it's not fair as you're asked very focused questions that point out the gaps in your skill set.

What's a newly-minted BA to do?

When this happens, the prep work you've done in developing your stories that demonstrate comparable skills will pay off. You never want to say, "I don't have any experience in that." You want to tell a story that pivots to an experience that is comparable in some way.

Your goal is to convince the interviewer that you can start contributing from day one and that you're a good fit with the company culture. Then ask the interviewer a question to get a dialogue going, and more importantly, gets them doing most of the talking. You'll find that the more you can get the interviewer to talk, the more likely you will get hired.

The art of interviewing is a learnable skill that will be critical to your success. You'll find that the more you practice and the more interviews you do, the better you'll get.

Chapter 6 Exercises

1. Set a timer for sixty seconds. Practice your elevator speech for a specific job you're interested in.
   - What's your brand sentence that positions you for the job in a memorable way?
   - What specific stories and examples can you bring to life?

2. Ask a friend or professional in your university's CSO to do a mock interview with you. Videotape the whole session, beginning with how you enter the room and greet the interviewer.
   - How good are your answers to interview questions? What stories do you share that demonstrate your abilities?
   - What is your body language? Are you doing high or low power positions?
   - Watch your video again, stopping it after the first ten seconds. How would you rate your first impression?

3. Do a mock Skype interview. How can you improve the lighting, room setup, or your appearance? How can you improve your performance?

4. Now do a mock telephone interview. How can you improve your voice quality and your answers?

CHAPTER 7

Creating a Personal Brand That's in Demand

Your professional image and reputation—your personal brand—is valuable. It's important for people to think well of you. In a competitive society, the best way to stand out is to have an appealing image and career identity. The image and perceptions others have about you matter—if you want to be hired, get promoted, and do just about anything that involves other people.

Now, you may think that your image, particularly your self-presentation, is superficial and shouldn't be an important factor in judging your worth. What about your grades, coursework, test scores, internships, and degree? How about your communications skills or your personality? How much should each of these things count?

You may even think that the opinion of others shouldn't count as much as your own self-assessment. I used to think that way, too. When I was growing up, a common refrain I heard was, "Don't pay attention to what other people say and think; what matters is what you think."

It seemed like good advice at the time.

Later I learned just how wrong it was.

In reality, your reputation is what other people say about you when you aren't in the room. What you want people to talk about is how impressive you are.

It's all about perceptions.
The perceptions of others are the perceptions
that count in your career.

Guess what? The most qualified person doesn't necessarily get the job.

Like it or not, perceptions are what count. A brand's image is based on the perceptions people have about it. At its core, branding is about tuning in to and creating positive impressions for a product, or in your case, for Brand You. In reality, nothing is sold until it's branded.

You can create positive impressions about yourself just as brands do through (1) a strong *visual identity*, including your self-presentation and presence; (2) a strong *verbal identity*, including your communications ability and the words and ideas associated with you; and (3) your *performance skill set*, which includes professional experience, skills, and accomplishments.

So the formula is:

Visual Identity + Verbal Identity + Performance Skill Set = Career Identity

All three variables are important in building a brand identity, but underestimate the power of visual identity and self-presentation at your peril.

Pictures vs. Words

The most powerful way to influence others and create positive perceptions is with visuals. That's because visual images burn into the mind better than words do. One study of both images and words found that after three days, people retained almost 65 percent of the visual information and only 10–20 percent of written or spoken information.

Why do visuals stay with us more than words? Visuals are processed by your long-term memory, where they are etched in the mind. Words are processed by your short-term memory, which retains a smaller amount of information. Not surprising given the power of visuals, the majority of people—65 percent—are categorized as visual learners.

Not only do visuals lodge in the long-term memory, they transmit messages to the brain 60,000 times faster than words and can trigger stronger emotions. Visuals and emotional responses are closely linked in the brain, and the two together form our memories.

Visual Identity: Your executive presence, appearance, clothes, posture, body language, facial expressions, visual marketing materials, the way you "perform" in interviews and meetings

Verbal Identity: Your words, messages, resume, elevator pitch, intellectual property, communications agility, stories, what you "say" in interviews and meetings

So how can understanding visual and verbal identity be useful to you?

Realize that the visual image people have of you—your visual identity— is equally important as the carefully crafted words of your resume, emails, or elevator pitch—your verbal identity.

Yet most of us focus on choosing our words more than on how we deliver them. When making a first impression, your visual identity is paramount because it happens before you've had a chance to say much of anything.

You'll find that two elements are critical to success in the workplace: your *visual identity*—how you "package" yourself through your clothes, body language, and attractive marketing material; and your *verbal identity*—the words you use and the career story you craft in your resume and elevator pitch.

If you combine beautiful words with a poor delivery, you are likely to fail. But if you deliver well, the words don't matter so much.

You'll want to weave the two together seamlessly as they do in the branding world. Your "look" should reflect your career identity. To stand out, you'll want a distinct look that's both different and appropriate for your career choice.

One way to stand out is with a visual trademark, such as a distinct hairstyle or pair of eyeglasses. It could be a color that's a dominant theme in your wardrobe. You should also develop visually appealing marketing materials and a resume that's well designed graphically. For competitive and highly creative fields, stand out with a well-designed website or a visually oriented infographic, short slide deck, or other leave-behind.

When you answer questions about your accomplishments, you should try to tell stories—visual stories—that people can see, and make the story come alive with your delivery. For example, if you're asked, "Tell me about a time when you led a team," you can answer, "I'm a very empathetic and collaborative leader. Let me tell you about . . ." Then launch into a story about a specific project. Tell the story like you were filming it in a movie by describing the scenario. Name key team members and who did what. Tell them about the obstacles you had to knock down. The more visual the story, the more likely the interviewer will remember it.

Judge a Book by Its Cover

It may seem superficial; it may be unfair. We may not like it. Why should you be judged by your appearance? Why should how you dress or look matter?

Self-presentation counts not only because visuals are so powerful. It is important because of people make instinctive links between what something looks like on the outside and what is inside. The power of looks is so pervasive that social scientists have names for it: the *what is beautiful is good* phenomenon and the *beauty premium*.

Good looks have a halo effect. Because something is attractive, we assign many other positive attributes to it that have nothing to do with looks. In fact, good-looking people are generally perceived to be better at just about everything.

This kind of thinking has a long history. The ancient Greeks and Romans felt that beauty of the body indicated beauty of the spirit. It persists even today. Something that is beautifully packaged is imagined to be of better quality than a competitive product that is less attractively designed. We even see it in business, where good looks give many people an advantage in the perceptions game.

> People who have a good self-presentation are viewed as smarter and more productive, along with a host of other positive attributes.

We make these snap judgments based on looks in spite of wise admonitions such as, "Don't judge a book by its cover," or, "Beauty is only skin deep."

The reality is that looks have a profound influence on our judgment of a brand or a person.

Don't you want to reap the rewards of its halo effect?

"Package" Yourself to Your Advantage

Clothes can help you project authority and attractiveness. Everyone can be "packaged' to create positive perceptions in the minds of others.

Attractive people make the most of what they have. Besides, today we have a much broader definition of what's appealing in terms of looks and style. Looking interesting and having a personal style is attractive. The tech whiz with large black-rimmed glasses is more likely to be viewed as hip than nerdy.

And good self-presentation pays off.

Two economists proved the attractiveness advantage in a study titled "The Beauty Premium." They created a mock labor market in which students were "employers" and "job seekers." The "job" was solving mazes.

Some employers considered only the resumes of job seekers. Others saw a resume and a photograph. Some received a resume and did a phone interview. Others got a resume, had a telephone interview, and saw a photograph. The last group received everything—resume, telephone interview, and in-person meeting.

Meanwhile another group categorized all the job seekers as "attractive" or "unattractive."

What was surprising was the power of looks. Attractive people got the jobs, were offered bigger salaries, and were expected to be more productive. All of the mock job hires benefited from the "beauty premium" and its halo effect.

The good news was that the attractive people were no better at solving mazes than the unattractive bunch! But when it came to job offers, unless hirers were only assessing resumes with no picture, the attractiveness advantage triumphed. Experts suspect that attractive people project more confidence because of the positive affirmation they've received throughout their lives, which comes across in their self-presentation in person, in photos, and over the phone.

The Power of Blink-of-an-Eye Impressions

We are branded in a matter of seconds: Hire/not hire, good/bad, smart/not so smart. Like it or not, your presentation affects how other people perceive you.

These snap judgments can happen in ten seconds—or less. We saw in the last chapter how recruiters and hiring managers can size someone up in the first ten seconds and decide whether they fit. If honest, they will even admit to it. A new candidate is barely in the door, and already the interviewer has them pegged.

It's all based on snap visual judgments: how you enter the room, how you look, your clothes, your posture, your expressions, your gestures—all the different elements of your physical presence. The visual images you present are messages that virtually scream at others. All of this cacophony is hard to resist. Interviewers make up their minds about who you are and whether you would fit into the organization before you have hardly even said a word. The same is true if you meet people at a networking event and they are deciding whether to get to know you better.

The interesting thing about these whirlwind impressions is that they are usually maintained even after longer exposure to someone. That's why you need to master making them. Throughout your career, you'll meet countless new people in meetings, networking events, over the phone, even online. The first impression you make will likely be the one that sticks.

In one study, students looked at a ten-second video of a professor teaching with no sound. These students were asked to rate each professor, none of whom they knew, for qualities like competence, honesty, likability, and professionalism.

Then their responses were compared to evaluations from students who had studied with those professors for an entire semester. Their opinions of the professors were remarkably similar, no matter whether they had taken a semester-long course or just looked at a ten-second video.

The study was repeated showing just two seconds of the videos.

Guess what? There were pretty much the same results. People can observe someone in two seconds and have the same read as others who interact with them for months. Amazing!

These snap first impressions are remarkably difficult to dislodge. That's why you want to create a positive first impression from the get-go.

Look the Part to Get the Part

Given that everyone makes these snap judgments about others, why not use it to your advantage? Your image counts, and you can improve it. Taking an interest in clothes can seem frivolous or bourgeois, silly or nonintellectual. But the fact is that looking the part is the price of admission in some careers, and often it will get you halfway hired. Looking the part works like a self-fulfilling prophecy: what you build in other people's minds through images has a way of coming true.

Style communicates confidence. People with style and presence feel more powerful than those who don't, and others recognize this power. Being well "packaged" will also increase your mood.

Each industry and individual company has a culture and a dress code that can be discovered and analyzed. In many businesses, meetings are the primary stage on which you perform. Meetings with clients are very special occasions. And if you're not invited to attend certain meetings, your image could be the problem, as Daisy discovered.

Daisy had an image problem and didn't know it. Her drive and smarts had gotten her an entry-level job in the supply chain at a large pharmaceutical company. She started noticing that she wasn't included in meetings with other departments, even for major projects where she had done a lot of the work behind the scenes.

Looking your best gives you a confidence boost.

She was good enough to do the work backstage but not to be with the rest of the team onstage. And fearing consequences in today's politically correct workplace, her boss hadn't pulled her aside as he might have for a male subordinate. Daisy had to figure it out herself.

It's important to tune in to the company uniform. The pharmaceutical industry is conservative, like many others including finance and law. Daisy was dressing too casually and didn't fit in. She was utterly clueless until a mentor took her aside and suggested she get a more professional wardrobe.

Daisy's makeover wasn't about spending a lot of money. It was about selecting clothing that communicated "talented, professional woman," what she wanted to stand for all along.

Professional Clothing Inspection

What's the impression you make in interviews? Clothes and self-presentation don't make the person, but they sure can help. Dressing the part (or not) can make or break you in an interview.

Identify outfits that make you feel great, but the byword for interviews is simplicity. Here are some tips:

- **Clothes:** Invest in a few classic working clothes and interview outfits. For men, that's a dark suit for traditional companies and business casual (khakis and buttoned shirt) for more entrepreneurial companies. Women should wear a simple well-cut sheath dress or suit in solid colors, not prints. Everything should be clean and neatly pressed. (It may seem obvious, but wrinkled clothing is a very common complaint recruiters have about young job applicants.)

- **Hair/makeup/accessories:** Keep your look simple, neat, and well groomed. Err on the side of dressing up a notch. Women: moderate makeup and accessories, closed-toe shoes, no sandals. Beware of looking like Alice in Wonderland with hair that's too long for a professional setting. Men: no canvas shoes.

- **Tattoos:** About 40 percent of millennial professionals have tattoos, more than any other generational group. Tattoos already have found a home in the trendy tech sector, and the barriers against body art are coming down in other industries. But visible tattoos can still limit you in many professions, which is something to think about.

Check your appearance right before an interview. One HR manager recently interviewed a woman with food caught in her front teeth. Fair or not, it was read as a lack of attention to detail, and it's hard to eradicate a bad first impression.

Hot or Cold?

During an interview, you'll be evaluated on many variables. Two critical ones are warmth and competence. According to research out of Harvard Business School, the first and most important interpersonal perception is, "Does this person feel warm or not to me?" This reaction on meeting someone new has roots in the "friend or foe" survival instinct.

Warmth accounts for a major portion of someone's overall evaluation of you. So don't be all business. The more open and conversational you are, the more other people will share and the more they will like you.

There are many ways to convey warmth. Greet people with a natural smile. Humor and appropriate openness also signal warmth. Use what psychologists call *immediate cues*, such as leaning in toward someone, facing them squarely, being at the same level, or being closer physically (the ideal distance varies greatly across cultures). These all signify warmth and openness.

Smart or Dumb?

Competence is assessed next. Academic measures like high SAT scores and grades can show competence, but companies favor internships and jobs that show mastery of specific skills and work environments. Having good answers to interview questions can signal intelligence.

Often companies ask for work "proof," such as writing samples for jobs in creative fields such as graphic design, communications, architecture, and the like. Many companies have potential hires take tests to determine competence in sales, computer science, and other disciplines.

Some people try to project high competence with a wonkish mastery of details and complex answers. Rather than impressing the interviewer, overexplanation usually has the opposite effect. It's counterintuitive, but using a grandiose vocabulary or talking too much actually lowers impressions of your brainpower. Your positive first impression can be destroyed as soon as you utter pretentious language that makes it difficult to understand what you're saying.

Simple, clear talk is best. It is hard to engage with someone throwing a lot of facts and figures at you. Complicated answers can betray low self-esteem or confidence, which is never good. Rather than spit out reams of data, convey your knowledge with a crisp reply or interesting story.

The physical cues that signal competence are similar to those that indicate dominance and power. Postures that are expansive, open, and take up more space mark you as capable, as does an organized briefcase.

Simply wearing glasses boosts people's perceptions of your IQ score. But you may not need glasses if you make direct eye contact while sitting up straight and listening. You also don't want to move too fast or too slow, which may lead people to view you as less competent.

People often see warmth and competence as opposites. If you're too nice, you must be incompetent or unintelligent, is how the thinking goes.

And vice versa. The trick is to be viewed as both warm and competent. Those are the people we admire.

High or Low

Ever notice how some people spread out and take up a lot of real estate at the conference table, while others sit so neatly and compactly that they are almost invisible? Well, those real estate hogs know a thing or two about projecting high status and power.

An important social dynamic in meetings is status hierarchy. Who's high? Who's low? In juxtaposition to your spoken words, which can indicate high or low power, there is a silent language—your body language, facial expressions, and overall bearing—that imparts high or low status. The physicality of your presence has a big impact on how you are *perceived*.

Standing tall and walking in confidently with good posture communicates power and confidence. Slumping or walking too fast or too slow conveys low power. Experts advise keeping your face and torso aimed solidly at the person as you listen, a pose called *fronting*.

Height also conveys power, giving men an advantage. When you meet with an executive in their office, take a high seat if you can. Choose one of the side chairs, not the sofa. Sinking into a low sofa screams low power.

Power poses tend to be open and expansive. They take up space and claim territory. Think head up, open chest, shoulders rolled back, and broad hand gestures. Lean in as you talk to someone.

Body language experts advise to use your hands, your *trust indicators*, by keeping them visible. One study of famous TED talks discovered that the ones that went viral featured speakers who used their hands a lot and had animated hand gestures.

Generally, you want to move your hands broadly but not flail your arms around. Keep your hands in the "strike zone." (Like in baseball, from your shoulders to your hips.) Don't hold anything in your hands. People find that distracting.

There's also visual dominance as a power tool. Look people directly in the eye while you're talking and when you are listening. This gives you what social scientists call a high *look-speak to look-listen ratio* that conveys power.

Speaking slowly and clearly indicates high status, while speaking quickly and tentatively (Umm, Ahh . . .) does the opposite. It can be powerful to stand up from the table when making an important point at meetings. Doing so sends an important message: "I have something to say and want your attention."

Power Poses = Better Performance

There's an added boost to high-status, power poses.

Expansive power poses can even change your body chemistry so that you perform better. They increase testosterone, the dominance hormone, and decrease the stress hormone cortisol. You'll feel more confident, composed, and energetic, and others will view you as more intelligent and skilled. And striking a power pose can reduce tension.

Crossing your arms, slouching, or taking up a small amount of space communicates low power to others and doesn't give you the testosterone boost. Constricted poses can spark feelings of powerlessness. They create a barrier and make it look as if you are withdrawing from the conversation.

You get the power pose boost whether you do the poses in front of others or by yourself before a meeting or important call. The effect occurs even if you do them for only two minutes, according to research by Harvard Business School and Berkeley's Haas School of Business. (To get the confidence boost before important phone calls or meetings, a good pose to do alone is arms upward in a V shape, like the victory gesture of winning athletes.)

If you're thinking that all this is unimportant at this stage of your career, think again: Power posing is linked to better performance in mock interviews. One Harvard Business School study had participants strike power poses for a few minutes by themselves before a mock job interview. Job seekers who did the poses privately got better job reviews and were more likely to be hired. Remember, the evaluators hadn't seen them doing the poses. Another study links power poses before a college entrance exam to higher scores.

Why not spark feelings of power before important meetings and conversations?

Don't hunch over a smartphone or laptop before an important meeting or interview, which automatically puts you into a low-power pose and state of mind. Take a couple of minutes to privately strike a power pose that broadcasts the right nonverbal messages—confidence, engagement, and leadership.

What's Your Q Score?

In branding, being liked counts a lot. That's why marketers look at a brand's or a celebrity's *Q Score*. The Q Score is a numerical ranking of the familiarity and appeal of a celebrity. Celebrities with high scores are not just well known; they are *well liked*. We feel a rapport with them, almost as if they were friends. They have strong *brand equity* that they can take to the bank. Likable celebrities are in demand and paid more than those with lower scores.

It's as if the celebrities with high Q Scores, such as Jennifer Aniston, Jennifer Lawrence, or Tom Hanks, bear a resemblance to the person we see in the bathroom mirror each morning. We feel an emotional connection and even see them as sharing our values and life experiences. It's all part of emotional branding. We buy things most often because of the way a particular brand makes us feel, not because of rational analysis.

> The secret of popular people is being emotionally available to others.
> Begin by liking others and see how they repay you by liking you.

You get a "Q Score," too, though it's not the kind you can look up on a ranking list. You are sized up in terms of authenticity, personality, and likability by others all the time. This virtual Q Score plays a vital role in interviews.

Especially in competitive markets, likability can make a big difference in getting hired and future career success. The best way to get someone to like you is to like them. Put the focus on others and empathize with them. Finding things in common also enhances likability. We like people who are similar to us, whether it is in style, political beliefs, national heritage, or school affiliation. One final factor in likability is authenticity—just being yourself makes you likable.

After a frustrating yearlong job search, Erin was in the final rounds of interviews at a women's fashion retailer, a well-known brand. "I met with six people in one day. It reminded me of sorority rush week," Erin told me. "All of these different personalities that you have to connect with and get them to like you—quickly. One fashion executive had spent a year abroad studying in France as I had done, and we had the best energy. After many misfires over the last year, I finally mastered interviewing and got the job offer."

Associate Yourself with a Word or Phrase

Brands try to own a word or short phrase in the minds of consumers. (Think Google and "search" or FedEx and "overnight.") If they succeed, people think of the brand when they hear the word. It usually takes a fair amount of time to lock in an association and have it go mainstream. Now, in the Internet era, going mainstream can happen rapidly; take the rapid adoption of a new word for the phenomenon of the "selfie."

Owning a word positions a brand with an important attribute in the minds of others, like Volvo and "safety" or Cartier and "luxury." They have meaning in a world where so many other brands do not stand for anything. It's like being the top result that comes up when you enter a keyword in a search engine.

Owning a word can help you, too. Your word could be a distinctive attribute that defines you and sets you apart from others, as "the creative MBA" does for Edouard, or reflects your career aspirations. A powerful phrase could help you dominate a niche, like Sheryl Sandburg does with her phrase "Lean In" and women's empowerment. Your phrase could indicate a special heritage that's part of your career identity: "She's the systems analyst who interned at Google."

The whole point of developing a USP pitch is to associate yourself with an idea and give people a memorable tagline so that they can easily remember what's different, relevant, and authentic about you. If you stand for something, you will stand out in a crowded job market. You're not just a run-of-the-mill engineer; you're Gwen, the top engineering graduate trained and certified in packaging engineering—from the only school in the US that offers this certification.

Become a Career Storyteller

Another important lesson to take from the Madison Avenue playbook is the power of story. Advertisers are adept at wrapping their brands in story.

Successful people tend to be good communicators and good storytellers, too.

Language is a uniquely human ability, and story gives language emotional power and pulls people into what you are saying. Don't just tick off your credentials and skill set you've achieved; tell a story that shows what you can do and the results you've achieved in a memorable way.

You'll need to develop stories for all your accomplishments and experiences that you can recount in interviews. The stories should not be about your job responsibilities, but about how you impacted and changed things. You may be thinking, "I haven't done much. My life is so ordinary." But that is just why stories can be so good: because people will relate to them.

Say you're asked in an interview, "Tell me about a time when you led a team to complete a difficult project." Begin by setting up a story. Talk about the difficulty of the task and the different strengths and weaknesses of the team.

Rather than taking them immediately to a successful conclusion, spend most of your time describing the journey. Maybe your team initially made a wrong turn and was beginning to get demoralized.

Then throw in some "magic dust." The magic dust moment is the turning point when something unexpected happened and the right solution to your problem became apparent.

When you wrap your accomplishments in story, you sell yourself in a more subtle and persuasive fashion than just ticking off a list of career highlights. You're not bragging; you're telling a story about what happened that involves the listener. Hiring managers and HR professionals are deluged with information. They need to decide who to hire. Being a good business storyteller gives them a reason to choose you.

The Sound of a Winner

The sound of your voice also affects the image people have of you. Your voice is twice as important as the words you say, according to a study by Quantified Impressions. A person's voice quality accounted for 23 percent of the listeners' evaluation, while the content of the message accounted for 11 percent. Other factors were the speaker's presence, passion, and knowledge.

Some young women have developed a bad habit called *uptalk* that makes statements sound like questions. (Think of Shoshanna Shapiro on

HBO's hit show *Girls*). Uptalk immediately brands you as weak, hesitant, and insecure—exactly what you don't want to project in a job search.

A strong, smooth voice communicates leadership and strength. If you are a man who covets the CEO title someday, you'll want to cultivate a deep voice with a 125.5 hertz vocal frequency, the median for successful CEOs according to a study by Duke University and the University of California San Diego. The highest paid CEOs had an even lower frequency on the hertz scale.

Women CEOs show a different pattern. With women, it's more about "vocal energy," which conveys authenticity and engenders feelings of trust.

Here are a few tips on how to project all the right things in interviews in terms of body language and communication style:

HIGH-POWER POSES AND COMMUNICATION

Strong posture/physical presence:

- Standing tall and leaning slightly forward with hands at one's side or taking a wide stance
- Leaning forward with hands planted firmly on the table surface and taking up more space at the conference table
- Facing another person directly and squarely

Power hand gestures:

- Showing your hands, your "trust indicators"
- Keeping your hands in the "strike zone" (shoulders to hips)
- Using broad open gestures with hands outstretched
- Keeping hands free with open palms

Clear communication style:

- Speaking more slowly with a lower voice
- Clear, concise language
- Projecting energy and authenticity

LOW-POWER POSES AND COMMUNICATION

Poor posture/weak physical presence:

- Leaning back or slumping
- Taking up very little space when standing or at the conference table
- Sitting at a lower seat than others

Contracted poses/jerky movements:

- Crossed arms in front of chest or crossed legs or ankles.
- Not showing your hands at the conference table or when speaking
- Flailing arms with too much movement or repetitive gestures
- Touching the face, neck, or hair

Embellished communication style:

- Too much detail, overexplaining
- Talking too fast
- Uptalk—rising pitch at the end of sentences

Establishing Your Career Credentials

We've talked a lot about *soft power* skills such as image and communications agility—the intangible assets built through visual and verbal identity. Soft power skills are critical in getting your first job and succeeding in the workplace.

That doesn't mean that *hard power* skills don't matter. They do.

Hard power is made up of the tangible things you can put on your resume, such as education, internship experience, skills, certifications, test scores, and the like. Hard power credentials are the price of admission to participate in the workplace. You must have a strong skill set to compete, and employers want to see actual proof of performance through relevant internships.

If you're missing key ingredients for your career aspirations, you need to fill in the gaps. With the wealth of information on the Internet, it's easy to see what specific skills and internship experiences employers are looking for.

Once you have your hard power credentials on par, soft power is the carrot that draws people to you.

The Power of Third-Party Endorsements

Marketers have always known that the best way to sell your brand is to get other people to do it for you. That's why marketers seek testimonials and endorsements from satisfied customers.

The *expert testimonial* and *celebrity endorsement* are successful ploys in the advertising business, too, because the touch of a well-known person can make a brand take off. When you have an influential person recommend you, you will get a sprinkling of their magic dust on you, too. "Gee, this person must really be good if she has a strong recommendation from Ms. Big," is how the thinking goes.

> If you say it, it's bragging.
> If someone else says it, it's an expert opinion.

You should solicit endorsements from your own "celebrities" and "experts"—the senior people you worked with in internships, summer jobs, and volunteer organizations. Your experts are your professors, college career professionals, mentors, and work colleagues.

Now with social media, it's easy to leverage the power of endorsements. Seek out people to write a recommendation on your LinkedIn profile or your one-page achievements addendum. And make sure to bring your a references one-pager to interviews.

No Time to Be Modest

A popular staple of our world today is the awards ceremony. There are a host of honors, rankings, and awards that signal achievement and special status in every industry, such as the Academy Awards in film and the *U.S. News and World Report* rankings of colleges and universities.

Everyone says they don't pay attention to awards, but this is simply untrue. US companies jockey to get on the *Fortune* list of the "100 Best Companies to Work For" just as actors promote themselves before the Academy Awards or UK brands vie for a royal warrant from the Queen.

Likewise, awards, rankings, and honors convey distinction—whether it's graduating with honors, being awarded a top prize, or heading up a school club. Websites and organizations dispense new awards, certifications, and badges by the minute. Include relevant distinctions in your marketing materials.

Modesty may be a virtue, but being known for something counts.

Here are the sorts of awards and prizes that can enhance your brand:

- Academic prizes and awards
- Awards for scientific research
- Achievement awards for women and minorities
- Community service recognition
- Awards from professional associations
- Awards for fraternity and sorority leadership activities
- Creativity awards (for example, in music or design)
- Sports awards

Cast Yourself in Leadership Roles

Most interviewers are looking for leaders, people who have the potential to rise in the company. In fact, one of the questions you can count on is, "Tell me about a time when you played a leadership role in a project." Many new grads have told me this is an unfair question because they hadn't had much opportunity at this point in their lives to be a leader.

That means you'll have to be a bit more creative in looking for your leadership stories. This could mean being a leader in a small pond (leading up a charity drive at your fraternity) or a big pond (leading the university golf team to victory in the national competition). It could be leadership of a club or a nonprofit where you spearheaded an important fund-raising event.

For each of these leadership and teamwork achievements, present your accomplishments in a format that builds suspense as you take others through the experience. Always shine the spotlight on the project, event, or obstacles, not on yourself. Always make your professional stories about something larger than yourself.

Guard Your Image

The image you worked so hard to build can come crashing down in a second. A brand's reputation is built by repetition over a long period of time, and your reputation will be built incrementally over time as well. Yet one bad act that's played out on the Internet can smash your reputation to pieces in seconds.

> Reputations take a long time to build and a short time to destroy.

A carefully cultivated professional image can be undermined by party photos on social media, a funny email address such as partyguy@gmail. com, or an unprofessional voicemail message.

Why chance it?

What's worse, a bad story can be magnified on the Internet. What do you do if a bad story appears about you online and comes up prominently when people Google you? The good reputation you've worked so hard to create can go up in smoke in a flash.

You'll find that it's hard to erase things from the Internet. That's why you must play a strong role in creating your story—the one you want told, not the story that someone else assigns to you. One tactic for exerting control is to post Internet content frequently. Search engines give more weight to real-time updates, so if you are active on social media and new media, posting and connecting frequently, your media updates will impact organic search results and push down the negative story on page rankings. You can also ask people to write positive recommendations and endorsements on social media sites as well. That way the bad story will look oddly out of place.

Leave a Role for Lady Luck

When you're pitching and selling yourself, it's easy to feel awkward tooting your own horn and recounting all your wonderful deeds. Here's where luck can come in. While I believe that you create your own luck, that doesn't mean you can't add a generous dollop of luck to your stories. Smart people often make luck a key element in their stories of achievement. If you attribute it to luck, it makes you look humble.

> Luck is not a good strategy for finding a job.
> You prepare for good luck by working hard.
> You prepare for bad luck by having a Plan B.

You might say, "Gee, I just got lucky. The architecture firm where I did my internship got a new project, and they needed someone who was fluent in German. My junior year abroad in Germany really paid off since they made me a good job offer after I graduated."

Be Consistent at Every Touchpoint

You will want to step back from time to time to look at your career identity holistically. What are all the places where people come into contact with you, both online and offline? What is the experience like, and is it consistent? How do prospects find out about you? What do they learn?

Do you know?

Examine your brand from a 360-degree perspective. You need to step into the shoes of all of your different "customers," just as marketing professionals do.

When you do that, you'll find many contact points, what marketers call *touchpoints*, both in person and online: your LinkedIn profile and social media presence, your resume, your pitch letter, your email signature, your voicemail message, and, of course, your self-presentation in person.

> Touchpoints: All the contact points—both real and virtual—
> where people come into contact with Brand You.

You want every one of your touchpoints to convey a consistent, positive impression. Brands, like reputations, are built through repetition. You want to repeat a consistent brand image at every touchpoint.

Managing your image is a skill you must master if you want to build a personal brand. The key to building your image well is to make it appear effortless. You want to be known for something but not for being a self-promoter.

And that indeed is an art worth learning.

Chapter 7 Exercises

1. What are the main touchpoints or contact points where people can access your brand? Are they all consistent?

2. Videotape yourself giving a mock interview and ask two or three friends to critique it. Then play it again for them with the sound off. How can you improve the image you project?

3. Before your next interview, do one or two power poses for two minutes by yourself. Consciously try to adopt some power poses in the meeting such as leaning in toward the interviewer.

4. How can you project a stronger image that's right for the job area you are exploring? Do you need to change up your clothes or hairstyle?

CHAPTER 8

Your Career Identity on the Internet and Social Media

Conveying your career identity is just a Google or a Bing away. The professional identity that you've worked hard to create at college can be made more valuable with online tools or be destroyed in a nanosecond if something negative starts trending.

If people want to know about you, they're going to search the Internet to find out. That's true whether they're considering you for a job interview, a date, or as a networking contact.

If you have a weak profile online, recruiters and hiring managers are likely to discount your abilities. "John must be better than Sally since he has a strong career identity online," is how the thinking goes. If you don't show up on major search engines at all, that sends a message about your brand, too—that you don't exist!

Your Online Career Identity

The decision to hire you or not is based on perceptions, and the Internet, particularly social media like LinkedIn, Facebook, Twitter, and Instagram, is a big factor in molding professional perceptions today. That's why you need to take charge of building and nurturing your career identity online as you do offline.

Look at the numbers. A whopping 78 percent of business managers say they Google prospective employees. Recruiters research prospects online after posting jobs on their company website, social media like LinkedIn and Twitter, and conventional job sites like Indeed.com, Glassdoor.com, and SimplyHired.com. And recruiters take social profiles seriously—70 percent have reconsidered candidates after seeing their social profile.

Job seekers are camping out on social sites in droves, too. Some 86 percent of job seekers have an account on at least one of the major social sites, according to Jobvite.

People don't even have to know you personally to "like," "friend," "endorse," or "follow" you online. These are the good things that people can do to you online, but they can also do not so-good-things—like post a picture of you drinking at a party and tag your name to it. Then it's up to you to untag yourself before it hurts your brand.

> A weak digital footprint is like a weak reputation.
> People won't think you're as good as someone with a strong
> online brand.

Social media takes word of mouth to a whole new level, magnifying and dispersing buzz as never before. And it's something that you should capture, too: word of mouth has always been the best (and cheapest) tool for branding.

After all, your career identity isn't just what you say; it's what others say about you when you're not around. And the more quality content, connections, and recommendations you have on social media sites like LinkedIn, the stronger your brand will be.

Make That 3.0 Degrees

Social media connects us as never before.

We've all heard of six degrees of separation: the idea that any two people can be connected using only six hops. The concept was based on research in the 1960s by American social psychologist Stanley Milgram, made famous by John Guare's 1990 play *Six Degrees of Separation* and popularized by the parlor game Six Degrees of Kevin Bacon.

Well, six degrees is now outdated, thanks to social media. Several studies prove social media takes fewer than six steps to connect us. According to a 2014 study by Facebook and the University of Milan of over 721 million users, the average number of hops it takes to connect any two people on Facebook is 4.74, including even far-flung users in the Siberian tundra. Twitter did a similar study that shows their number is 4.67 degrees.

On LinkedIn, the world's largest professional site, it's just 3 degrees. Here's their math:

- You know them
- You know someone who knows them
- You know someone who knows someone who knows them

The Art of the "Follow"

If imitation is the sincerest form of flattery, following people and companies on social media isn't far behind. As an aspiring job seeker, you can follow your dream companies, hiring managers, and influential people on Twitter, LinkedIn, and other such sites. On LinkedIn, go to the company page, click on the yellow Follow button at the top, and do an advanced people search to find interesting people to follow.

Begin to build relationships on Twitter by searching directories for potential contacts, commenting on posts, retweeting, and posting @Name or @Company with a question or a comment. Following a company's Twitter account lets the hiring manager know that you really want to work there. It can even lead to a job offer, as Byron Cordero discovered.

An aspiring publicist, Byron quickly learned at his first internship after graduation that his college public relations courses were good for learning theory, but not for the practice of PR. His initial emails were long and formal. What works in PR is short texts that are spot-on and provocative. He began to rely on social media communities, such as PR, Marketing, and Media Czars on Facebook, which featured an active exchange of tips and ideas among peers.

During the internship, Byron went to an event where he met the head of a public relations boutique, so he started following Ms. PR Director on Twitter. He retweeted a few of her tweets and gradually got on her radar screen. She returned the favor and started following him. Byron sent direct messages with articles he thought might be of interest, and a Twitter relationship was born.

So how do you build a professional relationship with an influential person on Twitter? Here is a sampling of the tweets between the PR head and Byron—Twitter handle: @NYCPRboy. Note that Byron purposely didn't use his name for his Twitter handle. He chose one that reinforced his career aspirations. Their tweets will show you how a social media relationship can build and lead to a job offer:

Byron
NYCPRboy

Thanks for the follow. Fab blog. Loved work-life-balance post!

← Reply   ⇄ Retweet   ★ Favorite   ••• More

1:33 PM   15 Feb

Ms. PR Director
@TwitterHandle

Thank you! Would love to have male perspective on the blog – please consider submitting a guest post

← Reply   ⇄ Retweet   ★ Favorite   ••• More

10:05 AM   17 Feb

Byron
NYCPRboy

Loved your latest blog post. Would love for you to read my bits and my tumblr, maybe we can colab

← Reply   ⇄ Retweet   ★ Favorite   ••• More

4:24 PM   05 Mar

Ms. PR Director
@TwitterHandle

I would LOVE it. I have actually viewed your tumblr quite a few times and I like it so much! Let's keep in touch

← Reply ⇄ Retweet ★ Favorite ••• More

9:35 AM 07 Mar

 Ms. PR Director
@TwitterHandle

Hello! Thank you, can you tell me a bit more about yourself? We are always looking for ambitious and exciting new talent

← Reply ⇄ Retweet ★ Favorite ••• More

4:33 pm 01 Apr

 Byron
NYCPRboy

All experience lies in fashion/lifestyle PR. I absolutely love traditional tactics coupled with innovative social media campaigns. #PR101

← Reply ⇄ Retweet ★ Favorite ••• More

8:22 AM 03 Apr

 Ms. PR Director
@TwitterHandle

Great! Are you currently working for a firm?

← Reply ⇄ Retweet ★ Favorite ••• More

8:22 AM 03 Apr

Shortly afterward, when someone left the PR boutique, Ms. PR Director tapped Byron for the job. Byron was successful in using Twitter as a job-hunting tool not only because it was a modern way to stand out from the crowd, but because the tone of his banter and verbal shorthand was perfect for the PR field and Twitter. If you're following someone in a more traditional field, look at their tweets to set the right tone.

@, #, and Other Social Stuff

At its core, social media operates on the concept of reciprocity. In short, give and you shall receive. In the world of social media, that means:

- Follow to be followed
- Comment to be commented on
- Ask, retweet, and like to join in the conversation
- Tag specific people to get their attention

You can really get on someone's radar screen when you tag them, as the exchange with the PR director demonstrated. Use *@Name* and *@CompanyX* to signal to people and companies your interest in them and their content. You'll increase your reach, too, since your post will appear on their page and also be seen by their network.

LinkedIn has made it easier to tag people. Go to your homepage and click the "Share an update" button or click "Comment" on someone else's update. Type @ and then begin typing a name, and you'll see a list of companies or people you can tag. Click the name you want and type your post.

If you're active on Twitter, you no doubt have mastered retweeting. A *retweet* (RT) is when someone on Twitter decides to share your tweet with their followers. When you retweet, the tweet is repeated in your timeline with the original person's attribution. It's an easy way to share news, messages, and information. Retweets will flatter people and are a good way to build relationships. If you add a sentence at the beginning of the retweet, you'll convey a little of your personality and point of view to further the relationship. Example: "This is the best advice on job hunting I've ever read RT@TwitterHandle."

Facebook's *like* button is one of the most valuable buttons in social media. It makes it easy to give posts a virtual thumbs-up with one click when you don't have time to write a message or comment.

Comment on the posts of people and companies you're following if you have something relevant to say. If you're adding value or saying something interesting, you're likely to get a response and maybe even a new follower or friend.

You can use the #, or *hashtag symbol*, before a word or phrase about any topic to label it. Social messages with the same hashtag are bundled together for easy subject-specific browsing that you can access by clicking on a hyperlinked text. If you use too many hashtags, your message will start to look like spam. Limit yourself to three hashtags per message. Hashtags are often used to show that a message is related to an event or conference. Check out hashtagify.me to locate the most popular hashtags in every category.

Here are a few hashtags every job seeker should know about:

#joblisting: A good source for job listings

#jobopening: Job listings in various industries

#IBMjobs: Many large companies have their own hashtag for job postings

#Techjobs: Most industries and fields have special hashtags for jobs and advice

#Graduatejobs: Has entry-level jobs for new grads

#JobHuntChat: For chats on job-hunting advice

Go Big or Go Home

To build your career identity online, begin by owning your name's real estate on the Internet. Buy your domain name even if you don't have a website or blog set up yet. Owning *yourname.com* is great for job hunting because you will be completely search engine optimized.

Register on popular social media sites such as LinkedIn so you have a customized URL with your name (www.linkedin.com/in/JohnSmith), not the default meaningless string of numbers and letters. That way recruiters and hiring managers won't have to go through hundreds of different profiles to find you.

Claim your digital real estate:
Your Name.com, LinkedIn/in/YourName, etc.

If you have a common name, don't be surprised if another person owns the domain or has staked it out on sites like LinkedIn. To differentiate yourself from a duplicate user name, consider using a nickname, a middle initial, a middle name or a double-barreled last name to set yourself apart. On Twitter, it's @JohnKSmith, not be confused with @JohnQSmith. You can also put a hyphen or underscore between your first and last name to own your domain.

Above all, you want to make sure that your website name or Twitter handle is easy to remember. You can use a modifier (@TheJohnSmith) or tie in your career choice (@SalesJohnSmith or @JohnSmithCPA). If you just got your MD, use @DrJohnSmith; if you've earned a PhD, use @JohnSmithPhD. Or you can flag your career aspirations with @MarketingMaven.

LinkedIn: The One Place You Have to Be

You may think LinkedIn is for old people, but when it comes to careers, it's number one. LinkedIn is for building your professional identity, enjoying organizations and groups, and finding out about jobs of interest.

LinkedIn is where recruiters do most of their employee-seeking activity. According to CareerGlider, 95 percent of recruiters search using social networks, and the network of choice is LinkedIn. Recruiters use it when searching for candidates, contacting candidates, vetting candidates preinterview, and posting jobs.

LinkedIn is where your "customers" are—the hiring managers, HR people, and recruiters you want to attract. Students and new graduates are catching on and are now the fastest-growing demographic on LinkedIn. Not surprising, since in addition to being the hot hunting ground for recruiters, the site has over a million and a half student jobs and internships.

To job hunt, go to the search bar and type in the functional area you've targeted, such as "sales assistant." If you click on a job at X Company, you will get a list of other jobs at X Company along with similar jobs at other companies. You can also get a list of jobs that people who viewed this job also looked at. Plus, LinkedIn is constantly adding new features to help you manage your career identity and look for jobs.

LinkedIn has added a number of features to make the site work better for students and new grads. They created the Alumni Tool, a searchable database of people who went to your university, and other cool stuff like University pages, Field of Study pages, and Decision Boards.

LinkedIn is a resume that works 24/7 and comes up high in the results when someone Googles you. (Check it out.) So it's smart to customize your LinkedIn page to make public the parts you want. Then use your personal URL (linkedin.com/in/YourName) as a link on your resume, email signature, business card, and other marketing pieces.

LinkedIn also has a mobile app that does everything the laptop version does. You can connect with people and put your two cents into group discussions. It even has a job board where you can save jobs of interest.

Warning: Turn off your activity broadcast completely in Privacy and Settings. Otherwise, every time you tweak your LinkedIn headline, your network will receive a message like, "Say congrats on the new job." That's not the message you want to have go out when you are still looking and actively interviewing.

Ace the LinkedIn Profile

If you've ever marketed yourself on dating sites like Match.com or eHarmony.com, you know how important a great profile and flattering picture are to dating success. The same is true for building your brand on LinkedIn.

The LinkedIn profile is integral to building your career identity on social media and is a powerful branding tool. Many employers won't take you seriously unless you have a professional-looking profile, so you'll want to craft yours carefully.

LinkedIn is a great opportunity to showcase your experience and expertise in detail through text and visuals. You're at an early stage in your career, so you may have to get creative in developing a profile that sells your abilities. You will have to think of comparable examples from your internships, jobs, and club activities.

You can include rich media such as slide presentations, videos, and documents in the Summary or Experience sections. Look outside of your resume. Is there a college paper in your field of study you could use? A picture of you on a school panel or receiving an award? LinkedIn gives you the opportunity to highlight awards and achievements in more detail than you would put on a one-page resume.

Never forget that branding always involves curating. As a brander, you want to put your best self forward, shining the spotlight on what burnishes your brand and dimming the lights to camouflage the gaps.

Did you know that LinkedIn gives you a great way to do that? You can rearrange the content sections in your LinkedIn profile in a different order. Let's say you don't have relevant work experience and internships but have unusual certifications and coursework in your specialty. Why not put those sections at the top under the summary, rather than begin with work experience as everyone else does? Be selective: emphasize job and internship details that position you for the direction you're heading in with your career, not the missteps or menial work you did along the way.

What Are Your Competitors Up To on LinkedIn?

Good marketing begins with *competitive analysis.* You'll want to look at how other people starting out in your field market themselves on LinkedIn. Look at the profiles of people you admire to get ideas. Study leaders who have strong, large audiences or who are active in the groups that you've joined.

We're not talking about copying, but competitive research will provide ideas and inspiration about how to make your profile as strong as it can be.

LinkedIn also has premium features that give you additional fields and controls. The site offers a free trial month, so you can test it out or do your competitive research up front and move back to the free service. In doing your competitive analysis, you want to change your view setting to "anonymous" so that your name won't be flagged to the people you're looking up.

Master the LinkedIn Headline

As in a print ad, the two most important elements on your LinkedIn profile are the headline and picture, so take time to craft a good headline and get an attractive picture. In fact, those are the first things recruiters see. Recruiters will read your profile headline with great care. LinkedIn only gives you 120 characters (about the length of a tweet), so you can't go into detail. That's for your summary.

Your headline should convey the one thing you want a hiring manager or anyone else to know about you. Chances are they won't go further if your headline lacks the right keywords or an engaging value proposition that makes people want to learn more.

Headlines should be punchy but informative. You want to convey something specific about the job you are seeking and an engaging power statement to differentiate you from everyone else. It should contain keywords that recruiters might use in finding candidates for target entry-level jobs. Your power headline can be your USP sentence, the brand differentiator that is part of your pitch.

Here is the headline from Erin's LinkedIn profile:

"Marketing Assistant: ABC University Graduate in Psychology with Pulse on the Consumer Mind-set"

And here is Edouard's profile headline:

"Business Development Assistant, International Business MBA—the mind of a businessman and the soul of a creative"

Here are a few more profile headlines for college students, new graduates, and young professionals:

- "Innovative Computer Programmer: Known for Building Next-Gen Software, C++, Python, Java"
- "Honors Graduate in Engineering: Minor Packaging Design, Winner of Prize for Innovative Design"
- "Entrepreneurial Accountant Specializing in Start-Ups, Dual Degrees: MBA, CPA"
- "Homeland Security–Certified Information Security Analyst with Internships in Public and Private Sectors"

The Right Picture = Priceless

Don't underestimate the importance of the profile picture. Having a photo makes the whole virtual experience real. And for some hiring managers, not having a photo is a disqualifier.

> A page with a profile picture is fourteen times more likely to be viewed.

Your picture will be scrutinized more than you realize. Get a high-quality picture that lets your personality and brilliance shine. If you're a DIYer and want to take a selfie, here are some guidelines for taking the best #workselfie:

- **Put the focus on you.** Select a head-and-shoulders shot of you alone, not a picture with your dog, significant other, or a scenic view in the background. Use a frontal shot or one turning to your left so you lead into your summary on LinkedIn.
- **Use one picture across all social media.** From a branding perspective, it makes sense to use the same picture across all social media channels so you have a consistent, recognizable brand image everywhere online.
- **Dress the part.** It's important to dress the part for your career and industry. Dress professionally and simply. Ditch the glam unless you are in the fashion industry and the jeans and T-shirt unless you want to work at a tech start-up or creative agency.
- **Show some personality.** Don't think a head shot and appropriate dress means that you need to opt for a dull, lifeless "corporate" shot. Although many industries prefer a corporate look, that doesn't mean you have to be expressionless. The best photos have a natural feel and project warmth and openness.
- **Compose the shot.** Look up at the camera; that angle will show you in a more flattering way, emphasizing your eyes. Natural light will also give you the best results.

Another way to make your profile stand out visually is to upload a customized background color or image behind your LinkedIn headline and head shot. Take advantage of this freebie option for making your profile look more graphically interesting.

Summary: Set Up Your Career Future

Recruiters and hiring managers will read your LinkedIn Summary carefully, so don't post a boring, slapdash statement that's dull or says too little. You get 2,000 characters to market yourself, the "story" of your experience, and communicate your vision for your future.

The best profiles tell a career story that ties all the pieces of your life together—your academic career, your professional journey, and where you want to go—into a coherent whole that's compelling and different. Write conversationally so your Summary is personal and engaging. Describe your accomplishments, what excites you, and what makes you different.

A complete Summary gives you an opportunity to use keywords that might come up on searches. Think of the words that hiring managers might search for, such as computer programmer, marketing assistant, assistant engineer, graphic artist, sales trainee, and the like.

It's smart to begin your Summary with your name and a brand sentence or USP that communicates quickly who you are and your differentiator. Recruiters often copy just the summaries, so having your name at the top will ensure your Summary is tied to you. Since LinkedIn doesn't reproduce bold type, use all caps for subheads to make them stand out.

The body of the Summary should bring your career future and your strengths to life in a captivating narrative flow. Weave in internships, credentials, and turning points in your career so far. Use bullets, action verbs, and metrics to highlight key accomplishments.

Downplay aspects of your academic or career journey that distract from your brand or lead people in the wrong direction unless you can make them part of your story. Avoid insider jargon so that your value is understandable to a broad audience.

One way to end your Summary is with a paragraph on your expertise that lists all skills and areas of interest for your future career. This gives you a further opportunity to include keywords and focus your brand. You can also end with your contact email address if you want to make it easy for people to contact you.

Here's a sample Summary by new grad Erin, a psychology major looking for a job in marketing:

MARKETING ASSISTANT: PSYCHOLOGY GRAD WITH PULSE ON THE CONSUMER MIND-SET AND EXTENSIVE INTERNSHIP EXPERIENCE

Today's consumer marketplace is very social, but it's not because of particular platforms like Twitter or Facebook. The products and companies that are most successful will adopt a model that puts people—not technology—at the forefront of products and marketing strategies.

My mission: To market to consumers in the brave new world of the "Internet of everything"—social, mobile, machine to people, and other new technologies. As a marketing intern, my passion is understanding what makes people tick and applying psychology to business to develop new and better marketing strategies and platforms to connect with consumers. I thrive on the thrill of challenge in a competitive, ever-changing marketplace.

Key Accomplishments

- Researched strategic options and developed a PowerPoint presentation to position ABC Company competitively in the digital era at XX Company internship

- Conducted market research and competitive analysis to identify target acquisitions and prospective clients, which increased market share by 20 percent

- Assisted in developing product promotions for key clients in the beauty, fashion, and lifestyle divisions at XYZ Company, including (list of products)

- Helped develop promotion giveaway gift bags and developed relationships with celebrity influencers, including the staff of Y magazine

---

Expertise/Areas of Interest

Marketing, Marketing Strategy, Consumer Behavior, Consumer Psychology, Market Research, Digital Marketing, PR, Promotion, Events, Social Media, New Media, Consumer Products, Brand Positioning, Merchandising, Digital Marketing, Analytics

Skills: Microsoft Office, Adobe Photoshop, WordPress, IT skills, budget spreadsheets, database entry, statistical analysis, reports

Show Your Stuff in Multimedia

On the Summary and Experience sections on LinkedIn, you can attach or link to rich media to showcase work samples and marketing materials. Take the time to design graphically interesting cover pages for important projects and documents so they pop as a thumbnail visual. You can feature a short video resume, slide presentation, or relevant school project.

Try including creative elements, such as a screen shot of tweets you sent at a conference or a visual infographic on your career story. If you're in a creative field, upload a creative portfolio of your design work that viewers can click on.

For the Experience section on LinkedIn, you can literally cut and paste from your resume. LinkedIn doesn't limit your word count in the Experience section, so it's an opportunity to supply critical details about your internships, work history, and computer skills.

As a student or recent graduate, it pays to think holistically about your experience. Write up your volunteer activities in the Volunteer Experience and Causes section. Try to include performance metrics for each volunteer activity. (Helped develop fund-raising bike race "Cycle for Hope" for Habitat for Humanity, which brought in $10,000 in one day.)

After the Experience section on LinkedIn, there are a number of sections that can add dimension to your brand. You can list relevant part-time consulting and contracting work. You can highlight grants and fellowships you received. You can name philanthropic or industry organizations you support. In the Honors and Awards section, you can list the prizes, recognition, scholarships, certificates, team projects, relevant classes, and even the languages you speak.

The Education section is your chance to list all degrees, study-abroad and summer programs, courses, certifications, and distinctions.

What's the Buzz on You?

We humans like to make decisions based on social proof. What do people say about you professionally? What do you want them to say?

LinkedIn Recommendations and Endorsements allow you to share the buzz on you through recommenders from your internships and jobs. Here's how to take advantage of this opportunity:

- **Put together a target list of recommenders.** Reach out to former bosses and professional colleagues, professors and college friends, and friends and acquaintances who think highly of your abilities.

- **Space out your requests so they appear organic.** LinkedIn time-stamps your recommendations, so don't ask eight people at once. Make it look like the recommendations built up naturally over time.

- **Approach each person with a specific request.** Approach your recommenders with a clear-cut request that outlines specific projects and tasks you were responsible for and how well things went. Don't use the default request, which is too generic a message. When you make a detailed request, you give your recommenders copy they can adapt for their recommendation.

Here's how you might approach someone:

Hello James,

I hope that everything is going well in Atlanta. I'm writing to ask if you could write a recommendation for me that highlights the PR and product promotion skills that I developed at my internship last summer. As you know, my role was to write press releases and prepare press kits for the launch of XYZ product. We had a tremendous response. Three of the four Atlanta stations did TV coverage, and we had a front-page story in the *Atlanta Times*. I helped set up over ten radio interviews.

I am so grateful for the internship experience that I had last summer. At college I learned a lot about PR and marketing promotions, but it's theory until you handle an actual event. I am also working hard to locate a full-time job in PR after graduation, and LinkedIn is the focal point of my job hunt, so your recommendation is particularly valuable to me.

Thanks in advance.

Best,

Elizabeth

LinkedIn Endorsements make it easy for people to put in a positive word without having to write a thing, only click a button on a skill or expertise. Recruiters don't put much weight on endorsements because endorsers don't have to put much thought into it, yet having no endorsements doesn't speak well of you, either. See if you can reach out to your friends so that important strengths and abilities are endorsed the most. Consider eliminating endorsement topics that can lead recruiters in the wrong direction.

What Is Your Philosophy Toward Connections?

Are you going for broke aiming for the maximum number of LinkedIn connections? (It will appear as 500+ near the top of your profile, but the current cap is 30,000.) Or should you limit your connections to people you know? While Twitter encourages bingeing on followers, many people feel that LinkedIn should be focused on people you know in some professional capacity, no matter how vaguely.

For networking, whether online or in person, a large group of connections beats a small group—not that you need to be an *open networker* and say yes to everyone. The ideal network is broad but selectively deep. When recruiters look for someone with your qualifications, your name will likely appear near the top on searches if you have a large number of Level 1 contacts.

My philosophy is to be semiselective. If someone reaches out to you, browse their profile to see if there is synergy. And you can connect with people in jobs or at companies that appeal to you by sending a short invitation. You'll have much better results if you send a customized note rather than the default message.

The Power of Facebook

Facebook is a great place to find a job. Because of the size of its audience, over 1.5 billion active monthly users and counting, a whopping 76 percent of social job seekers found jobs through Facebook.

Consider taking a two-faced approach on Facebook: dedicate your main feed for family and friends (use the Just Friends privacy setting) and the other for your career. Begin by adding your professional history to your Facebook profile (under Work and Education in the About section) to create a strong work and academic profile.

Now, go to your list of Friends, and then from the pull-down menu go to Add to Another List and select Professional for your career contacts. It takes a little time at first, but you'll end up with a list of professional contacts that you can use for status updates. You can "like" their updates and comment on what they're doing. It's a way of maintaining informal relationships, as you would do in person.

You should "like" the Facebook fan pages of companies that interest you and start commenting on their posts. You can also reach out to target companies on their Facebook fan page, as Edouard did. For each of his dream companies, he put together a PowerPoint presentation of why he wanted to work there and why they should hire him. But he didn't send them the whole presentation; instead, he launched *teaser campaigns*. Edouard took a screen shot of the cover slide and posted it to the company page with a message such as, "Hello Z Company, I created this presentation on why I want to work at Company Z and would love to send you the full presentation." Try it and see if it works for you.

Twitter: Brevity Is the Soul of Wit

Twitter is the pulse of the Internet, where new topics start trending and politicians, celebrities, and people of all types announce their news. A tweet is short and sweet. How can you resist a communication tool that limits you to a handful of words?

Well, tweeting takes practice and a little wit to master the short quips that get noticed. As a personal branding tool, you can use Twitter to promote events in your life, big and small, from conferences you're attending to interesting articles to what's on your mind. It's not a sin to repeat tweets or other digital messages. Use the # symbol before a word or phrase to label the tweet and help it appear on Twitter searches. For example, if you are tweeting about job search tips, use #jobsearch or other popular hashtags for job hunting. (Try Googling "Best job search hashtags.")

At the beginning of the chapter, Byron showed you how to use Twitter to follow hiring managers, retweet (RT) their tweets, and reach them directly using the "@" symbol and their Twitter handle or through a direct message (DM). Edouard used Twitter to take his teaser campaign directly to hiring managers, similar to efforts on Facebook. He created short, graphically interesting PowerPoint presentations on why he wanted to work at the company, and just tweeted a message with the cover slide, asking the hiring manager to respond directly if she would like the full presentation.

You can use Twitter to stand out from the crowd at college fairs and events. Tweet, "Plan on attending the @XCompany event at Z University next week." After the event, you can tweet, "Thank you @XCompany." Many companies have Twitter feeds for job listings that you can tap, in addition to job listing sites and feeds like @craigslistjobs.

Beyond the Big Three Social Giants

While the big three—LinkedIn, Facebook, and Twitter—see most of the action, social platforms such as Instagram, Pinterest, YouTube, Google +, and SnapChat can play an important role in personal networking and landing jobs. Don't forget about niche sites targeted to an industry or job function, either. Even dating apps such as Tinder can guide you to a job lead, if not romance.

First off, make sure that your Instagram profile reflects the professional image you want to portray. If you're interested in architecture, post pictures on Instagram of your favorite architects, your design work, or being on location at an internship. If you're interested in a particular company, look for a visual way to show your engagement and interest. For example, you could take a picture of yourself using a product and write a short caption about your customer service experience or why you like the product.

#DreamCompany or #CompanyEvent: Mimicking the hashtags a company uses is a great way to get noticed and build relationships at your target companies.

Find the most important people in a company or industry and begin following them on Instagram or other social media. You can also "tag" a company or individuals in your posts to get their attention. Mimicking the hashtags a company already uses is another way to get noticed. But don't be a hashtag junkie with seven hashtags in a row; keep it to three, max.

Pinterest is all about beautiful images and inspiration, so it's a great vehicle for creative people. You can easily create an up-to-date repository of all of your design work or writing clips by putting together a Pinterest portfolio. Pinterest also gives you a creative way to display your resume. Rather than "pinning" your resume, you can create an entire board that shows each of the different parts of your resume with a picture and text. For example, in the section on internships, you can include a photo of yourself on location with copy underneath about the experience.

Videos on YouTube let you show your personality, communication ability, and what you can do. But YouTube is more than a place for a video resume; you can create a channel and post videos on your area of expertise. If you're an accounting or business major, you can make a video of tips on how to get through college on a tight budget. Try to keep your videos short—one to three minutes—and put relevant tags and keywords on all your videos in the description to aid search.

Don't make a sales pitch in your videos. Make your videos entertaining or enlightening or designed to inform or educate. Research shows that videos that are passed on have *high arousal*, meaning that people get emotionally involved. Many companies hold video contests online to find potential candidates, particularly in the performing arts. These have become so popular that YouTube has a page dedicated to video contests.

The Secrets of Bloggers, Tweeters, and Social Media Mavens

Blogging, tweeting, and social media stars have something in common. They know that the more real or useful the content, the bigger the online following. They realize that social media provides a way to connect with people directly and often.

Rather than trying to sell anything, even trying to sell themselves for a job, they share articles, experiences, and useful tools that might be of interest to others.

Make your posts and tweets about sharing what's interesting to you, since it might be of interest to others on a similar journey.

As a student or new graduate, be the storyteller of your career journey by sharing relevant articles or describing conferences you attended. Share what you're doing and who you're meeting. Reveal what others are thinking and why it intrigues you. Try to repurpose every piece of content you create into other social and Internet formats so that all of your hard work as a content creator pays off.

You don't have to be an online expert to build a brand online, but you do have to understand the basics:

- **Develop a consistent, quality online career identity across all channels.** A cardinal rule of branding is to have a consistent brand at every touch point. You don't want to be Professional Paul on LinkedIn and Party Paul on Facebook. Everywhere you appear in public online should convey the same career identity, with the same profile picture and summary. All this should match your self-presentation in person.

- **Establish your message and keywords.** Put yourself in the shoes of people who might search for you and your job skills. Research the most commonly searched keywords in your industry and job function. Make sure that those keywords are used in your online profiles so that search engines will pick you up. Keywords evolve and change, and you'll need to keep your keywords up to date.

- **Utilize social media's powerful networking and job-hunting capabilities.** LinkedIn is king and totally focused around careers, but Facebook, Twitter, Instagram, Google+, Pinterest, and YouTube all offer distinct advantages in the personal branding and job-hunting game. Learn how to make them work for you by mastering job search, following, tagging, hashtagging, sharing, and all the other tactics that make social media so hot for building relationships and finding a job.

- **Automate your online career identity.** You can't do it all, so use social media management sites such as TweetDeck and Hootsuite, which allow you to manage all of your social media in one place. Many sites allow you to schedule blog posts or tweets in advance so that you can do a week's worth (or a month's worth) at once. You can always come back and add something topical. Or you can use tools so that every tweet you do automatically appears on other social media sites like Facebook and LinkedIn.

- **Develop a website or blog if you're serious.** While your LinkedIn profile can serve as an ad hoc website, if you're serious about building a strong career identity online, and I hope you are if you're reading this book, a website or blog is a must. If you're in a creative field, your website should have a unique look and feel along with samples of your work. But as a personal brander, you should always tweak a website template so the design, look, and feel are unique. It is easy to set up a blog on WordPress and other sites, but it's important to blog regularly, at least twice a week, if you want to use it as a brand-building tool. Think of how you can reuse all of your material effectively in other formats.

- **Express your personality, but sidestep controversy.** As a blogging or tweeting careerist, you've got to be interesting, and guess what? It's not as hard as you think. Share what you know. Tell people what you're doing. Remark on something you saw. Explain a complicated idea. Above all, be yourself. It's good to reveal your personality, but you need to avoid controversy that can alienate prospective hiring managers or your current boss and clients. Ask yourself, Is this enhancing my career identity? Controversy is an asset only if you're in a highly creative field where a maverick image is par for the course, or you're a brash entrepreneur and going against the grain is part of your brand persona.

- **Monitor your virtual image.** Set up Google Alerts for your name and relevant keywords so you can check what is being said about you and your interests as you build your career identity online. There are a number of reputation management tools you can use to track your online reputation and keywords such as Trackur, BrandsEye, Klout, and My Reputation. Gradually, Brand You, not the copycats with the same name, will rise to the top of search engine results.

Effective job hunting today needs more than just traditional, in-person networking and marketing, as powerful as that is. Instead, employ a holistic approach using all the tools at your disposal to build a strong personal brand both in person and online. What works best is standing for something and building a community with your professional colleagues, prospects, and like-minded people through traditional and virtual touch points.

Leverage the new social media world. Social media like LinkedIn gives you tools to make your professional identity more valuable and new ways to land a job. Unlike the old media world, where you had to pay dearly or know the gatekeepers to gain entry, social media is low cost and democratic. But you have to make the time to take advantage of it.

Chapter 8 Exercises

1. Spend time crafting a complete LinkedIn profile with all sections filled out. Here is your checklist:

   - **Headline:** Write down your LinkedIn headline. How can you make your headline more compelling?
   - **Picture:** Is it appropriate and flattering?
   - **Summary:** Try to use the complete word count so that you have a powerful career identity and room for relevant keywords. Do you have any rich media you want to attach to your Summary, such as a short slide presentation?
   - **Experience:** Include your internships and summer and part-time jobs.
   - **Honors and Awards:** Do you have any awards or recognition you can cite?
   - **Publications:** Do you have any articles or blog posts published online?
   - **Education:** Include university and summer courses
   - **Interests:** Give companies a snapshot of who you are

2. Ask three people to write you a professional recommendation on LinkedIn.

3. Write professional recommendations for three former coworkers.

4. What keywords do you want to be known for? What keywords are recruiters likely to use in finding someone in the field you are targeting? Make sure your LinkedIn profile includes these keywords.

5. Google to find out the keywords or buzzwords in your profession. For example, search for "marketing keywords or buzzwords." Write them down. Which should you incorporate into your LinkedIn profile?

CHAPTER 9

Who Do *You* Know? Who Knows *You*?

You can't launch your career alone. Unlike in academia, where your work speaks for itself, in the real world your work and abilities are just part of the equation. Who you know and who knows you count for a great deal, as new law school graduate James discovered.

Smart and hardworking, James was worried. He had substantial student debt and was facing a tough job market for lawyers. He had read some alarming statistics about recent law graduates—some 20 percent were working in jobs that didn't require a law degree and only 40 percent had a job in a law firm. Even his degree from a good law school was no guarantee of a secure, well-paying law career.

James noticed a job posting at a law firm and made it into the final round of interviews with a committee of five partners at the firm. His academic background and internship experience were perfect. The interviews went so well James felt sure he had the job.

Of course, we know how this movie ends. The job went to Sylvie, a law school grad who attended a less prestigious law school and had fewer internship credentials than James.

How did Sylvie succeed when the better-educated perfect candidate, James, did not? It wasn't luck. It wasn't an accident.

The Power of a Network

James *interviewed* for the job, but Sylvie *networked* her way into the job!

Surprise, the most qualified person doesn't necessarily get the job. What tipped the committee in favor of Sylvie were phone calls from two lawyers—one from a senior lawyer at a firm where Sylvie had worked as a summer intern, the other from a friend of a law school classmate who worked at the the same firm where she was interviewing. Sylvie had called those lawyers and told them about her interest in the job. They offered to lobby for her candidacy (or maybe Sylvie politely asked if they wouldn't mind calling on her behalf). So Sylvie had a double whammy: an inside referral and an outside recommendation from a respected lawyer.

I asked James, "Do you know lawyers you worked with at summer internships whom you could have approached, or law school friends who might know someone who worked there?" "Sure," James said, "But I wanted to get the job on my own merits. Plus, I don't like to bother people."

> Networking is far and away the number-one way to get a job.
> Seventy percent of jobs are got through networking,
> according to the Bureau of Labor Statistics.

Then James said something interesting, "Gee, it doesn't seem fair. My credentials are better."

Of course it's fair. That's how the work world works. It's not school rules anymore. School and grades matter, but probably not as much as personal recommendations and how well you present yourself in interviews. As a personal brander, you must marshal all your assets, particularly recommendations by influential people or inside employees. There's nothing more powerful than positive word of mouth, particularly when it's from an influential person or company employee.

Don't feel, as James told me, "My accomplishments should speak for themselves." In an ideal world, perhaps they would have. But wouldn't you have been swayed to Sylvie's candidacy, too, if you were on the committee and received those glowing endorsements?

Cultivate a Network of Recommenders

Your recommender network is your secret weapon when you are looking for a job, because nothing counts more than the right person singing your praises.

When you have been introduced or recommended by someone, it means that you have been vetted. It says that you are a person who should be considered before the long line of other candidates. That's why over 60 percent of recruiters rate referrals as the number-one source of high-quality candidates.

As a new grad, you want to put together three to five (or more) people who will advocate for you in your job hunt. See if one or two professors who have contacts in your industry can be part of your network. Are there people you worked with at internships and jobs who could be recommenders?

On a more practical level, how do you ask for a recommendation or referral? Well, it starts by having a good experience working together. When the job or internship is ending, ask your supervisor or colleague if you can use them as a job reference when you start looking for a full-time job. Or ask if they could post a recommendation on LinkedIn. Or you could recommend them first on LinkedIn and see if they reciprocate.

When you ask for a recommendation for a specific job, give them phrases they can use in recommending you. Provide your value proposition and examples of how your work or other experience relates to the job at hand.

If you want a referral for a position you covet from Robert, your internship supervisor, don't say, "Robert, I think you know Sue Smith at ABC Company. She's the hiring manager for a job I'm really interested in, and I'm wondering if you could recommend me." That approach is all about you and what you want.

Better to say, "I'm interested in meeting Sue Smith at ABC Company. Her company is developing a cutting-edge technology, and I think I can be an asset there. I learned a lot about the field and got valuable experience at the summer internship I did with your team. We all pulled together to get the project successfully completed on time. Plus my double major in engineering and computer science will be an asset."

That way Robert will feel more comfortable making the referral since it will be mutually advantageous. Plus you're giving him sound bites he can use in discussing you with the hiring manager.

Advantage New Graduate

There are powerful networking tactics you can use to drive your job hunt success.

Master networkers get an "in" at each company they are targeting. Likewise, your goal should be to get an employee contact at each of your dream companies. Resumes from inside referrals go to the top of the pile and are reviewed more closely. Company recruiters know that the internal employee is likely to follow up find out how their referral is doing in the interviewing process. If you're rejected, they'll want to know why. The recruiter will try extra hard to see if there is a fit.

Young networking stars realize that they have a unique advantage. You are at the very beginning of your career, and the vast majority of people— some 77 percent—say they want to help out young people just starting their careers. When breaking the ice at networking events, identify yourself as a new or upcoming graduate in search of advice ("Hi, I'm Bob Jones, a new business grad from X University . . ."). Flag your status in email subject lines ("Upcoming X University graduate seeks informational interview") and pitch letters.

Networking pros also realize that we all know more people than we realize. You've already had a taste of networking at college mixers, job fairs, and the like, but now you need to graduate to advanced networking.

Make a list of every person you ever met at an internship, summer job, volunteer project, class, or school club, and you'll have a pretty good beginning professional network. Expand the list to include friends, classmates, your family and relatives, and people that you knew growing up. Pretty soon you'll have an impressive professional network.

Make Time for and Even Learn to Like Networking

The benchmark of your success as a job seeker and later as a professional is how many meaningful relationships you've made. You can't succeed alone or even with a small group of people. You need a large, diverse network of all types.

You may think, I'm shy, or, I don't like doing this. Networking makes me feel uncomfortable.

Do you?

It's helpful to move away from the idea that your goal in networking is just to make useful contacts. Instead, decide that your goal is to meet some interesting new people, expand your thinking, get advice for your career path, and maybe make some lifelong friends in the process.

Just this shift in emphasis makes a big difference. You'll be much more successful if your motive is to learn and get to know a wide variety of people, rather than to hustle contacts.

> Relationship building is probably the most important career skill of all.

College students and young professionals who have strong networks tell me that they allocate time to get out in the world, just as they allocate time to keep in touch or fill out online job applications. Connections are powered by curiosity and asking the right questions.

As one well-networked young professional told me, "In many ways, networking is like romance. It's about cultivating connections with what is going on in someone's life so you build a human connection. At a networking event, I try to keep the conversation lighthearted and maybe even funny if there's a natural way to do that. So I don't ask someone new I'm introduced to, 'What do you do?' I make conversation with things like, 'Where are you going for the holidays?' to kick off the relationship on a more personal level rather than a stiff professional one."

People can sense when you're genuinely interested in discussing ideas and experiences and when you're interested in knowing them just because they can help you. Network to expand your thinking by connecting with new people outside your normal orbit and outside the ivory tower. You're more likely to learn about the real world of careers from people who are doing it, not teaching it.

So many of the struggling new graduates I interviewed lamented that they wished they had spent more time networking while at school and on jobs and internships. Wherever you are, the best and only time to start is now.

Your Network Is Your Lifeline

You've probably spent the last four years growing up, pulling away from your parents, and getting them to let go. Well, now is the time to renew family ties!

Finding a job and making a successful transition from college to career is tough. Realize that no one wants you to get a good job and fulfill your destiny as much as your parents.

In today's job reality, you need all the help you can get. Tap them. If they don't have contacts, they can give you emotional support. If you've grown apart, reach out to them. An important caveat: Don't ever let your mom or dad call to set up appointments or pitch you for a job. It happens more than you might think and telegraphs all the wrong things to companies.

Staying in touch and helping others means you'll have people to tap when you are looking for introductions and referrals. Many people contact those in their network only when they are looking for a job, then ignore them. That's not networking; it's called using people.

While networking involves building relationships, it still has a transactional component. Networking isn't about meeting tons of people; it's about meeting like-minded people who can refer you and whom you can refer. Done right, networking results in the best kind of professional transaction, one where there is a win-win. Both sides feel good about the exchange because both sides feel that they benefited. Think of networking as an economy of favors. Just like any healthy economy, you want to have active trade back and forth. In the networking trade, there is the expectation of reciprocity.

For some, thinking this way may seem manipulative. But there's another way to look at it, what psychologists call "reciprocal altruism." You'll find that if you do a lot of favors and participate in the networking economy, you'll gain a reputation for helping others, and people will want to help you.

You'll discover that doing favors and giving small "gifts" attract others to you. I'm not talking about monetary gifts. It could be an article you email that you think might be of interest. It could be an introduction. It could be sharing what websites are best for a job search in your field. Your gift just has to show thoughtfulness. Being generous in this way will give you a strong network of contacts and career capital you can practically take to the bank.

While there's no formal quid pro quo system in the networking economy, favor givers are attracted to those who reciprocate and punish those who take favors and don't reciprocate. Believe me, word will get out if you're a taker and not a giver, too!

Conference Commando

Many professional associations have special programs for students and new graduates at their yearly or regional conferences. It's a worthwhile investment and a great networking opportunity. You'll learn more about the industry and meet players at all levels in the industry.

Before the event, use social media to reach out to speakers, panelists, and key attendees. At the event, go up to speakers and tell them how much you enjoyed the talk and exchange business cards.

The best networking takes place in the hallways, so make sure to move around during coffee breaks. All the conference attendees will be wearing name tags, so reach out and say hello when you see a fellow attendee in the hotel lobby or elevator. The dog tag is a natural icebreaker.

If you go to a conference with a friend, don't just stick together during the networking periods. Tag-team it by splitting up and coming back together from time to time. When you meet someone interesting, bring your friend over and introduce them. Make it a goal to meet at least five new contacts at each conference, and be sure to follow up.

Here's Erin's follow-up template to new people she meets at networking events:

> Fiona,
>
> It was great meeting you last night. I enjoyed our conversation about _____. I've attached a link to the article I was talking about. Let's stay in touch.
>
> Best,
>
> Erin

Go Big and Selectively Deep

Power networkers realize that you'll need a network with different kinds of contacts on the road to success—a large network with many people you know only superficially along with mentors, friends, and colleagues you know well.

Don't think the people you barely know are of little value. I got two jobs in advertising through people I had just met at networking events. It's often the connections outside your usual circles that provide the entrée to the new company or business arena.

Make a commitment to step outside of your circle by recognizing diversity. You'll find that the more varied your network and the more people you know, even casually or briefly, the more opportunities will come your way. So don't be afraid to speak up and share what you're looking for in your job hunt. You never know where the connecting link will come from.

Build Four Key Networks

Here are the four key networks that can play a significant role in your professional success. The two on the left, your core *career contacts* of professional associates and your *casual acquaintances network* of people you don't know very well, are your *wide/shallow networks*. They are "wide" because there are many people in each network, and while the depth of each relationship is "shallow," they are valuable just the same.

FOUR Key Networks

Career Impact →	**Career Contacts** Professional contacts from jobs, university, organizations in person and online	**Career Champions** Recommenders, allies, mentors, sponsors, and connectors
	Casual Acquaintances People you don't know well	**Close Confidants** Close friends and family who provide support

Relationship Strength

The two on the right, your *career champions*, or recommenders, allies, mentors, and sponsors; and your *close confidants*, your close friends and family, are your *narrow/deep networks*. While these networks are small in size or "narrow," they're "deep" in the strong relationships you have with the people in them.

Here are the special kinds of people who play a significant role in your professional networks.

Career Champions: This is your brain trust of influential recommenders, allies, mentors, sponsors, and connectors—your informal "board of directors." It is, no doubt, your most important network because these people can impact your career success dramatically.

Your *recommenders* are the people you will use to vouch for your performance on job applications. They can include professors, bosses, or other colleagues from internships and jobs.

Most *mentors* and *sponsors* are executives, professors, family friends, recruiters, and counselors. As seasoned pros, their advice is valuable. Don't wait to reach out. Mentoring can begin over coffee where you discuss an issue that's important to you, and the mentoring relationship gradually builds over time. You can follow people you admire on Twitter and other social sites as a first step in forming a mentor relationship.

When you have an exceptionally positive connection with a mentor or adviser, the person can become a *sponsor*, an advocate who calls people up and introduces you around. (There's nothing better than that!) Generally, sponsors offer to play a hands-on role in advocating for you, but I have known people who reach out to ask a former boss or mentor if they would feel comfortable making a call to advocate for them in a specific role. It just depends on how well you know the potential sponsor.

There are two other important types to have in your strategic network. *Allies* are groups of college friends and young professionals who share similar ambitions. The best groups form a tight-knit bond, sharing job tips, advice, and contacts. *Connectors* know a lot of people. Connectors may or may not have powerful job titles, but they are powerful nonetheless. Doctors, financial advisers, recruiters, and even hairstylists often are valuable connectors because they interface with so many different types of people. Bloggers and tweeters are strong connectors, and social media is a great place to tap into virtual connectors.

Career Contacts: This is your core group of professional connections. Most people think of networking as building contacts outside the job and neglect to cultivate an internal network, which is often the most valuable. Make sure you stay in touch with college friends and colleagues at internships, jobs, volunteer activities, and certainly with your professors. You can expand your core network dramatically by joining relevant groups on LinkedIn, Facebook, and Google+ and participating in the discussions.

Close Confidants: This is your fan club of close friends and family. They are people you trust and who know you well. What they may lack in prestige, they make up for in the support they provide. They are often the first group that new grads tap to set up informational interviews.

Casual Acquaintances: The people in this network are weak links because you don't know each other well, but don't ignore them. A casual acquaintance is often the source of a fresh job lead or introduction because you don't travel in the same circles. When I look back on my career, most of my job opportunities came through weak links, people whom I had just met through friends or at networking events. So if you're looking for a job, tell everyone you run across.

The bigger your network gets, the more it will multiply and the more valuable it will become. Getting a job is about access, and networking gives you access. But you have to realize the value of building and nurturing a network and make time for it.

The Secret to Attracting Recommenders, Mentors, and Advocates

Today, just about every student or new graduate has a mentor or two. Smart personal branders don't stop there. They build a strong group of advisers who function as their career brain trust.

Building a strategic network of recommenders, mentors, sponsors, and allies takes some finesse. Don't make a bold request such as, "Will you be my mentor?" I've had complete strangers ask me that. It feels like a big commitment, and few people will respond favorably unless there is an established relationship or the introduction comes through a trusted friend.

Set up interesting people meetings.
Every month set up a coffee with someone
who is on an interesting career path.

A more natural approach is, "I've admired how you've navigated your career and done different jobs. I'm trying to figure out how to launch my career and develop a career path, and I'd like to hear more about how you did it." Then, if you both hit it off, keep in touch periodically, and maybe the relationship can then turn into a mentor relationship.

What separates the networking A-listers from everybody else is their ability to attract and nurture sponsors or advocates. Mentors give you advice, but sponsors do something very special: they pick up the phone and advocate for you. Nothing will help you more than that!

Where can you find people who will do that for you? Likely candidates might be people with a long history of effectiveness, such as senior executives, retired executives, entrepreneurs, and professors. Mentors can develop a personal relationship with you and become interested in your future success. Another group might be friends of your parents or the parents of your college chums.

The Allied Forces

There's another group in your strategic network that can be as powerful as mentors and sponsors. These are your *allies*, a small group of your peers who are ambitious and want to succeed as you do.

What makes someone an ally? Allies are people you can call, text, or email weekends and evenings about just about anything. Your pact is to help each other on your career journey.

Allies are roughly your age and form a tribe of friends and future careerists who are on a similar journey. Allies are happy to do mock interviews with you and critique your performance. They'll double-check your resume for spelling and grammar. They'll help you refine your pitch for a specific job.

With your allies, it's okay to show your vulnerability, and you can ask them things you wouldn't dare ask your mentors and sponsors.

Good Hunting Grounds

Putting your network together will take some ingenuity at first. But it will take effort to keep it alive when you are busy. Like any ecosystem, your network must be kept healthy, with new blood coming in on a regular basis.

You need to infuse your network with contacts you meet in person as well as those you find through social media.

Here are some of the best in-person networking places:

- **Professional conferences:** Every industry, job function, and minority group has conferences, both national and regional. Many have special membership and conference pricing for students and new graduates. These are a great way to increase your network in your industry or functional area. Many professional conferences have career fairs with a wide range of companies present so you can build relationships right on the spot.

- **University alumni groups:** There is something very powerful about school ties. Alumni possess a willingness to help that many other professional network groups don't have, so get involved in alumni activities in your town or over the Internet. Reach out to alumni who are working in your field of interest for informational interviews, job shadowing, or internship experience, or just plain old advice over the phone.

- **Networking groups:** Explore different groups until you find ones that are the right fit. These groups can be daunting if they are large, so consider going with a friend and breaking up to network separately. Then come back together again from time to time. If you meet someone really interesting, pull your conference pal over and introduce them.

- **Gender- or ethnicity-based networking groups:** Take advantage of the shared interests of these groups and the natural bonding that takes place and often quickly leads to mutually beneficial and supportive relationships.

- **Nonprofit activities:** Meeting others who have a common goal can be a great way to connect with people in your community or across the country because you share values and a commitment to making a difference in the world.

- **College career fairs and events:** This is a great way to stop by the booths of companies you have targeted or want to learn more about. Be prepared with your elevator pitch, resume, and business card. Check out school events where outside speakers are brought in to talk about careers and job hunting. Often they are underutilized by students and offer great information and networking opportunities.

The Social Network

Social media is like in-person networking on steroids. The career network you've worked hard to build in person can be made more valuable through virtual networking. Social media like LinkedIn, Facebook, Twitter, Google +, and other platforms magnify networking as never before. Even if you live in the middle of nowhere, you can build a network of people anywhere in the world.

Don't be shy. Post your opinions and jump into the conversation. As in the "real" world, networking on social media starts with finding the right people. Reach out to employees at your target companies. Tell them you're a new graduate seeking advice. Chances are they will be willing to meet with you for an informational interview. If you hit it off, they can be instrumental in your job hunt.

How to Network on LinkedIn

LinkedIn is built on a series of powerful networking ideas: the power of connection, the value of an introduction, and the multiplier effect of virtual networking.

To make the concept of a personal introduction a socially powerful idea, the organizing principle of LinkedIn is *degrees of separation*. So you have first-degree (direct) contacts, second-degree contacts, and third-degree contacts. The best ones for networking are the first- and second-degree contacts since you either know them (first degree) or someone else who knows them (second degree).

What's astounding is how quickly your contacts can snowball when you tap into the contacts of your first-degree contacts.

> Use LinkedIn to link up with people, to keep in touch with your network, request and make introductions, and to tap into relevant groups.

To harness the networking power of LinkedIn, you'll need to master making requests to connect, asking for help, making introductions, and tapping into relevant groups. Otherwise, you've just got a list of names with contact information you'd find in a phone book.

Here are a few tactics for using LinkedIn to network:

- **Build your first-degree network.** You can begin by uploading your contacts into LinkedIn. When you ask someone to connect, write a short personal note instead of using the template. If it's someone new, you may want to remind them of how you met.

- **Ask first-degree contacts to introduce you to second-degree contacts.** When you want to meet someone in your extended network (a second-degree contact), request an introduction from a first-degree contact who knows the person. Just as with traditional networking, you need to ask directly for something specific and to focus the request on why you want to be introduced. Especially in social media, where it's easy to accept invitations to connect to people you barely know, your contact may not know the person well enough to introduce you.

- **Act like a networking pro and introduce people to each other.** If you think two people in your network should know each other, write a short note to each person explaining why they should collaborate.

- **Give and ask for recommendations.** Reach out to people you worked with on internships or other activities and offer to write recommendations for them. Most will want to reciprocate. Even easier is LinkedIn's endorsement feature, where you can click and endorse people for specific skills and abilities.

- **Use LinkedIn Groups to build relationships with new first-degree contacts.** Choose groups that are relevant to your university, the career you are targeting, or other interests. You can post questions, start a conversation, and comment on discussions. After you've participated in the group, you can reach out directly to members. One of the benefits of being a member of a group is the ability to reach out directly to members.

- **Reach out to executives and employees at your target companies or job function.** LinkedIn makes it easy to search for people, and you can reach out to them for advice as a new graduate. Here's the appeal in the subject line of emails sent by an enterprising MBA grad: "I'm a recent MBA looking for advice." And it clicked. One contact said he would be happy to meet as long as he wasn't used as a reference. Well, they hit it off in the meeting, and the contact passed the MBA's resume on to HR. That led to a meeting and a job offer.

How to Network on Other Social Sites

While LinkedIn is the one place you have to be for job networking, other social media have certain advantages, too.

- **Facebook:** With over 1.5 billion active monthly members, Facebook is a force to be reckoned with. You can connect with people who are not on LinkedIn or other social sites who can be important on your career journey. Join the groups that are the best fit for your aspirations and try to actively involve yourself in the social conversation. You can set up your notifications to get alerted every time a new post appears.

- **Twitter:** Twitter is also a great networking vehicle, particularly valuable for its ability to let you target specific people and build a relationship directly. Begin by following people of interest. Retweeting tweets is a great way of showing that you're interested in someone's content or point of view.

- **Google +:** The tie with Google gives Google+ certain advantages, such as being able to be picked up in Google searches. So when you share posts, they will appear in searches on the topic and your name will come up high on Google searches. For networking, you'll want to tap into Circles. After you upload your contacts, figure out who belongs in which circle. You can set up broad circles, such as a friends circle and a professional circle, and targeted ones, such as a hiring managers circle and marketing contacts circle. (You can find out more about social media for personal branding and job hunting in Chapter 8.)

Networking Across Cultures

Knowing how to network is critical for any new graduate, but it becomes more complex if you're pursuing a career on the international stage.

From an American point of view, it's perfectly fine to reach out with introductory emails to professionals you want to know or to speak positively about yourself. This open style of networking often doesn't play well outside the US. You must be formally introduced to break in, and talking yourself up can come across as way too self-promotional. Likewise, foreign-style networking in a US context can seem too polite or could be read as lacking confidence, which is not what you want to project, either.

How do you cross the cultural divide? Observe those around you to find out what networking style works and what doesn't. Fine-tune your own style so that it fits in but also reflects who you are. You'll find the more you practice different networking styles, the better you'll pick up cultural differences.

Getting a PhD in Networking

Here's how to network like a pro as a new graduate:

- **Appeal to old school ties.** Many alumni want to help out students and graduates from their alma mater, so searching the alumni database or LinkedIn can be very rewarding. Make sure you identity the alumni affiliation in the subject line of your emails and that you're an upcoming graduate. I've reached out successfully to alums who are authors to blurb my books, so I know that having a university tie means your email will be opened.

- **Make a human connection.** Find an area of common interest so a real relationship takes hold. It could be your hometown, sports, volunteer activities, major area of study, or the high school you attended. Ask open-ended questions that lead to a conversation and a connection.

- **Seek out people you admire.** It's more advantageous for your professional growth to meet successful people who work in your target industry or job function. Go to up presenters and panelists at industry events and talk to them. Follow people on social media and comment on their posts. Follow up afterward with an email or a request to connect on LinkedIn, or follow them on Twitter.

- **Don't neglect the finishing touches.** Most networking ends right after the first meeting or social media exchange. Follow up with an article, an introduction—whatever might be useful. Above all, stay in touch.

Let them know how your job search is going from time to time. Most people just contact people in their network when they are looking for a job, then ignore them.

- **Tag-team at conferences.** Networking events can be intimidating if you don't know anyone, but if you go with a friend, you're likely to stick together and not meet anyone new. That's why I recommend a tag-team approach. Go with a friend but split up to meet other people and then join up again from time to time. That way you have someone to fall back on if you feel awkward. Plus if one of you meets someone interesting, bring the other over to be introduced.

- **Join your industry association.** The best networking is where the right people gather, and what is more targeted than your industry association? Often there are even more targeted industry groups such as the Society of Women Engineers (SWE) or the Healthcare Business-women's Association (HBA) for women in these specialties. Make sure you attend regional meetings and national conferences where you can meet valuable career contacts.

- **Ask for something specific.** It's hard to respond to sweeping requests such as, "I'm looking for a job in marketing. Do you know anyone?" Ask for help with one or two companies, or ask the person in your network to do something specific (such as write a reference letter) and provide a time frame, if there is one.

- **Network and job hunt the modern way on social media.** If you're a millennial like new graduate Amanda Rigie, you know that the best (and fastest) way to network is through social media like Tinder, Facebook and LinkedIn. Amanda met a new friend on Tinder. They never dated but became friends and friended each other on Facebook. Shortly afterwards, her new friend posted a job opening at his company on Facebook. Amanda immediately reached out, went in for an interview the next day and left with a job offer as an account executive. Start-to-finish, she landed the new job in a handful of days, all because of meeting and greeting on social media.

- **Track your contacts.** Whether by using your computer address book, a spreadsheet, or specialized contact software, track your contacts and record specific personal and professional details.

Networking and community building are skills that anyone can learn. Self-branders embrace networking because they know they can't succeed on their own. And having a community of friends, colleagues, and advisers around makes the journey a lot more fun.

It's a big world out there, and you can be a big part of it with your virtual and in-person networks in tow.

Whatever you want to achieve, whatever relationships you want to develop, wherever you want to go on your journey, use your network to get you there.

Chapter 9 Exercises

1. What specific things can you do in the next three months to make more professional contacts?

2. What can you do to make more contacts in the specific field you are targeting?

3. Close Confidants network: Who are the people you can really count on? Do you need to add someone new to the mix?

4. Career Champions network: Who are your recommenders, mentors, sponsors, allies, and connectors? Which group needs to be expanded, and how can you attract new people?

5. Career Contacts network: Which organizations and events can you get involved with to increase your professional contacts?

6. List three to five LinkedIn groups that you plan to join and be an active member of.

7. Look at your target list of companies or organizations. Do a LinkedIn search to find people key people in each and reach out for advice or an informational interview.

8. Look at your first-degree contacts on LinkedIn (the people you have imported from your address book). Who do they know that you want to know? How can you approach your first-degree contacts for an introduction?

9. Look at the industry conferences in your field. Which conference do you plan to attend this year to expand your professional network?

CHAPTER 10

Closing the Deal and Launching Your Career

At the end of the day, don't forget that getting hired is a personal (and partly emotional) decision by a hiring manager. You can have great credentials and make a good impression in the interview, but you will jeopardize your chances if you fail to enthusiastically wrap up the interview by asking for the job. You must end with a statement proving why they should choose you and how much you want the job. Follow up immediately with a personal thank-you note.

Look at new grad Nicole DeMeo's story. After a year of internships while looking for a job after graduation, Nicole finally got an interview for her dream job in communications. Here's the email she sent me about what happened:

Whenever I have an interview in the city, I like to leave an hour early so I have enough time to primp in the bathroom and arrive fifteen minutes promptly before the appointment. The day of my interview, my train was canceled. I had to take the next train, which got me in with not enough time to arrive early. I emailed HR and apologized, saying I will most likely be a little late.

When I got into Penn Station, I was panicking, and in my panic, I did something very stupid and decided it would be fastest to take a cab across town. I was wrong. The cab barely crawled down 7th Avenue. I hopped out, wasted about five dollars and ran to the subway. Because I was rushing, I was not thinking about what subway I needed to get on. I got on the M train and had to walk from 50th

Street to 55th and 3rd Avenue. I arrived to the interview sweating, exhausted, and on the verge of tears.

Despite the drama of getting there, my interviews went fantastically well! Later that night, I wrote my thank-you notes and realized after I had emailed them that I misspelled "communications" in the thank-you to my prospective supervisor.

Oh, the irony! For a job in communications, I misspelled the keyword. After all of the frustration looking for a communications job for over a year, I could not believe I did that.

A few days later I got an email from HR with the subject line "Good News."

Fast-forward to the company holiday party. I was speaking with the creative director and copywriter, two of the people I had interviewed with and they said, "Did your boss ever tell you how you got the job?" They proceeded to tell me that I was in the running against another well-qualified candidate, but what made me get chosen for the job was my enthusiasm and personalized thank-you notes.

I interrupted and said, "Are you kidding? I misspelled a word in one of them!" Thankfully, no one had noticed. They were impressed that I sent the thank-yous the same day as the interviews and personalized each one, referencing something each person said in our meetings. For my new boss's thank-you in particular, I mentioned something about her son and Halloween. So in the end, getting my dream job was about connecting with the team, telling them how much I wanted the job, and taking the time to write old-fashioned, personalized, and heartfelt thank-you notes.

Last Impressions Can Make the Difference

You know how important first impressions are, but last impressions are crucial, too, as Nicole's story shows. It may seem obvious that you should enthusiastically tell the hiring manager that you want the job, but some college students and young professionals are too polite and just say thank-you, shake hands, and leave without having a clue about whether they got the job or not. You must directly ask for the job at the end of the interview, reinforcing your USP and your ability to hit the ground running.

Inquire about the next steps. You'll learn valuable information about whether there are other candidates, the time frame, and if you can provide something additional to help your candidacy. Ask for the decision date. Make sure that you know the key contact person you should keep in touch with during the decision process. You can even say something disarming at the end of the interview such as, "What's your feeling about where my candidacy stands?" or, "Is there anything you've seen in other people on your short list that you haven't seen in me?"

Don't underestimate the power of sending personal thank-yous to every person—and do it immediately. That means sending out thank-you emails to each person the same day as the interview. Don't just send a note to the "important" people, but to everyone you met with. I know it takes a little more time, but personalize each note with something specific that came up in each interview. It shows you care enough to go the extra mile. You can easily avoid misspelling someone's name or getting their title wrong by asking each person for their card at the end of the interview. You can follow up your emails with a handwritten thank-you note or marketing piece for added impact.

Impress Them with Your Passion

Your passion for the company might even overcome your lack of work experience or the perfect academic background. Companies thrive on passionate people. Chances are your interviewers are passionate, too.

How do you show passion?

Successful job seekers go beyond a cursory glance at the website and know the organization inside out, its philosophy, culture, and latest news. Make sure to use online resources like Vault.com that give you inside intelligence on the company and what to expect in an interview.

Tell them how excited you are about the job and the company. Projecting positive emotions like confidence and passion are important not only because you'll perform better (and that's good reason enough), but because you will make others feel better, too! We have mirror neurons in our brain that make us predisposed to mimic what others are doing or feeling. So if you smile and are enthusiastic, that will make others smile back, feel warmth toward you, and even feel happier.

Displaying these positive emotions sends essential nonverbal messages. One study by Boston College was of venture capitalists pitching investors to fund their project. What made the difference was not their brilliant slide presentations or the words of their pitch. Success turned on nonverbal factors such as how "charismatic" and "comfortable" the presenters were. Strong predictors of success were factors such as "calmness," "confidence," "passion," "eye contact," and "lack of awkwardness."

Remember, your goal in the interview is to get a job offer. So, even if you're unsure, you can't be wishy-washy and say you don't know if the job is right for you. You'll always have the choice of whether or not to take the job later. You must convey passion and conviction in every interview.

Plug and Play

Hiring managers want to know how you can immediately help the company. They want to be able to plug you right in, and off you go.

If you have internship or job experience that allows you to hit the ground running, emphasize that in the interview. Outline your marketable skills and tell stories about specific projects. Tell your teamwork and leadership stories, whether from school, work, or sports. Think of relatable volunteer or school activities that demonstrate how you are a self-starter and learn new things quickly.

Go over the key responsibilities in the job specs and why you are confident you can handle the work and fit into the culture. Whip out your leadership or accomplishments one-pager outlining three key projects in a mini case study format. Hand out a one-page list of references right on the spot.

As was mentioned in Chapter 5, if you're competing in a highly competitive job market, you can hand out a more ambitious marketing piece, such as an infographic resume that outlines your abilities in a more engaging, unusual, and artistic way than the typical resume. Or you could hand out a brag book, an attractive binder full of key accomplishments, recommendations, awards, and the like. You could send a follow-up email with a short PowerPoint slide presentation on why they should hire you. (Remember: It's not because you are brilliant but because you can help the company.)

Don't laboriously take someone through these handouts in an interview. That's boring. You need to internalize ahead of time the message and points you want to make. Say them directly to the interviewer as you hand her the marketing piece, and say, "This will give you some additional details on how I can add value." Then top-line a few of them.

The Long Wait to Hear Back

The interviews went great. You've been called back for additional interviews two times. You even got to the point of discussing salary range. Everything seems good, and you are really excited about working there. Then silence. This can happen even when your HR contact repeatedly tells you that you were the "top candidate" and insinuated that you had the job.

One new grad, Tom, was told, "'I'll let you know either way by next week." Two months later he received an email letting him know that there was a delay. Periodically, he would check in and get the same story: "Delays in the process," or, "We're tied up with budgeting and haven't been able to focus on this, but we're still really interested in you." Tom eventually took another job.

Many interviewers make the promise that they'll call either way and then don't follow through. The business world is very dynamic, and people are busy, so don't take it personally.

Here's what you can do during a long waiting period. First off, write a personalized thank-you note within twenty-four hours of the interview. Here's a sample:

Hello John,

It was great meeting with you and the rest of the team. What a dynamic group of IT professionals! I was impressed with the exciting challenges you face and the important role IT plays in ABC Company's businesses. I am particularly interested in contributing to the new Z project we discussed and developing new software systems to improve customer satisfaction. My internship at XYZ Company gave me practical understanding of working on projects like this, so I'm confident I can quickly add value to the company.

Best regards,

John Smith

You need to follow up after your thank-you email, but don't be a pest. If you haven't heard back from your main contact in ten days or so, send a follow-up email. Don't complain about not hearing back. Many people are just very busy. Often, companies have a number of people who must weigh in first, and budgets might be put on hold. There are many reasons for delays in hiring. In your keeping-in-touch emails, you should try to say something new—maybe comment on a recent news story or a new fact about the company that makes you interested in jumping on board.

If your follow-up email doesn't get a response, a good strategy is to leave a voicemail after hours when your primary contact is not likely to be there. Your message should be friendly and upbeat, reinforcing your interest and inquiring about possible next steps. If the person does pick up, introduce yourself and politely ask if this is a good time to talk. If it is a good time, reiterate your interest and then let them respond.

Above all, don't communicate with many people outside of close confidants that you're close to something. Candidates have lost jobs over announcing prematurely that they had something in the bag. But if you're a smart brander, you won't be sitting around waiting, you'll keep busy looking, pitching, networking, and refining your interview performance. You'll soon have other irons in the fire and quickly get back on your feet.

To Negotiate or Not to Negotiate

Finally, you get the call you've been waiting for so long—a final meeting to discuss a job offer.

Do your homework beforehand so that you are prepared and know what the industry norm is for the position. You can check out websites that have competitive salary information like Glassdoor.com, PayScale.com, and Salary.com, or consult with people in the business.

One danger point in job offer meetings is determining who should go first in throwing out a salary number—you or the interviewer. As a rule of thumb, you want the interviewer to go first. Here are two ways it can play out:

Scenario one: Ask the interviewer, "What is the salary range for this position?" The best strategy is to get the interviewer to toss out a number first. It may even be higher than what you had in mind. Begin with, "If I understand the job correctly . . ." and then go over the key job responsibilities and weave in your USP and elevator speech. You want to show that you understand the job and are qualified for it.

If the number lies in the middle or at the high end of the pay range you researched, graciously accept the offer: "Great, I'm very excited about working here!" If the salary is below what you expected, convey the research you've done for comparable positions and ask, "How much flexibility is there?"

Scenario two: The interviewer wants you to suggest a salary first. Don't give a specific number. This is your chance to give a salary range based on your research. You may want to increase the upper end of the range a bit so you have negotiating room. Reiterate the job responsibilities and the value you can bring to the organization. Then listen to the interviewer's response.

But it's important to put your negotiation in perspective. This is your first job. You can't drive as hard a bargain as a seasoned employee with lots of experience or someone who already has a job. If you negotiate too hard, you can be replaced by one of the other candidates waiting in the wings. Offers from large organizations, the government, and certain specialties like management consulting are often set in stone, and all entry-level people receive the same package.

At other companies, you should try to negotiate for the best offer. You're not *asking* for more. Think in terms of *presenting a case study* based on your research and the value you would bring. Cite specific experience and credentials that make you stand apart. If the salary you are offered is firm and on the low side, see if there are other perks that can improve the offer such as an extra week of vacation.

Many employers bring in new hires initially on a contract basis. Tiffany was originally brought in on a six-month contract in the operations area of a large entertainment company. Then she was offered a regular position with a big salary increase. Here's her email about her salary negotiation: "I gave a range on my application but did not negotiate during the interview, as I thought the salary offered was very good for someone with little experience and just starting out. I was originally hired on a six-month contract basis and actually was just hired permanently as of this week! I received a $9,000 increase in pay since I am going from assistant to coordinator. Honestly, I was not sure about coordinator's salary because the promotion was a happy surprise. The HR person asked me if I was okay with the salary and I said yes, but I do plan to research salary ranges more and ask the HR department about the average pay for my new position."

Know Your Value

Realize that you have some leverage in your first salary negotiation, but not much unless you are in a hot field where there is a shortage of talent. Hiring officers expect you to negotiate to some extent and will be impressed if you know your value. Do your research so you know the parameters. Negotiating shows you're self-confident, always an important trait in the career world. The caveat is that for most first-time job seekers, there will be little room to negotiate unless you're in a bustling economy. You'll have many other opportunities to negotiate throughout your career.

If you're a lucky job candidate like Cole, our real estate analyst, and have more than one job offer, you have a great opportunity to negotiate a strong package even if you're just starting out. Don't make the mistake of turning down a job that's your second choice unless you have a written offer and have gone through all the prescreening for your dream job. You never know for sure until everything is finalized.

If you're negotiating an offer for a start-up like our equestrian engineer, Gwen, you'll be negotiating salary plus equity options. Start-ups are exciting and can offer tremendous upside potential if the company takes off, but they are riskier than more established companies. Often there will be more back and forth at start-ups over the salary and options than for more established companies.

The arts of interviewing and negotiating well are learnable skills, and they will be just as critical to your success as networking and marketing. In deciding whether to accept a job offer, always ask yourself, What is the experience I will gain? How interested am I in the position? How interested am I in the company? Am I willing to walk away from the job offer? Think about other "perks" that you can ask about, such as vacation days or relocation expenses.

Realize too that you'll likely have many job changes over the course of your career. This won't be your last job offer and salary negotiation. You want to get the best offer possible, but you're not in a position to squeeze every last dollar out of a negotiation unless you're willing to walk away. And unless you have another solid job offer, it's probably unwise to do so.

Measure Your Progress

One last lesson from the branding playbook: measure your personal branding and job-hunting efforts. You're spending a lot of time on both, so how do you gauge how you're doing? Here are some online tools that can help you keep track:

- **Look at your LinkedIn profile stats regularly.** LinkedIn gives you statistics on profile views over a period of time, how often your name has appeared in search results, and how many of those people visited your profile. You can test out different profile headlines and summaries to see what attracts the most views.

- **Set up Google Alerts.** You probably have set up Google Alerts for your dream companies, but make sure that you track how your name appears online. Use quotation marks ("Your Name") to get exact matches. (www.google.com/alerts)

- **Monitor your Klout score.** Klout measures your popularity on social media based on a scale from 1 to 100. Klout accounts for 400 different factors and will give you a good understanding of your personal branding efforts. You can watch your score go up over time as you are more active blogging and posting. (www.klout.com)

- **Set up bit.ly links.** You can use bit.ly not only to shorten standard URLs (especially important on Twitter), but also to track the links you include in your web articles, blog, tweets, even the links in your pitch email. For example, in your email pitch, include a bit.ly link to your online resume, infographic, or slide show. You'll be able to see in real time how often your links are clicked. By knowing what works and what doesn't, you can adjust your "offer" as brands do.

It's Up to You

There is a lot that is difficult, even terrible, about finding your career direction and launching your career after graduation. Your college group is about to scatter. You may be confused about your calling in life. Then there are the unreturned phone calls and the litany of disappointments, both big and small.

The future doesn't just happen. Nothing is written. There's no secret algorithm that will tell you where the job market is going or the perfect career path for your talents and sensibility (though online assessment tests are trying to help you do that). There is no "right" way to launch a career. It took me a while to find my own way and even longer to find my voice.

But there is something profoundly empowering and liberating about launching your career. It's an attitude that comes from struggle, from facing adversity and bouncing back. It's now easier to dismiss annoyances that once would have knocked you off your perch. You've found a new power from strength, from taking action, from realizing that there is no one right path. The goal of your searching is to find work that gives you pleasure or hope. Does it strengthen your spirit? Is this the ending of your story, or the first step in the journey?

One thing I have found in working with all types of clients is that practically anything is possible. This is true whether your goal is a great first job, launching a business, or getting into the right school. Think of your goals. Brainstorm. Take baby steps first. Create a chain of links. What is one little thing you can do to get yourself moving in the direction of achieving your goal? What else can you do? Start building links on a chain to get yourself from one point to the next. Apply the branding mind-set and the branding process. Take advantage of the opportunities and changes in each cycle, and try not to box yourself in or sell yourself short.

If what you're doing isn't working, try something else. Branders change tactics all the time. Even if a tactic is working great for you now, at some point it will start to wear out. Like a brand manager, you will have to change and refresh the experience. Marketers refresh the brand experience all the time. They might try a new advertising campaign, a new promotion, a special event, new packaging, or a celebrity tie-in. As Erin told me, "You can be prepared, on time, well educated. You can be analytical and write well. But are you perfect? Nobody can really be perfect. You have to figure out how to present your best self."

The best way to come up with a good idea for your career is to think of many ideas. You may not be able to use them all, but some will be worthwhile. Focus on the best ideas and see where they lead you. Try a different tactic and see where it takes you.

When things are going well and you're on a roll, that is the time to push for more. That is the time for bold actions and new projects. Ask for the big raise or the promotion. Seek out more visibility.

Your Career Is a Lifelong Endeavor

Few of us have one calling, a single purpose discovered in college or earlier that becomes the theme for our entire life. Few have it all figured out.

You'll find that your purpose and passions evolve and change as you have new experiences, travel, make new friends, or start a family. What was once the most important thing in your life may no longer hold the same meaning a few years later.

Don't worry so much about finding the one perfect job. This is your time to try new things and see what works for you. Look for experiences where you can learn as much as possible in as short a time as possible. If your first job seems disappointing, don't waste time feeling discouraged. Test out different environments. Even when you realize that a particular job or sector or culture is not the right fit, don't see it as a failure. You learned something valuable from the experience.

Throughout your career, look for short-term experiences so that you can keep evolving. These can take the form of internships, freelance work, consulting, or short courses that give you growth and mentorship.

While you want to develop a strong personal brand, it shouldn't be a static thing that limits you from taking risks and seeking new opportunities. Try to find a balance between your career identity and new possibilities, between the known and the new. Lila, a new graduate from France interviewed with a global company that offered her the choice of an entry-level job in Paris, Berlin, or London. All were great cities, how could she choose? But as she talked with people in the various offices, Lila discovered that the UK culture would give her the most autonomy and ability to lead her own projects. Therefore, she decided to cross the Channel and launch her career in the London office.

The Power of Personal Branding

Each of us is unique. Our individual brains, strengths, and experiences are powerful assets. In careers, as in life, success is much more likely if you feel positive about yourself and stay in the moment, rather than feel negative about the way things are now.

To succeed, you must cultivate positive perceptions in the minds of others about who you are, what you've done, and what you can do. You need to tap into the power of being yourself. You need to attract people to your ideas and abilities. You need to create your own special sauce so that people want you and no one else. To pull it off and successfully launch Brand You, you need a plan for getting your first job and for staying in the game.

Keep a Side Hustle Going (Just in Case)

No one will care about your career as much as you, not your boss (who may have to let you go when the economy goes south), not your friends (who have their own career worries), or your teachers (who have a new batch of graduates to launch). Your parents may be your next closest champions, but in truth, your career success depends on you; on your skills and your brand; your hard power and your soft power.

Will you ever feel perfectly secure?

In today's job market, few people will. But, if you're like most young professionals, you don't follow traditional career paths and definitions of success as much as previous generations—at least at this stage of your career.

You realize that the only person you can count on is you—and that's not depressing—it's reality and it's powerful. Many companies are not likely to employ you long term, and savvy young professionals are prepared for that. Many millennials want to move on after a few years anyway. The median job tenure of young adults, ages twenty to twenty-four, is sixteen months.

That's why you shouldn't stop hustling when you get a full-time job. Explore a start-up idea or two on the side or cultivate a transition to a new job in the future that will give you additional credentials to expand your network and your brand footprint.

No one can create the best career journey for you but you. You must take ownership. Personal branding will help you make the most of your important assets. You have to start wherever you are. You have to start today.

Chapter 10 Exercises

1. For your next interview, plan what you will say to close the sale and ask for the job. Write down your ideas.
2. Think of the jobs you are seeking. What is the going rate of pay based on your research? What is the salary range? Why might you deserve pay on the higher end of the salary range?

3. Set up an account on Klout or other social media that helps you track your brand strength and monitor it every few months. What specific things can you do to increase your brand strength, such as posting content online?

4. Set up a plan to measure and track your personal branding progress with Google Alerts and LinkedIn profile views. If you have a website, set up Google Analytics to measure site visitors. Set up bit.ly links to see who is clicking on your links and which messages are getting the most traction.

Acknowledgments

First off, I would like to thank the smart, talented, and candid students, new graduates, and young professionals who opened up and shared their career and job-hunting journeys with me so that students who follow them will have a better chance to graduate to a great career.

I would like to thank Gary Andrew Gulkis, who has the poet's appreciation of words. He generously read every page and shared his wordsmithing suggestions and ideas for improving the book. Gary always pushes me to think more originally and write more concisely. Alas, I still have much progress to make on those endeavors.

In conceptualizing this book, I spoke to more than one hundred students, recent graduates, and young professionals about their college-to-career journeys. What a treasure trove of passion, stories, and advice. I can't list them all here, but I want to thank the following who generously shared their stories and point of view: Nicole DeMeo, Edouard Bellin, Cole Ungar, Gwendolyn Campbell, Ben Prawer, David Mullett, Alexa Herzog, Byron Cordero, and Amanda Rigie.

There were many others who shared their stories but wanted to maintain their privacy. You know who you are. Thanks again for sharing your stories and tips. I also interviewed a number of HR directors, hiring managers, and recruiters, as well as university Career Services professionals, and want to specifically thank Carrie Weaver, Tom Blanco, and Mark Presnell for their insights. I also want to thank Madeleine Cohen at the New York Public Library for her research assistance.

I am so grateful to the amazing people at John Murray, an imprint of Hachette, particularly Nicholas Davies, and at Nicholas Brealey Publishing: Nick Brealey, who has supported me now through four books. Michelle

Morgan, head of production, who is always responsive and on top of everything. Special thanks to Melissa Carl, who has led the sales effort with thoroughness and a personal touch. I also want to thank Janet Crockett, who makes everything run smoothly, and Graham Green for his efforts on the book. Thank you to Tom Willkens at Tom Willkens Literary and Media Services for his thorough copyedit and attention to detail. Enormous thanks to the PR team, particularly Meryl Zagarek and Marina Mortimer in the US, and Rosie Gailer, Lucy Hale and Ben Slight in the UK.

A final thanks to friends and family who have encouraged me in this writing endeavor. Most of all, I would not have written a word without the support of my husband, Michael. I owe more to him than words can say.

About the Author

Catherine Kaputa
President, SelfBrand (www.selfbrand.com)
Personal Brand Strategist, Speaker, and Author

From Madison Avenue to Wall Street to the halls of academe, Catherine Kaputa perfected her ability to market products, places, and companies. She learned brand strategy from marketing gurus Al Ries and Jack Trout before leading the award-winning "I ♥ NY" campaign at Wells, Rich, Greene ad agency. For over ten years, she was SVP, Director of Advertising and Community Affairs, at Citi Smith Barney. She has taught branding at New York University's Stern School of Business.

Yet Catherine discovered that one of the most important applications for branding is not for products or companies—it's for individuals to define and own their career identity and create their own performance success. That's why Catherine launched SelfBrand LLC, a New York City-based branding and professional development company, and started speaking to groups of young professionals, executives, employees, and new graduates on personal branding and career success.

A High-Energy Speaker

Catherine Kaputa cut her teeth in branding in three of the most demanding and innovative environments: Madison Avenue, Wall Street, and a top business school. Now Catherine shares those experiences with others.

Catherine is known for her compelling content and entertaining style, using storytelling, branding insight, and humor in keynotes tailored for each audience. Her topics are:

- **Personal Branding**, based on ideas in her award-winning book *You Are a Brand: In Person and Online, How Smart People Brand Themselves for Success*

- **Launching Your Career and Brand You for New Graduates and Young Professionals**, based on the ideas in her book *Graduate to a Great Career: How Smart Students, New Graduates, and Young Professionals Can Launch Brand You*

- **Women's Leadership**, based on the ideas in *Women Who Brand: How Successful Women Promote Themselves and Get Ahead*

- **Breakthrough Branding for Entrepreneurs**, based on the ideas in her award-winning book *Breakthrough Branding: How Entrepreneurs and Intrapreneurs Transform a Small Idea into a Big Brand*

In addition to keynote presentations, Catherine also conducts highly interactive workshops on personal branding designed so that attendees leave with actual work done on their own brands. Often, companies bring her in when launching a women's initiative or a professional development program for high-potential employees, new hires, or midlevel executives. She speaks at entrepreneur conferences on transforming a business idea into a big brand. Universities and organizations bring her in to talk to students, new graduates, and young professionals on launching Brand You in the career world. All her presentations use vivid case-study examples and branding principles in an interactive format.

An Award-Winning Author

Catherine wrote the definitive book on personal branding, *You Are a Brand!*, which was winner of the Ben Franklin Award for Best Career Book, a bronze IPPY Award, and a Top Ten Business Training Book in China. It has been translated into ten languages and is now out in an expanded and updated second edition. (www.youareabrandbook.com)

Catherine's book *Breakthrough Branding*, on innovation, branding, and creativity, won the Silver Medal in *Foreword* magazine's 2012 Book of the Year awards, Business/Economics category. (www.breakthrough-brandingbook.com)

Catherine is passionate about women's leadership and creating more female leaders, the topic of her book *Women Who Brand*. (www.womenwhobrand.com)

Personal branding is a particularly important message for university students, new graduates, and young professionals who need to empower themselves to find the right career path and entry-level job in a highly competitive job marketplace. This is the topic of her latest book, *Graduate to a Great Career*. (www.graduatetoagreatcareer.com)

Catherine has been featured on CNN, ABC, NBC, MSNBC, the *Wall Street Journal*, the *New York Times*, *USA Today*, the *Financial Times*, *Fortune*, *Harvard Business Review Online*, and other media. Catherine has a BA from Northwestern University, a MA from the University of Washington, and was a PhD candidate at Harvard University.

Corporate Sales

Catherine's books are an excellent gift for employees or clients, for young professionals or new graduates, for entrepreneurs or business owners.

You Are a Brand is for anyone—customers, employees, executives—who wants to learn how to apply the principles and strategies from the commercial world of brands to your most important product, Brand You.

Graduate to a Great Career is for university students, new graduates, and young professionals who want to empower themselves to find the right career path, and for their parents who want them to find a good job.

Women Who Brand is for high-potential and other women employees and female professionals who want to empower themselves and their organizations to create more female leaders.

Breakthrough Branding is for entrepreneurs and innovation-based companies, where everyone must be a growth agent and know how to transform ideas into brands.

For information about Catherine Kaputa and her keynote talks, visit her website www.selfbrand.com, her blog www.artofbranding.com, or contact Catherine@selfbrand.com.

Resources

There are hundreds of books on job hunting, interviewing, finding your career path, and related topics for new graduates, not to mention the wealth of information online on job sites, forums, blogs, and the like. Here is my short list of required reading for new graduates:

Bock, Lazlo, *Work Rules: Insights from Inside Google That Will Transform How You Live and Lead*, New York: Twelve, 2015.

Bolles, Richard N., *What Color Is Your Parachute? 2016: A Practical Manual for Job-Hunters and Career-Changers*, Berkeley: Ten Speed Press, 2015.

Buckingham, Marcus, *Now, Discover Your Strengths*, New York: Free Press, 2001.

Carpenter, Ben, *The Bigs: The Secrets Nobody Tells Students and Young Professionals about How to Find a Great Job, Do a Great Job, Be a Leader, Start a Business, Stay out of Trouble, and Live a Happy Life*, New York: Wiley, 2014.

Cuddy, Amy, *Presence: Bring Your Boldest Self to Your Biggest Challenges*, Boston: Little, Brown and Company, 2015.

Frankl, Viktor, *Man's Search for Meaning*, Boston: Beacon, 2006.

Hoffman, Reid, *The Start-Up of You*, New York: Crown, 2012.

Johnston, Keith, *Impro: Improvisation and the Theater*, London: Routledge, 1987.

Levit, Alexandra, *They Don't Teach Corporate in College, 3rd Edition*, Wayne, NJ: Career Press, 2014.

Lore, Nicholas, *The Pathfinder: How to Choose or Change Your Career for a Lifetime of Satisfaction and Success*, East Hampton, NY: Touchstone, 2012.

Pollak, Lindsey, *Getting from College to Career: Your Essential Guide to Succeeding in the Real World, Rev. Ed*, New York: Harper, 2012.

Pink, Daniel H., *A Whole New Mind: Why Right-Brainers Will Rule the Future*, New York: Riverhead, 2006.

Tieger, Paul D., and Barbara Barron, *Do What You Are: Discover the Perfect Career for You Through the Secrets of Personality Type*, Boston: Little, Brown, 2014.

Yate, Martin, *Knock 'Em Dead, 2015: The Ultimate Job Search Guide*, Avon, MA: Adams Media, 2015.

Notes

Chapter 1

1. Much been written about the difficulty of the job market for new graduates and their high rate of "underemployment." For a study of the rising percentage of new graduates who are unemployed or underemployed, see Jaison R. Abel, et al., "Are Recent College Grads Finding Good Jobs?" Federal Reserve Bank of New York, *Current Issues*, Volume 20, Number 1, 2014, http://www.newyorkfed.org/research/current_issues/ci20-1.pdf.

2. For the unemployment rate of millennials and young adults entering the workforce, see Bureau of Labor Statistics: http://www.bls.gov/web/empsit/cpseea10.htm, and a new report by the Economic Policy Institute: Alyssa Davis, et al., "The Class of 2015: Despite an Improving Economy, Young Grads Still Face an Uphill Climb," *Economic Policy Institute*, May 27, 2015, http://www.epi.org/publication/the-class-of-2015/. See also: Hilary Wething, et al., "The Class of 2012: Labor market for young graduates remains grim," *Economic Policy Institute*, May 3, 2012, http://www.epi.org/publication/bp340-labor-market-young-graduates/. Sarah Ayres Steinberg, "The High Cost of Youth Unemployment," *Center for American Progress*, April 5, 2013, https://www.americanprogress.org/issues/labor/report/2013/04/05/59428/the-high-cost-of-youth-unemployment/.

3. For more on the job difficulties of new grads, see also Douglas Belkin and Mark Peters, "For New Graduates, Path to a Career is Bumpy," *Wall Street Journal*, May 23, 2014, http://www.wsj.com/articles/SB1000

1424052702303749904579580263397059866; Jordan Weissmann, "How Bad Is the Job Market for the Class of 2014?" *Slate*, May 8, 2014; Leah McGrath Goodman, "Millennial College Graduates: Young, Educated, Jobless, *Newsweek*, May 27, 2015.

4. According to the US Government Accountability Office, 40 percent of workers have "contingent" jobs. For a discussion, see Elaine Pofeldt, "Shocker: 40% of Workers Now Have 'Contingent' Jobs, Says U.S. Government," Forbes, May, 25, 2015, http://www.forbes.com/sites/elainepofeldt/2015/05/25/shocker-40-of-workers-now-have-contingent-jobs-says-u-s-government/.

5. For the UK report on 58.8 percent underemployment of new grads, see the CIPD report, "Over-Qualification and Skills Mismatch in the Graduate Labour Market," CIPD, cipd.co.uk. Note: underemployment is defined differently in the UK than in the US and also includes employed workers who want to work more hours. See the Office of National Statistics, ONS: http://www.ons.gov.uk/ons/search/index.html?newquery=underemployment&newoffset=0&pageSize=50&sortBy=&sortDirection=DESCENDING&applyFilters=true

6. For the Oxford study predicting that 47 percent of US and one-third of UK jobs are vulnerable to automation, see Carl Benedikt Frey and Michael A. Osborne, "The Future of Employment: How Susceptible are Jobs to Computerisation?" September 17, 2013, http://www.oxfordmartin.ox.ac.uk/downloads/academic/The_Future_of_Employment.pdf

7. For an interesting article on the threat of automation, also see Derek Thompson, "A World Without Work," *The Atlantic*, July/August 2015, p. 51 ff., http://www.theatlantic.com/magazine/archive/2015/07/world-without-work/395294/.

8. The different values of millennials and baby boomers, see Allstate/National Journal Heartland Monitor project, see: http://heartlandmonitor.com/americans-local-experiences.

9. Also see Gillian B. White, "Millennials in Search of a Different Kind of Career, *The Atlantic*, June 12, 2015, http://www.theatlantic.com/business/archive/2015/06/millennials-job-search-career-boomers/395663/.

10. The assertion that a millennial will change jobs every three years is based on the Bureau of Labor Statistics 2014 Job Tenure Survey. The higher number of jobs held by the eighteen to twenty-four age bracket is reflected in "The National Longitudinal Survey of Youth," Bureau of

Labor Statistics, September 2015, http://www.bls.gov/opub/mlr/2015/article/the-national-longitudinal-surveys-of-youth-research-highlights.htm.

11. According to the Bureau of Labor Statistics, one in three workers—some 53 million Americans—earn income from work that's not traditional nine-to-five jobs, http://www.bls.gov/opub/mlr/2015/article/freelancers-in-the-us-workforce.htm. The fact that one-third of the workforce in the US comprises freelance workers has been true for a while. The Freelancers Union statement that 42 million, or one-third of the US workforce, are already freelancers is based on a 2006 Government Accountability Office report, which said that there were 42.6 million "contingency workers," including temps, on-call workers, day laborers, contract company workers, independent contractors, self-employed, and part-time workers.

12. The vagaries of the way the government defines occupational categories has made determining the number of contingency workers difficult indeed. Hence there has been some debate over what percentage of the US workforce are freelance or contingency workers and how to define them. For an overview of this issue, see Justin Fox, "Where Are All the Self-Employed Workers?" *Harvard Business Review*, February 7, 2014, https://hbr.org/2014/02/where-are-all-the-self-employed-workers/.

13. For an article on the reclassifying of workers to cut costs, see Lauren Weber, "Bosses Reclassifying Workers to Cut Costs," *Wall Street Journal*, June 30, 2015, http://www.wsj.com/articles/bosses-reclassify-workers-to-cut-costs-1435688331

14. For the move toward hiring more liberal arts majors in Silicon Valley, see George Anders, "The Revenge of the Philosophy Majors," *Forbes*, August 17, 2015. There is a growing movement to STEAM, with the "A" for the arts over STEM. The fact that people with a balance of social and math skills make about 10 percent more than their counterparts is based on research by Catherine Weinberger, an economist at UC, Santa Barbara.

15. To learn more about coding boot camps, see Steve Lohr, "As Tech Booms, Workers Turn to Coding for Career Change, *New York Times*, July 28, 2015, http://www.nytimes.com/2015/07/29/technology/code-academy-as-career-game-changer.html; John Lauerman, "Nice Ivy League Degree. Now if You Want a Job, Go to Code School,"

Bloomberg Businessweek, May 7, 2015, http://www.bloomberg.com/
news/articles/2015-05-07/coding-classes-attract-college-grads-who-
want-better-jobs. Also see "The Ultimate Guide to Coding Bootcamps:
The Exhaustive List," http://www.wsj.com/articles/SB10001424052702
303749904579580263397059866.

16. "The New Anti-College," *Bloomberg Businessweek*, May 11, 2015, http://
resourcecenter.businessweek.com/reviews/the-new-anti-college-oh-
sure-harvards-great-but-whered-you-go-to-coding-cam/.

17. The jobs/skills mismatch story is also under debate, see Gary Burt-
less, "Unemployment and the 'Skills Mismatch' Story: Overblown and
Unpersuasive, Brookings Institution, July 29, 2014.

18. For the finding that 70 percent of the jobs don't entail sitting in
front of a computer screen and programming in high tech companies, see Professor David Klappholtz, "Attracting Young Women and
Minorities to Computing," http://blog.acm.org/archives/csta/2009/04/
attracting_youn.html. Also see, https://docs.google.com/viewer?a=-
v&pid=sites&srcid=ZGVmYXVsdGRvbWFpbnx0aGVycHJjY2luaXR
pYXRpdmV8Z3g6MzQ3NmNiOTFkNDIxYjgzYQ.

19. The fact that people with a balance of social and math skills make about
10 percent more than their counterparts is based on research by Catherine Weinberger. "The Increasing Complementarity between Cognitive
and Social Skills," *The Review of Economics and Statistics*, January 16,
2015, http://www.econ.ucsb.edu/~weinberg/MathSocialWeinberger.pdf

20. For the high percentage of STEM graduates not in STEM careers, see
"Census Bureau Reports Majority of STEM College Graduates Do Not
Work in STEM Careers," US Census Bureau, July 10, 2014, http://www
.census.gov/newsroom/press-releases/2014/cb14-130.html.

21. For the shift to the "Hollywood model," see Adam Davidson, "What
Hollywood Can Teach Us about the Future of Work," *New York Times*,
May 5, 2015, http://www.nytimes.com/2015/05/10/magazine/what-
hollywood-can-teach-us-about-the-future-of-work.html?_r=0.

22. For an article and research on the slowness of the hiring process,
see Lauren Weber and Rachel Feintzeig, "Why Companies Are
Taking Longer to Hire," *Wall Street Journal*, September 1, 2014,
http://www.wsj.com/articles/companies-are-taking-longer-to-hire-
1409612937.

23. For a discussion of the rise of personality and pre-hire assessment tests, and the lengthening of the job recruiting process, see: Lauren Weber, "Today's Personality Tests Raise the Bar for Job Seekers," *Wall Street Journal*, April 14, 2015, http://www.wsj.com/articles/a-personality-test-could-stand-in-the-way-of-your-next-job-1429065001.

24. For studies on millennials' addiction to their smartphones, see the Zogby Analytics Millennial study and the 2015 Jobvite Job Seeker Nation survey, http://www.jobvite.com/wp-content/uploads/2015/01/jobvite_jobseeker_nation_2015.pdf.

25. Statistics on employee tenure show employees ages twenty-five to thirty-four have a fairly constant three years of tenure with current employer. See: http://data.bls.gov/cgi-bin/print.pl/news.release/tenure.t01.htm.

26. For discussion of how opportunity cost can multiply tuition and the study of four fictitious eighteen-year-olds done by Professor of Economics, Laurence Kotlikoff at Boston University, see Chris Bowyer, "Do the Math: How Opportunity Costs Multiply Tuition," *Forbes*, June 21, 2014, http://www.forbes.com/sites/thecollegebubble/2014/05/21/do-the-math-how-opportunity-costs-multiply-tuition/.

27. For the noncorrelation between elite universities and career success, see Frank Bruni's book, *Where You Go Is Not Who You'll Be: An Antidote to College Admissions Mania*, New York: Grand Central Publishing, 2015. See also, Jeffrey J. Selinge, "Forget Harvard and Stanford. It Really Doesn't Matter Where You Go to College," *Washington Post*, March 16, 2015, http://www.washingtonpost.com/news/grade-point/wp/2015/03/16/forget-harvard-and-stanford-it-really-doesnt-matter-where-you-go-to-college/.

28. For the detailed study of the earnings of graduates ten years after graduation at nearly every college in America based on matching data from the federal student financial aid system to federal tax returns, see https://collegescorecard.ed.gov. See also the article, Kevin Carey, "Gaps in Earnings Stand Out in Release of College Data," *New York Times*, September 13, 2015, http://www.nytimes.com/2015/09/14/upshot/gaps-in-alumni-earnings-stand-out-in-release-of-college-data.html?_r=0. See also Richard Fry, "For Millennials, a Bachelor's Degree Continues to Pay Off, but a Master's Earns Even More," Pew Research: http://www.pewresearch.org/fact-tank/2014/02/28/for-millennials-a-bachelors-

degree-continues-to-pay-off-but-a-masters-earns-even-more/ch Center, February 28, 2015,

29. For the study with "Joe the Plumber" and "Jill the Doctor" see, Laurence Kotlikoff, "Study This to See Whether Harvard Pays Off," *Bloomberg Businessweek*, March 8, 2011, http://www.bloomberg.com/news/articles/ 2011-03-09/study-hard-to-find-if-harvard-pays-off-commentary-by-laurence-kotlikoff.

30. For the study of career earnings by major, see the Brookings Institution's Hamilton Project: http://hamiltonproject.org/earnings_by_major/. See also the report on college majors and earnings by Georgetown University's Center on Education and the Workforce, https://cew.georgetown .edu/report/whats-it-worth-the-economic-value-of-college-majors/. For an article on the topic, see Melissa Korn, "College Majors Figure Big in Earnings," *Wall Street Journal*, May 7, 2015, http://www.wsj.com/ articles/college-majors-figure-big-in-earnings-1430971261.

31. For the $1 million ROI of a college degree, see the US Census Bureau, and for the global study done by the Organization of Economic Cooperation and Development, http://www.oecd.org/washington/whatarethe returnsonacollegeeducationandhowaffordableisit.htm. For the PayScale study done for *Bloomberg Businessweek* and Georgetown University's methodology, see http://www.bloomberg.com/bw/articles/2012-04-09/ college-roi-what-we-found.

32. For a study of the value of a college degree and how young people (particularly black graduates) have borne the brunt of the job market downturn, see Janelle Jones and John Schmitt, "A College Degree Is No Guarantee," CEPR (Center for Economic and Policy Research), May 2014, http:// www.cepr.net/publications/reports/a-college-degree-is-no-guarantee

33. See the Pew Center for Research for the finding that new household formation is at a forty-year low: http://www.pewsocialtrends.org/2015/07/29/ more-millennials-living-with-family-despite-improved-job-market/.

34. To read more about the rise of college tuition, read Paul F. Compos, "The Real Reason College Costs So Much," *New York Times*, April 4, 2015, http://www.nytimes.com/2015/04/05/opinion/sunday/ the-real-reason-college-tuition-costs-so-much.html?_r=0; for the cost of studying in the UK, see http://www.topuniversities.com/student-info/student-finance/how-much-does-it-cost-study-uk; Harry Dents,

"Will College Ever Stop Increasing?" *The Economist*, February 4, 2015, http://economyandmarkets.com/demographic-trends/education/economist-says-college-tuition-will-stop-increasing/.

35. To read more about whether a prestigious university is worth the cost, see Douglas Belkin, "Are Prestigious Private Colleges Worth the Cost?" *Wall Street Journal*, March 1, 2015, http://www.wsj.com/articles/are-prestigious-private-colleges-worth-the-cost-1425271052. See also Mohamed A. El-Erian, "Opinion: The US Education Bubble is Now Upon Us," *Marketwatch*: http://www.marketwatch.com/story/the-us-education-bubble-is-now-upon-us-2015-11-09?dist=beforebell.

36. For more on the student debt crisis: "The Student Debt Collection Mess," *Bloomberg Businessweek*, June 8, 2015. The average student debt in 2012 was $29,400, according to College Access & Success.

37. For the *Chronicle of Higher Education* research with employers on the importance of internships over courses and grades, see "The Role of Higher Education in Career Development: Employer Perceptions," *Chronicle of Higher Education*, December, 2012, https://chronicle.com/items/biz/pdf/Employers%20Survey.pdf; also see Derek Thompson, "The Thing Employers Look For When Hiring Recent Graduates," *The Atlantic*, August 19, 2014, http://www.theatlantic.com/business/archive/2014/08/the-thing-employers-look-for-when-hiring-recent-graduates/378693/; For the NACE study on internships including the percentage that lead to job offers, see 2015 Internship and Co-Op survey, https://www.naceweb.org/uploadedFiles/Content/static-assets/downloads/executive-summary/2015-internship-co-op-survey-executive-summary.pdf.

38. For the Bentley University study of hiring managers and new graduate's preparedness for the job market: *The Prepared U Project*, https://www.bentley.edu/files/prepared/1.29.2013_BentleyU_Whitepaper_Shareable.pdf; for the DeVry University study of hiring managers and new graduate's preparedness: *The Career Advisory Board Job Preparedness Indicator Study*, http://careeradvisoryboard.org/public/uploads/2014/12/2014-JPI-Executive-Summary.pdf; for Adecco's survey of employer's perceptions of the job readiness of young adults, see "2013 Way to Work Survey," http://www.adeccousa.com/about/press/Pages/20130425-Way-to-Work-Survey.aspx.

Chapter 2

1. For the difficulty in getting on a career path, see Douglas Belkin and Mark Peters, "For New Graduates, Path to a Career Is Bumpy," *Wall Street Journal*, May 23, 2014, http://www.wsj.com/articles/SB10001424 052702303749904579580263397059866.

2. Economist Neil Howe estimates that only about 5 percent get their career choice right the first time; see Neil Howe and William Strauss, *Millennials Rising: The Next Great Generation*, New York: Vintage, 2000.

3. The study showing that 80 percent of workers in their twenties and more than half of all workers wanted to change careers was a Harris survey done for the University of Phoenix; see http://www.phoenix.edu/news/releases/2013/07/more-than-half-of-working-adults-are-interested-in-changing-careers-and-nearly-three-quarters-are-not-in-the-career-they-planned-reveals-university-of-phoenix-survey.html.

4. See the American Bar Association's annual survey for the finding that the majority of lawyers wouldn't recommend their career to others: http://www.americanbar.org/publications/youraba/2015/june-2015/regret-your-career-choice--it-might-be-due-to-the-expectations-r.html; for information on similar results in the UK: http://www.lawgazette.co.uk/practice/dont-choose-law-as-career-say-4-in-10-lawyers/5041120.fullarticle.

5. My formula for determining your career was influenced by the formula used by career counselor Richard Leider, though it is different in important ways, particularly my emphasis on gauging opportunities in the work marketplace and downplaying passion as a driver.

6. There are many articles on "T" and "I" professionals. Look at Andy Boynton, et al., "Are You an 'I' or a 'T'?" *Forbes*, October 18, 2012, http://www.forbes.com/sites/andyboynton/2011/10/18/are-you-an-i-or-a-t/.

7. For the 85 percent uptick in the number of students doing a double major, see the Department of Education statistics. For an article on the pros and cons of a double major, see http://www.quintcareers.com/multiple_majors_minors.html.

Chapter 3

1. For a more detailed discussion of how to position yourself using the ten positioning strategies outlined here, see my first book, *You Are a Brand: How Smart People Brand Themselves for Success, 2nd Edition*, Boston: Nicholas Brealey, 2012.

Chapter 4

1. The estimates for the size of the hidden job market vary. For years, a number of career experts have claimed 75–95 percent of jobs are hidden or unadvertised. This seems to be too high. The Bureau of Labor Statistics says that "employers fill the majority of job openings through the unadvertised, or hidden, job market," in its *Occupational Outlook Quarterly*. Its JOLTS Report (Job Openings and Labor Turnover), issued periodically, also measures the hidden job market.
2. To read more about phantom job listings and the hidden job market, see Lauren Weber and Leslie Kwoh, "Beware the Phantom Job Listing," *Wall Street Journal*, January 8, 2013, http://www.wsj.com/articles/SB10 001424127887323706704578229661268628432.
3. My discussion of how to approach job rejection was influenced by David Burns, *Feeling Good*, New York: William Morrow, 1980, p. 314.
4. For avoiding the "black hole," see Liz Ryan's articles in *Forbes*: http://www.forbes.com/sites/lizryan/; for thinking of your career like an entrepreneur, see Erika Fry, "How to Approach Your Own Career Like an Entrepreneur. Startup: You," *Fortune*, January 1, 2015, p. 83 ff.
5. Seventy percent of jobs are found through networking, according to the US Bureau of Labor Statistics. The 70 percent number is inferred through data in the JOLTS, or Job Openings and Labor Turnover Survey, by looking at three items that, when combined, create the 70 percent number: number of hires, open positions, and previously open positions filled by someone the employer already knew. See the analysis of the math written by Kimberly Beatty, at http://blog.jobfully .com/2010/07/the-math-behind-the-networking-claim/. See also, "January 2015 Press Release," *Bureau Labor of Statistics*, March 10, 2015, http://www.bls.gov/news.release/archives/jolts_03102015.htm.

6. For the CareerXroads survey that only 15 percent of jobs are filled through job boards, see its Source of Hire Report 2014: http://www .careerxroads.com/news/2014_SourceOfHire.pdf.

7. The Ladders study on the need to respond to a new online job posting within three days was done by Alexandre Douzet, "You Only Have 72 Hours to Land Your Dream Job!," *The Ladders*, June 10, 2013, http://info.theladders.com/inside-theladders/you-have-only-72-hours-to-land-your-dream-job.

8. The NACE study on higher salary for those who got involved with Career Services is "The Class of 2014 Student Survey Report," http:// career.sa.ucsb.edu/files/docs/handouts/2014-student-survey.pdf.

9. The statistics on paid versus unpaid internships are according to NACE's Class of 2013 Student Survey.

Chapter 5

1. Statistics from National Association of Colleges and Employers on recruiting at job fairs can be found at https://www.naceweb.org/surveys/ current-benchmarks.aspx.

2. For The Ladders research on recruiters spending an average of just six seconds per resume, see "Keeping an Eye on Recruiter Behavior" by Will Evans, *The Ladders*, July 6, 2012, http://cdn.theladders.net/static/ images/basicSite/pdfs/TheLadders-EyeTracking-StudyC2.pdf; and "You Have 6 Seconds to Make an Impression" posted anonymously on *The Ladders*, March 21, 2012, http://info.theladders.com/inside-theladders/ you-only-get-6-seconds-of-fame-make-it-count.

3. Preptel did the study on how many resumes make it through the ATS; see http://www.preptel.com. See also Lauren Weber, "Your Resume vs. Oblivion, *Wall Street Journal*, January 24, 2012, http://www.wsj.com/ articles/SB10001424052970204624204577178941034941330.

4. For the study on pre-hire assignments from 2010 to 2013 see Lauren Weber, Today's Personality Tests Raise the Bar," *Wall Street Journal*, April 14, 2015, http://www.wsj.com/articles/a-personality-test-could-stand-in-the-way-of-your-next-job-1429065001.

5. BeHiring did the study that showed that an unprofessional email address will get your resume discarded 76 percent of the time. There are many articles citing this research and the problem with unprofessional

emails; see "Interesting Facts about Interviews, Job-seeking and Resumes, *LinkedIn*, July 1, 2015: https://www.linkedin.com/pulse/interesting-facts-interviews-job-seeking-resumes-info-solutions.

6. The article about using one resume for every application can be found by Dr. John Sullivan, "Why You Can't Get A Job … Recruiting Explained By the Numbers," *ERE Media*, May 20, 2013, http://www.eremedia.com/ere/why-you-cant-get-a-job-recruiting-explained-by-the-numbers/.

7. The website research was done by Workfolio; see Jacquelyn Smith, "Why Every Job Seeker Should Have a Personal Website, and What It Should Include," *Forbes*, April 26, 2013, http://www.forbes.com/sites/jacquelynsmith/2013/04/26/why-every-job-seeker-should-have-a-personal-website-and-what-it-should-include/.

Chapter 6

1. John Pollack's description of his interview in his book; see John Pollack, *Shortcut: How Analogies Reveal Connections, Spark Innovation and Sell Our Greatest Ideas*, New York: Gotham, 2014.

2. For the University of Toledo study of the quick ten-second "read" interviewers made in assessing job candidates, see Lazlo Bock, *Work Rules*, New York: Twelve, 2015.

3. Also see Jacquelyn Smith, "Google HR Boss Explains Why Most Job Interviews Are a 'Waste of Time.'" *Forbes*, March 17, 2015, http://www.businessinsider.com/laszlo-bock-interviews-are-a-waste-of-time-2015-3.

4. There are hundreds of articles on interviewing and how to answer interview questions, such as Thomas Kulenbeck, "It Pays to Ask Smart Questions at a Job Interview," *Wall Street Journal*, January 16, 2015, http://www.wsj.com/articles/it-pays-to-ask-smart-questions-at-a-job-interview-1421543154; and Liz Ryan, "How to Answer 'Tell Me about a Time When' Questions," *Forbes*, December 20, 2014, http://www.forbes.com/sites/lizryan/2014/12/20/how-to-answer-tell-me-about-a-time-when-questions/.

5. For a paper on clicking and mimicry, see Amy N. Dalton and Tanya L. Chartand, "Nonconscious Mimicry: Its Ubiquity, Importance and Functionality," Duke University.

6. The Huffington Post mention of casual dress in a job interview was written by Nate C. Hindman, "Millennials' Biggest Interview Mistake Is 'Inappropriate Attire,' According To Hiring Managers," *Huffington Post*, September 25, 2012, http://www.huffingtonpost.com/2012/09/24/millenial-biggest-interview-mistake_n_1910103.html.

7. The Adecco research on millennials and clothing attire is on Adecco. com and PR Newswire. "Adecco Staffing US Survey Reveals Hiring Managers Highly Value Today's Mature Workforce," September 26, 2012, http://www.prnewswire.com/news-releases/adecco-staffing-us-survey-reveals-hiring-managers-highly-value-todays-mature-work-force-171326501.html.

8. The Stanford Graduate School of Business course "Acting with Power" is taught by Professor Deborah Gruenfeld; see: https://www.youtube.com/watch?v=6mLFUtv0pCo.

9. My discussion of story types was influenced by Nick Morgan, *Give Your Speech, Change the World*, Cambridge: Harvard Business Press, 2005.

Chapter 7

1. For statistics on the power of visuals, Dale E. 1969, "Cone of experience," *Educational Media: Theory into Practice*, Wiman RV (ed)., Charles Merrill: Columbus, Ohio, https://www.etsu.edu/uged/etsu1000/documents/Dales_Cone_of_Experience.pdf. See also, "Reaching the Visual Learner: Teaching Property Through Art" by William C. Bradford, September 1, 2011, *The Law Teacher* Vol. 11, 2004.

2. For more on quick impressions, see the person who put thin slicing on our radar screen: Malcolm Gladwell, *Blink*, Boston: Back Bay Books, 2007.

3. There have been multiple studies on the "beauty premium." Rosenblat T. "The Beauty Premium: Physical Attractiveness and Gender in Dictator Games." *Negotiation Journal*. 2008;24(4):465–481.

4. The study that had students looking at a ten-second video of a professor teaching with no sound see, "Half a minute: Predicting teacher evaluations from thin slices of nonverbal behavior and physical attractiveness." Ambady, Nalini; Rosenthal, Robert. *Journal of Personality and Social Psychology*, Vol. 64(3), Mar 1993, 431–441.

5. The statistic that 40 percent of millennials have tattoos is supported by the article by the Pew Research Center, "Millennials: A Portrait of Generation Next," February 2010, http://www.pewsocialtrends. org/files/2010/10/millennials-confident-connected-open-to-change .pdf.

6. For power poses, see Harvard Business School professor Amy Cuddy's TED talk, "Your Body Language Shapes Who You Are," viewed by over 29 million and counting. Also see Craig Lambert, "The Psyche on Automatic, *Harvard Magazine*, November/December 2010, http:// harvardmagazine.com/2010/11/the-psyche-on-automatic. See also Amy Cuddy, et al., "The Benefit of Power Posing Before a High-Stakes Social Evaluation," Harvard Business School, September 2012, http://dash .harvard.edu/handle/1/9547823.

7. See also, Sue Shellenbarger, "How 'Power Poses' Can Help Your Career," *Wall Street Journal*, August 20, 2013, http://www.wsj.com/articles/SB1 0001424127887323608504579022942032641408.

8. For HBS research on warm/cold, smart/dumb, Cuddy, A. J.C., S. T. Fiske, and P. Glick. "Warmth and Competence As Universal Dimensions of Social Perception: The Stereotype Content Model and the BIAS Map." *Advances in Experimental Social Psychology* 40 (2008): 61–149.

9. For supporting information on how your voice is twice as important as the words you say, see Noah Zandan, "WSJ: Is This How You Really Talk?" *Quantified Communications*, http://www.quantifiedcommuni cations.com/wsj-is-this-how-you-really-talk/. Sue Shellenbarger, "Is This How You Really Talk?" *Wall Street Journal*, April 23, 2013, http:// www.wsj.com/articles/SB10001424127887323735604578440851083674 898. "Voice Pitch and Labor Market Success of Male Chief Executive Officers" by William Mayhew, et al, April 12, 2013, http://tippie.uiowa. edu/accounting/mcgladrey/winterpapers/mpv_ehb_accepted%20-%20 mayew.pdf.

10. For the "look-speak to look-listen ratio," see John. F. Dovidio and Steve L. Ellyson, "Decoding Visual Dominance," *Social Psychology Quarterly*, Vol. 45, No. 2 (June, 1982) pp. 106–113.

11. Sue Shellenbarger, "The Sound of Your Voice Speaks Volumes," *Wall Street Journal*, April 24, 2013, http://blogs.wsj.com/atwork/2013/04/24/ the-sound-of-your-voice-speaks-volumes/.

12. For the high/low status divide, see Professor Deborah Gruenfeld, https://www.youtube.com/watch?v=6mLFUtv0pCo; and Keith Johnstone, *Impro: Improvisation and the Art of the Theatre*, Routledge, 1987.

Chapter 8

1. For further guidance on how to leverage your LinkedIn profile, see the many articles on LinkedIn.com.
2. 78 percent of business managers say they Google prospective employees. "Online Reputation in a Connected World," *Cross-Tab*, January 2010, http://www.job-hunt.org/guides/DPD_Online-Reputation-Research_overview.pdf.
3. Jobvite's statistics on social media accounts can be found in the 2012 Social Job Seeker Survey, http://web.jobvite.com/rs/jobvite/images/Jobvite_JobSeeker_FINAL_2012.pdf.
4. For Stanley Milgram research see Milgram, Stanley, "The Small World Problem," *Psychology Today* 2: 60–67, (1967), http://snap.stanford.edu/class/cs224w-readings/milgram67smallworld.pdf.
5. The 2014 study of Facebook and the University of Milan: L. Backstrom, P. Boldi, M. Rosa, J. Ugander, S. Vigna, "Four Degrees of Separation," January 6, 2012, http://arxiv.org/abs/1111.4570, http://arxiv.org/pdf/1111.4570v3.pdf. The Twitter study can be found at, "Six Degrees of Separation, Twitter Style,"April 2010, https://sysomos.com/inside-twitter/twitter-friendship-data.
6. Ninety-five percent of recruiters search using LinkedIn and social networks. Siofra Pratt, "How Recruiters and Job Seekers Use Social Media in 2015 (Infographic)," *Social Talent*, February 18, 2015, http://www.socialtalent.co/blog/how-recruiters-and-job-seekers-use-social-media-in-2015.

Chapter 9

1. The article on law firm jobs in 2010 can be found at: Elizabeth Olson, "Law school class of 2010 struggling in job market," *Boston Globe*, April 27, 2015, https://www.bostonglobe.com/business/2015/04/26/burdened-with-debt-law-school-graduates-struggle-job-market/40N9Zr8Jw4tUgpSpQX1zeL/story.html.

2. Sixty percent of recruiters rate referrals as the number-one source of high-quality candidates according to the "2014 Jobvite Job Seeker Nation Study," http://web.jobvite.com/rs/jobvite/images/2014%20Job%20Seeker%20Survey.pdf.

3. The nationwide survey conducted by Fairfield Inn & Suites showed that 77 percent of adults are willing to help college graduates find work. See also Robin Mandell, "Networking 101 for New Grads," *US News & World Report*, June 10, 2014, http://money.usnews.com/money/blogs/outside-voices-careers/2014/06/10/networking-101-for-new-grads, and http://news.marriott.com/2014/05/a-message-to-the-class-of-2014-connecting-is-the-key-to-igniting-your-career.html?aff=MARUS&affname=10l1110&co=US&nt=PH.

4. For an in-depth look at how to network on LinkedIn, see the cofounder's book: Reid Hoffman, *The Start-Up of You*, New York: Crown, 2012.

Chapter 10

1. For additional closing tips, see Lisa Quast, "Job Seekers: How to Close an Interview with Class," *Forbes*, March 17, 2014, http://www.forbes.com/sites/lisaquast/2014/03/17/job-seekers-how-to-close-an-interview-with-class/.

2. The Boston College study of 185 venture capitalists was done by doctoral student Lakshmi Balachandra; see http://www.simswyeth.com/20101104-how-to-raise-money-from-venture-capitalists-and-other-investors/. For winning traits of successful venture capitalists' pitches to investors, see "The 6 keys to making a killer venture-capital pitch," *CNBC*, http://www.cnbc.com/2015/03/25/the-6-keys-to-making-a-killer-venture-capital-pitch.html.

3. For the new world of work for millennials and the importance of self-reliance, see Claire Groden, "A Millennial's Field Guide to Mastering Your Career," *Fortune*, January 1, 2016, pp. 82 – 88.

Index

Ungar, Cole, 20, 40, 49, 59, 142, 222
unique selling propositions, vii,
      10–11, 53–60, 65–67
   differentiation with, 104, 163
   launching of, 79
   on LinkedIn, 183, 185
United Kingdom, 6, 17, 30
universities, 15, 40
University of California, San Diego,
      165
University of Chicago, 14
University of Milan, 175
University of Toledo, 128
University of Washington, 57
uptalk, 164
Urban Fellows, 43
US Bureau of Labor Statistics, 76
US Census Bureau, 10, 18
US Department of Education, 19, 50
USP, *see* unique selling proposition

V

values, 5, 35, 47
VentureLoop, 41
verbal identity, 129, 152–53
video interviews, 15, 145–46
video resumes, 187, 192
virtual pitch, 54
virtual reality, 37–38
visual identity, 129, 152–53
visual pitches, 66–67

visuals, 102, 152–3
vocational knowledge, 6
voice, 164–65
voicemail, 120–21, 220
Volvo, 55

W

wage advantage, ix
wages, viii
waiting periods, 219–220
Wall Street, 47, 64
Wall Street Journal, 1
warmth, 158–9
weaknesses, 45–46
websites, 41, 122–23, 153
wide/shallow networks, 204
word association, 163
Wordle, 95, 100
wordplay, 67
WordPress, 194
Workforce Solutions Group, 23

Y

Yale, 16
YouTube, 191, 192, 193

Z

Zuckerberg, Mark, 133